Black Star

BLACK STAR

Britain's Asian Youth Movements

Anandi Ramamurthy

PlutoPress
www.plutobooks.com

First published 2013 by Pluto Press
345 Archway Road, London N6 5AA

www.plutobooks.com

Distributed in the United States of America exclusively by
Palgrave Macmillan, a division of St. Martin's Press LLC,
175 Fifth Avenue, New York, NY 10010

British Library Cataloguing in Publication Data
A catalogue record for this book is available from the British Library

ISBN   978 0 7453 3349 6   Hardback
ISBN   978 0 7453 3348 9   Paperback
ISBN   978 1 8496 4945 2   PDF eBook
ISBN   978 1 8496 4947 6   Kindle eBook
ISBN   978 1 8496 4946 9   EPUB eBook

Library of Congress Cataloging in Publication Data applied for

This book is printed on paper suitable for recycling and made from fully managed
and sustained forest sources. Logging, pulping and manufacturing processes are
expected to conform to the environmental standards of the country of origin.

10   9   8   7   6   5   4   3   2   1

Typeset from disk by Stanford DTP Services, Northampton, England
Simultaneously printed digitally by CPI Antony Rowe, Chippenham, UK and
Edwards Bros in the United States of America

Contents

List of Illustrations

The codes at the end of each caption are references to the catalogue entries in the Tandana archive (www.tandana.org).

Acknowledgements

Thank you, Tariq, for sharing your experiences of political activism with me throughout the 24 years I have known you.

This book first started life as the development of an archive and I am thankful to all those who shared their materials with me. Matloob, your belief in the importance of preserving history for the future has left documents which are testimony to the activities of activists in Sheffield, Bradford, Birmingham and Manchester. Thank you to Anwar (Qadir), Jani and Marsha for sharing documents from the Saathi Centre. Anwar (Ditta), your need to collect everything as evidence when you found the state unwilling to believe you has left an archive which will keep your struggle alive for the future. Thank you also to Tariq, Mukhtar, Jayesh, Greg, Steve, Fahim and Zulfi for sharing what they had.

Many others gave their time through allowing me to interview them and consult with them. A number of activists who gave me advice and shared their experiences with me have died during the research for this book. I would like to give them special thanks for sharing a past which I hope lives on through the book. They are Saeed Hussain, Anwar Qadir, Quamrul Kabir, Marsha Singh, Vasant Patel, Dave Stark, Geoff Robinson, Steve Cohen. Other people who shared their experiences through interviews and conversations are Jani Rashid, Noorzaman Rashid, Gurnam Singh, Jayesh Amin, Shanaaz Ali, Harjinder Gata Aura, Mohsin Zulfiqar, Nilofer Shaikh, Kuldeep Mann, Anwar Ditta, Matloub Husayn-Ali-Khan, Mukhtar Dar, Jasbir Singh, Anne Singh, Bhupinder Bassi, Balvinder Bassi, Sheera Johal, Naeem Malik, Amrit Wilson, Sarbjit Johal, Balraj Purewal, Ruth Bundey, Francis Webber, Gareth Pierce, Dave Harrison, Paul Kelemen, Mike Loft, Suresh Grover, Bharat Mehta, Ruchi Tandon, Fahim Qureshi, Aki Nawaz, John Boolten, Greg Dropkin, Dilip Parmar and Aleema Svoo.

Thank you also to my children, Neelam, Mishaal and Waris, for putting up with a very distracted mother.

Abbreviations

ANL	Anti-Nazi League
ARA	Anti-Racist Action
ARAF	Anti Racism, Anti Fascism
AUEW	Amalgamated Union of Engineering Workers
AYM	Asian Youth Movement
AYO	Asian Youth Organisation
BBS	Birmingham Black Sisters
BCG	Black Consciousness Group
BCM	Black Consciousness Movement
BDFC	Bangladeshi Divided Families Campaign
BYMER	Bangladeshi Youth Movement for Equal Rights
CADRIL	Campaign against Deportations and Racist Immigration Laws
CAIL	Campaign Against Immigration Laws
CARF	Campaign Against Racism and Fascism
CARL	Campaign against Racist Laws
CBGB	Communist Party of Great Britain
CPI (M, ML)	Communist Party of India (Marxist, Marxist–Leninist)
CRC	Community Relations Commission
CRE	Commission for Racial Equality
FBYO	Federation of Bangladesh Youth Organisations
HCAR	Hackney Committee Against Racialism
IPYA	Indian Progressive Youth Association
IS	International Socialists
IWA (GB)	Indian Workers' Association (Great Britain)
KWA	Kashmiri Workers Association
NALGO	National Association of Local Government Officers
NAYM	National Asian Youth Movement
NF	National Front
NGO	non-governmental organisation
NMP	Newham Monitoring Project
OWAAD	Organisation of Women of African and Asian Descent
PFLP	Popular Front for the Liberation of Palestine

PWA (GB)	Pakistani Workers Association (Great Britain)
RAAS	Racial Action Adjustment Society
RAR	Rock Against Racism
RCG	Revolutionary Communist Group
RCP	Revolutionary Communist Party
SASG	South Asia Solidarity Group
SBS	Southall Black Sisters
SDC	Southall Defence Committee
SWP	Socialist Workers Party
SYM	Southall Youth Movement
TGWU	Transport and General Workers' Union
UBYL	United Black Youth League
UCPA	Universal Coloured People's Association
UFFC	United Family and Friends Campaign
US	United States
WAF	Women Against Fundamentalism
ZANU–PF	Zimbabwe African National Union – Patriotic Front

1
Introduction

Over the last 20 years there has been a transformation in the way in which the South Asian community has been constructed by mainstream public discourse as well as in the way it has seen itself. The primary identity with which South Asians are framed in Britain today is a religious one. Academic scholarship research on South Asians has been focused within religious or cultural identity discourses (Ahmad 1998, Benson 1996, Handa 2003, Maira 2002, Sharma et al. 1996), its varied political traditions rarely recalled. The development of this book was motivated by the desire to give expression to forms of political and cultural identity amongst South Asians that hailed from a left and anti-colonial tradition but were rooted in a concern for the transformation of British society. In 2003, following the start of the 'war on terror', the ways in which South Asians were represented became further entrenched to the point where the representations felt so discordant to myself and many others of my generation that I decided to collect the history of the Asian youth movements (AYMs) in Britain in order to represent a different picture of South Asians – one in which identities were focused around a commitment to a set of political beliefs and values that had increasingly come under attack since the collapse of the Soviet Union. As someone who was involved in the anti-racist movement in the late 1980s and early 1990s, I knew many of those who had been active in the youth movements of the mid 1970s and early 1980s – a period which marked the height of the anti-racist movement in Britain. Constructing a digitised archive of extant materials was to leave these documents as proof of a different political identity and history. This book makes use of this archive as well as oral histories that I later collected to present the history of a movement that was the first organisation of South Asian youth in Britain, a movement that was driven not by religious or cultural identities but by a left tradition and anti-imperialism.

Such a history challenges the 'notion of coherent ethnic communities [that] lie at the heart of mainstream liberal understandings of racial and ethnic difference' (Rattansi 1992:12). Culture amongst South

Asians has often been represented as unchanging tradition rather than a dynamic process impacted by political values. The AYMs expressed the concerns of a second generation of South Asians in Britain who did not have the same ties to their countries of origin as their parents. Their political activity was based on their desire to be accepted as equal citizens and to belong in Britain.

Youth are often understood as a symbol of change and of crisis' (Alexander 2004:24). Like all young people, those involved in the AYMs wished to shape their future. In the context of widespread racism and economic hardship suffered by black communities, the AYMs struggled to change their situation and address the major domestic and international political issues of the time. They wished to influence the development of British society, its culture and its politics. They were part of a host of black organisations that played a key role in the development of a broader anti-racist movement.

This period signified a shift in British society, which although never homogenous, had changed culturally and ethnically more rapidly as a consequence of post-war migration than in any previous period. Scholarship on the anti-racist movement in Britain has referenced the contribution of South Asian youth but there has been no systematic study of the movements to date (Ramdin 1987, Renton 2006, Shukra 1998, Sivanandan 1982). This book seeks to fill this gap and to analyse their pivotal contribution to the anti-racist struggle and to the political black identity that was forged in Britain at that time.

The late 1970s saw the children of the post-war migration, who were brought up in Britain, reach adulthood. The AYMs that formed in Bradford, Sheffield, Manchester, Coventry, Leicester, Birmingham and London, as well as in small towns such as Bolton, Burnley, Luton and Watford, were mainly made up of young men. While many members were of college age, they included individuals that were as young as 15 and others that were in their late twenties with experience of political organisation and the workplace. The AYMs did not have fixed age restrictions but wished to create organisations to represent the concerns of young South Asians and their families. In this sense they were organisations of youth but not simply for youth. They took up issues that impacted on their communities as a whole to respond to the climate of racism, which young people and their families experienced in a period of rising unemployment caused by an economic downturn that led to the decline of the manufacturing sector in Britain.

They understood racism as being more than prejudice and saw it as embedded in the power relations of the British State and imperialism worldwide. In Britain in the 1970s, the state through its policies fuelled the notion that black people were a problem. Interpreted as 'a problem', young children were being bussed to school outside of their areas. Immigration laws were also brought in to restrict black immigration which caused heartache with families divided across continents, and large sections of the police viewed men of African and Asian origin with suspicion. Life on the street was also more violent fuelled by frustrations over the lack of jobs that was felt by all sections of society. 'Paki-bashing' became a pastime for racists and fascists – an activity rarely and reluctantly investigated by the police. As organisations the youth movements cut across the stereotype of the Asian as victim that was so frequent in the press during these decades and provide an expression of self-help by the youth of communities who felt disenfranchised. In organising themselves as a movement, they were different to the other new social movements of the time, since they did not wish to challenge the importance of class as the basis for political organisation but to highlight the importance of tackling racism within the class struggle (Melucci 1980, Touraine 1981). The period was one in which black self-organisation was seen as a key method in the struggle against racism and the search for equality.

The AYMs present an image of the youth that challenges the image of them as problems and explores the way they mobilised and organised to change the conditions of their lives. While focused on Britain, these young people saw a direct connection between the global political context and their own experiences. They were inspired by both the anti-colonial struggles of the previous decades as well as the civil rights and Black Power movement in America. The global needs of capital had led to the movement of their families and communities and the impact of colonialism was directly felt by the youth and their families. Anti-colonial struggles were still being waged in Palestine, Zimbabwe and South Africa and the youth felt these experiences related to their own. The Iranian Revolution of 1979, the Latin American struggles in Chile, the Soviet invasion of Afghanistan and the subsequent US funding of the Mujahideen were also processes the youth were keenly aware of and impacted on their motivations to create a better world. They were inspiring to those around them as Gareth Peirce, solicitor for six of the Bradford 12, remembers: 'It was for many of us the happiest time of our life, ...

because we were fighting a war on the same side and when you are involved in that fight, the bonds you make are the strongest bonds you will ever make in your life... we owe to them that line of history that gives us still some hope in saying that whatever the language used, however the false narrative is sustained where ever it is in the world that we are party to the same disgraceful injustice of calling self-defence something different, we absolutely owe it to you our thanks for teaching us how to struggle for the truth' (Peirce 2011).

The AYMs along with other anti-racist organisations fostered an inclusive 'black' political identity, 'where *black* was a *political colour that could only exist in a white world*' (Mehmood 2008). It was the fermentation of a very British kind of identity and as such offers an opportunity to explore the way in which youth forced society to look at changing realities and identities. 'Come what may! We're here to stay!' and 'Black people must unite, here to stay here to fight!' were chants that resounded on the streets of many British towns and cities in the late 1970s and early 1980s. Previous expressions of political involvement such as the Indian Workers' Associations (IWAs) were rooted in sub continental politics. As British based organisations, the AYMs represented a force that recognised Britain as their home and wanted to be treated as equal with other members of the society. They were not 'unwilling citizens' but unwilling to be treated as inferior (Thomas & Sanderson 2011). Most members, if not born in Britain, had spent the formative years of their childhood here. They did not wish to jettison their cultural and historical pasts, but wanted to be accepted for who they were and the cultural hybridities and political experiences that shaped their lives. They challenged the state's policies of assimilation, integration and multiculturalism as solutions to racism, arguing for an understanding of racism as an expression of power inequalities. They were motivated by political ideas and strategies from organisations across the world such as the Black Consciousness Movement in America and Southern Africa, communism in China and anti-colonial struggles. They were an outward-looking movement concerned to make links with groups with similar beliefs in Britain and abroad.

Yet within a matter of a few years this broad-based identity was marginalised in the 1990s surge towards identity politics and the concept of political blackness which the AYMs adopted was even represented as hegemonic (Modood 1994a, 1994b). Political blackness had aimed to create a feeling of unity between all those that had experienced racism and colonialism. The identity politics of the 1990s represented a very different agenda in which debates shifted from class based politics to cultural politics (Mercer 1998:47). America's global strategy disseminated by the dominant media also began to feed into attitudes towards Muslims to create feelings of difference between groups that previously searched for similarities fuelling anti-Islamicism amongst not just whites but also amongst Asian Hindus, Sikhs and Christians. 'Culture and religion became conflated and "Muslim" became the new "ethnicity"' (Wilson 2006). The construction of South Asian identity as faith based, while encouraged by external forces was also grasped by some sections within South Asian communities in the space provided by the attack on radical left-wing politics. The promotion of faith based organisations by the state ensured the privileging of conservative voices through the formation of religious based councils amongst Hindus, Muslims and Sikhs. This fragmented the previous socialist voice that found expression in organisations such as the Asian youth movements (Kundnani 2008, Sivanandan 1991). The AYMs continued a radical tradition that stretches back to the latter part of the nineteenth century, with Indians in Britain centrally involved with the communist party of Britain, for example, and organising Indian workers and migrants in welfare and anti-colonial forums (Visram 2002). The recent resurgence of interest in Marxist analysis makes an analysis of such a movement embedded in class and anti-imperialist thinking relevant and valuable (Eagleton 2011).

In defining this radical tradition, my first approach was to assert the existence of secular political histories within our communities (Ramamurthy 2004). The first paper I wrote on the AYMs spoke of their secular identity, yet the adoption of the AYM political history to attack Muslims by libertarian writers such as Kenan Malik with minimal reference to the impact of geopolitical shifts that have given rise to such a development, demanded a re-assessment of such an approach and an acknowledgement that while the AYMs were secular, secularism was not an identity that they felt the need to profess. Their advocated identity was with an anti-imperialist blackness which was secular through its inclusive nature.

Today we cannot separate all religious organisation from anti-imperialist actions, since there has been an emergence of a radical anti-imperialist Islamic identity in the last two decades. At a thirtieth anniversary commemoration of the Bradford 12, former members of the youth movements recognised how the new context of Islamaphobia demanded the right of Muslims to organise as Muslims. They focused on the importance of understanding struggles against racism in the contemporary context and as such reasserted the importance of organisations independent of the state, challenging the drive for funding that divided communities through the struggle over resources.

The book makes use of documents that were collected for the Tandana archive, which stores materials relating to the youth movements and campaigns with which they were involved (www.tandana.org). It focuses on movements in the North of England, partly because these movements have been left largely undocumented but also because AYM (Bradford) was one of the largest, most organised and influential of the youth movements. Extant files for AYM (Bradford) and AYM (Sheffield) were also the best preserved and form a large part of the Tandana archive. The focus on Bradford is also appropriate because it is clear that not only were they the largest and most organised but they were also one of the most disciplined groups and had a commitment to creating a national organisation. While the archival material provides evidence of the campaigns with which they were involved, minutes of meetings that could have given a detailed understanding of how decisions and policies were reached are mainly missing. The book therefore relies on interviews and conversations with former members from the youth movements in Bradford, Manchester, Sheffield, Birmingham, Southall, Bolton, Haringey and Luton to whom I had access to explore how the movements developed and organised. The book explores the innovative strategies for action that the youth adopted to further their struggle for justice in a movement where politics was not limited to symbolic actions but was driven by a determination to win campaigns and create lasting change. All the people I interviewed, regardless of their current political perspectives, all looked back on this period as one of intense inspiration and dynamism. The interviews also support an understanding of the contradictions and conflicts that ensued as the movements consolidated and the visions of people within them shifted as the state adopted a strategy to buy activists off the streets (see Chapters 7 and 8). Most importantly, however, the AYMs offer a spirit of resistance the history of which can inspire young people today.

Chapter 2 explains the context within which the youth movements were formed. It considers the social and political climate of the period, the experiences of racism by families and young people that were later involved in the youth movements as well as the influence of previous political organisations such as the IWAs in Birmingham,

1.1 Photograph of AYM members from 1984 taken in Sheffield (courtesy Mukhtar Dar), MD11.

Southall and Bradford on the formation of the first movements. Chapter 3 explores the network of organisations that emerged across the country in the late 1970s. It highlights the experience of Bradford in particular to consider the relationship between the movements nationally as well as to provide an understanding of the ways in which local histories and environments impacted on the youth. Chapter 4 steps out of the historical narrative to explore the political identity which the movements as a whole forged in the late 1970s and early 1980s. It looks at the literature and culture that influenced them as well as the complex nature of an inclusive black political identity that sought to make links across communities nationally and internationally. It highlights the anti-racism of the youth movements as inherently anti-imperialist, an important issue when we think about their legacy today. The chapter also explores the involvement of women within the movement and why women felt the need to establish their own organisations in some cities.

Chapters 5 and 6 focus on two key aspects of AYM activity, the campaign against the immigration laws and the right to self-defence. The chapters explore these issues through specific campaigns, to highlight the way in which the AYMs often worked to make cases into issues and thereby used an individual's story to humanise a broader issue and offer an understanding of the plight of a community. This strategy was particularly powerful in the anti-deportation and divided family campaigns with which the youth were involved, where they adopted innovative strategies for action that were rooted in community participation. Chapter 6 focuses entirely on the case of the Bradford 12, as an example of a self-defence campaign. The case made legal history in arguing the right of a community to defend itself in law and was a symbol of communities' challenging the state's response to the rebellions of 1981. The chapter was written with access to legal as well as campaign documents and gives insight into the power of a strong relationship between a campaign and a legal team. It also highlights the difficulties and conflicts that often arise in campaigns and the importance of keeping unity. The legacies and lessons of the Bradford 12 are drawn out through the final chapters.

Chapter 7 considers the inspiration of the Bradford 12 case for youth in cities like Sheffield and Birmingham who established movements in the early 1980s. It also explores the parallel shift away from the independent anti-racist organisations embodied by the United Black Youth League as many youth movements began to apply for funds to set up youth centres and got more and more involved in the delivery of services to the community. It explores the difficulties and conflicts that arise as movements establish themselves and highlights the impact of funding on changing priorities and directions that were not always understood by members when they first applied for funds. It considers why independent voices such as those that the early youth movements encapsulated are so crucial in the struggle for change.

Chapter 8 looks at organisations that were established in the mid 1980s in an attempt to maintain the anti-imperialist anti-racist position of the early phase of the Bradford and Manchester youth movements and explores the shattering of the broad black political identity as cultural and religious identities began to be used as legitimate criteria for state funding and as Anglo–American imperialism changed its focus from the Soviet-as-demon to Islam as demonic. The final chapter explores the way in which Muslims as the 'new black' have attempted to struggle against victimisation and oppression as the 'war on terror' made it increasingly difficult to build broad-based alliances. It highlights the way in which the next generation of South Asians have argued for exactly the same things as their parents generation – the right to belong. It considers the different response required by anti-imperialist anti-racists in the climate of Islamaphobia today. It questions the ideas of secularism as an inclusive strategy and highlights its ideological nature. Finally, the chapter considers how South Asians today involved in politics still embody attitudes and motivations of the Asian youth movements from the 1970s and 1980s.

2
The Birth of the Youth Movements

'Come what may, we're here to stay!'
  (slogan of the Asian Youth Movements)

When workers from a variety of areas of the Commonwealth and Empire were needed to fill the factories for post-war Britain, they experienced all forms of racism. These included attacks on the street, as well as exclusionary practises in housing and the workplace, despite this being a period of relative prosperity (Ramdin 1987, Fryer 1987). This chapter will outline some of these experiences and the ways in which migrant workers organised for social and political rights before the AYMs were formed. These histories of resistance were seen by the youth as a tradition of which they were a part. Balvinder Bassi recalls how when Sivanandan's pamphlet 'From Resistance to Rebellion' was published in 1982, they would carry it around with them, 'almost like a campaigning manual.' 'I remember it cost £1 and we would sell it at our meetings.' The youth's own experiences of violence in school and on the street were also a fundamental motivation for organisation as this chapter outlines. I make use of interviews from former members of the youth movements to provide an understanding of the experience of racism which encouraged their belief in direct action that was to mark their future organisational strategies.

RACISM AND RESISTANCE IN 1960s BRITAIN

South Asians have a long history of involvement in political organisation in Britain. In 1916 the communist party member Shapurji Saklatvala set up the Workers Welfare League of India, and in 1922 and 1923 the Lascar's Welfare League and the Indian Seamen's Association were established. Indians also developed organisations concerned with Indian independence such as the hostel India House that became the centre for political meetings and the dissemination of revolutionary ideas (Visram 2002). Indians were also integrated into British politics with Rajne Palme Dutt holding a leadership position in the Communist Party of Great Britain (CPGB) for 40 years, acting as a key ideologue and as a central figure in developing links with Indian communists in the struggle against colonialism (Callaghan 1990). Prior to Indian independence, organisations representing Indian peddlers were also established in the 1930s in Coventry. Setting themselves up as an Indian Workers' Association they supported the struggle against colonialism. Following the Second World War and the establishment of independence for India, an IWA was re-established in Coventry in 1953 with connections to the Indian Communist Party. Other less formalised forms of organisation also existed as a result of the 'colour bar' in housing. Exclusion forced community systems of support, where extended families and former village networks established 'mortgage committees' in order to share resources to purchase housing. Such committees still exist today. However, in their belief that they would return to their home countries many of the early IWAs fell into acting predominantly as social and welfare organisations.

The 1962 Commonwealth Immigration Act hailed the 'nationalisation' of racism (Sivanandan 1982:12). It led to many migrant workers inviting their families to Britain in the fear that they would be left divided by the changing laws. By inviting their wives and children, their desires and expectations for life in Britain changed. At the same time the rise of an aggressive street racism led to IWAs and other groups beginning to show 'vigour and initiative in combating racial discrimination and opposing racist immigration policies' (Hiro 1991: 139–40). In 1961 the Coordinating Committee Against Racial Discrimination was formed by Jagmohan Joshi of the IWA and the anti-fascist campaigner Maurice Ludmer. Acting as an external pressure group, it campaigned against the Immigration Bill and adopted an anti-imperialist perspective, with protests against the death of Patrick Lumumba in the same year. The following year another pressure group, the Conference of Afro–Asian–Caribbean Organisations was established, mainly playing a lobbying role in conjunction with the Movement for Colonial Freedom and the Labour Party against the Immigration Act and racism in Britain. Peter Griffith's racist electioneering campaign in 1964, 'If you want a nigger for a neighbour, vote Labour', saw the public articulation of racist attitudes by MPs. Following their victory in the general elections, the Labour Party, however, did not repeal the 1962 Immigration Act, but was later to strengthen it with the 1968 Kenya Asian Act that aimed to prevent Kenyan

Asians with British passports from entering the UK. The militant Racial Action Adjustment Society (RAAS) was also set up in 1965 following the visit of Malcolm X to Britain. These organisations represented a variety of conflicting approaches to organisation from lobbying to the radical external pressure group approach (Sivanandan 1982:11–16).

The increasing violence that was experienced by South Asians can be seen from documents such as the secretary of East Pakistan House's letter in *Peace News* in 1965, which noted that there was 'a growing mass hysteria against the Pakistanis' (Kabir quoted in Leech 1994). The rising racism is also discernible through the establishment of the National Front from the British National Party and the League of Empire Loyalists in 1967. The same year the Universal Coloured People's Association (UCPA) created another strong anti-colonial/'Black Power' organisation that offered a voice of resistance against the rising tide of racism and fascism which was crystallised in Powell's 1968 'Rivers of Blood' speech. The speech was a turning point in the mobilisation of a racist and fascist political agenda and fuelled the belief by racists in the legitimacy of their beliefs. The sight of dockers and workers at Spitalfields marching in support of Enoch Powell increased the demand for a strong anti-racist voice. It led to the establishment of the umbrella organisation, Black People's Alliance that marched against racism as the dockers marched for it. After 1968, levels of violence escalated and 'Paki-bashing' could not be seen simply as a pass time attributable to extremist groups. Paul Kelemen who was active in anti-racist politics in Sheffield in the 1960s recalls a Pakistani taxi driver who was knifed in 1968 and attacks on Yemeni workers in 1969 which the police did nothing to investigate (Kelemen 2006). In 1970 Derek Cox, a youth worker in Spitalfields wrote: 'The current racial problem in Spitalfields, and possibly the worst, is the growth of resentment against the Pakistani community... There is considerable "Pakibaiting" and "rolling" (robbing with violence) by some of the local young people. The situation is becoming both violent and unhealthy and is evident in the schools as well as the streets' (Cox 1970). Derek Cox's observations were not over stated. In 1969 and 1971, Pakistanis were murdered and robbed in East London. Despite appeals, the East London MP Peter Shore made no attempt to address the problem. This led the Pakistani Progressive Party with support from the Universal Coloured Peoples' Association to organise a demonstration in 1971 outside the House of Commons against the MP to try to raise awareness of the issue. Violence on the streets of Bradford was also apparent as Noorzaman Rashid, a member of AYM (Bradford) recalls: 'Before I was seven ... there was a huge demonstration in Bradford organised by the Muslim community about an accident, so-called accidental shooting of a Pakistani boy that pulled out a toy gun and was shot.'

Racist violence despite the term 'Paki-bashing' was not simply experienced by Asians, although South Asians were stereotyped as meek and docile and were seen as easy targets. Racist violence was also not simply perpetrated by gangs on the street but also by the police and state institutions. David Oluwale's story in Leeds is an example of institutional involvement in this aggressive racism which was perpetrated against non-whites in general. David was a Nigerian stowaway who came to Britain in 1949. After three years in Britain he was arrested and charged with disorderly conduct and assault on a police officer. Later he was sectioned and spent eight years in an asylum. David's experience with the police and hospital authorities was riddled with racism. His charge nurse pictured him as a brute with superhuman strength, and his nationality was recorded in police files as a Wog (Athwal 2007). It is no coincidence that David was first arrested by the police who were eventually implicated in his death in April 1968, the same month in which Powell made his inflammatory 'Rivers of Blood' speech against immigration. In 1969, the involvement of the state in racist violence was combated by the United Coloured People's Association with a march in Brixton against 'organised police brutality' (Sivanandan 1982:32). It was in this climate of increasing racism by the state and on the street, fuelled by the economic downturn of the early 1970s that the young people who were to form the AYMs grew up.

FIRST GENERATION ASIAN CHALLENGES IN THE WORKPLACE

As the state and the street became more violent, the parents of these young people also began to feel the brunt of the economic crisis in the work place as employers tried to change pay and conditions. Racism in employment had already been experienced by workers who were forced to accept the lowest paid, most dangerous jobs and unsociable working hours. Racial divisions in the labour force remained strong throughout the post war period. Asian and African Caribbean workers were often kept apart with ethnic groups being defined as good at certain types of activity (Miles 1982). In the textile industry the belief that Asians were 'nimble fingered' encouraged employers to recruit Asians. Racist concepts such as

Asians being 'plodders' and more docile were also applied (Jackson 1992). Such stereotypical attitudes led employers not to expect Asians to confront exploitation and inequalities. There is evidence that trade unions were complicit in the racialised division of labour with white workers operating the 'craft' sections of woolers and dyers and Asians doing the 'unskilled' machine minding jobs. This meant that in standing up for rights in the workplace, South Asian workers often took on conflict with both the employer and the trade unions (Ahmat et al. 1983). The first 'immigrant' strike at Red Scar Mill in Preston in May 1965 saw Asian workers, supported by the IWA, challenge management who were forcing them to work more machines. The strike exposed the collaboration of white workers with the union management. As such, black workers brought politics back into trade union struggles. The IWAs with their communist roots in workers' struggles influenced this focus on industrial struggles against racism, which were to become some of the most powerful acts of resistance in the 1970s. Strikes at factories such as Mansfield Hosiery, Imperial Typewriters and Grunwick Film Processing Laboratory became symbolic struggles for union recognition as well as being significant in the anti-racist struggle.

All three strikes were to expose union racism that had failed to protect the rights of black workers. At Mansfield Hosiery in Loughborough in 1972, Asian women workers had been denied promotion to the better paid jobs. In their struggle they had to confront the hostility of white workers in the factory as well as struggle independently for two months to force the National Union of Hosiery and Knitwear Workers to support them. It was only through local community action, political organisations and the support of Asian workers from other factories that the women were able to win their demand for access to promotion. J. Naik, a member of the strike committee commented on the lessons and experience for organising: 'If we have learned one thing in our years here, it's that we – are strong only when we stick together... All the time we tried to get unity with the white workers, but if we can't get that, we must first have unity among ourselves.' As Bunsee has commented, it became clear that '"unity" could never be achieved on a basis of racial inequality, on privileges for some and imposed inferiority for the rest. Racism therefore was not seen as something superficial or secondary which could be removed "at a stroke" by the application of a few "facts" but as a cancer embedded in the working class with deep, historical roots' (Bunsee 1973).

Some of the young people that formed the AYMs witnessed and supported the industrial disputes of the 1970s. In supporting strikes in the mid 1970s at Imperial Typewriters and at Grunwick, these young people saw the way in which their parents' generation confronted both the racism of the employer as well as the racism of the Unions. While the strike at Imperial Typewriters started on a conflict over pay, its focus soon shifted to confront the racism of the local Transport and General Workers' Union (TGWU) branch whose first response to the strike was to try to encourage the initial 38 workers back to work. Within a week, however, 500 workers were out on strike because as the Sunday Times reported, 'more than payslips, their complaints are about dignity'. As one worker commented: 'every morning when we come to work... we have to stand in a long queue to clock in... white women push past us and clock in first... The setters (all white) set the white women's machine first... We asked for waiting time but they wouldn't even give that to us. White women also get jobs of their choice. We have to do what the setter gives us' (Moore 1975 in AYM Manchester 1981a). The union continued to put pressure on the strikers to return to work. The overt racism of the union served to encourage the National Front to organise against the strikers. The mass pickets that were organised became a confrontation with racism and attracted support from anti-racist activists nationally. In challenging the racism of the unions, the workers at Imperial Typewriters and their supporters never contemplated establishing separate trade unions, 'Our struggle', they declared, 'has taught us that black workers must never for a moment entertain the thought of separate black unions. They must join the existing unions and fight through them' (CIS Report in Mahamdallie 2007). Mohsin Zulfiqar, who was later to help establish AYM (Manchester) in 1980, was studying in Nottingham and involved with a Black liberation organisation called Quatcha that organised support for the strikers. For Mohsin the strike was a prime example of 'community action – cum industrial action'. They raised substantial funds for food and basic necessities for the strikers. For students such as Mohsin Zulfiqar there was no choice but to mobilise the communities because the trade union officials were so hostile to the strikers and their demands (Zulfiqar 2006). Asian students organised alongside the Indian Workers' Associations and others to support the strikers.

By the late 1970s many of the trade unions had shifted their position and attitude towards Asian workers. They had little choice, as Mike Loft, an anti-racist and anti-fascist activist from Oldham, comments, 'As the textile unions went into decline the only potential for membership were the Asian workers because they then became the majority of the workers. So, [the unions] were quite pleased to accept the dues but they weren't at all keen on defending their jobs.' At Arrow Mill in Lancashire, for example, the management wanted speed-ups and shorter coffee breaks on the shifts that were essentially all-Asian shifts. 'The union rep was quite prepared to sell out the Asian workers if he could get a marginal advantage for the white workers.' Often Asian workers that had been drafted into the union would try to sell these deals to the shift, arguing that at least they had a job. Building links between white and Asian workers was difficult because the workforce was so segregated between shifts, with Asians primarily working 'the dead man's shift' which at one point even became called 'the Paki shift'. It was only in the final stages of decline when jobs were scarce that integration began to occur between Asian, white and the by then few African Caribbean workers in the industry (Loft 2006).

The strike that was to have the greatest impact on many of the young men who would later establish the AYMs was Grunwick's. Grunwick's was a strike not simply for wages or better conditions but for union recognition. As such, the dispute brought politics back into trade union struggles. It ran for two years between 1976 and 1978. The strike was led by Jayaben Desai – an East African Asian migrant whose passion and defiance towards the management of Grunwick's inspired her fellow workers as well as both the young and old who attended the picket line. While this was the first strike involving mainly Asian workers that the trade unions supported, community mobilisation again played a key role and was to inspire the young people that went down on the picket line. It was during this period that young Asians began to organise and set up their own organisations. Many actively supported the strike at Grunwick's, mobilising and attending pickets. Jayaben Desai's final speech to the strikers before it was called off epitomises values that the AYMs were to stand for in the future: the importance of resistance not just for an immediate cause but for future generations; the right for all human beings to live with dignity, and the importance of workers of all colours and creeds standing together: 'We have shown,' she said, 'that workers like us, new to these shores, will never accept being treated without dignity or respect. We have shown that white workers will support us' (in Dromey 2010).

SCHOOLING AND YOUNG ASIANS IN THE 1970s

The inequalities and degradations experienced by their parents at work was mirrored in the experiences of young people in school in the 1970s. Intimidation and violence in the playground went hand in hand with racism and colonial indoctrination by the educational establishment. The policy of the local council bussing Asian school children to schools outside their community to ensure that no school had 'too many' black kids and the relegation of most South Asians to 'immigrant' classes that focused entirely on the learning of English constructed black kids as a problem. The playground, like the street was also tinged with a general level of violence which left the youth with no alternative but to learn to defend themselves. The lessons that they learned about solidarity, self-organisation and resistance were ones that they took into the Asian Youth Movements.

Policies of bussing and the introduction of English language tuition were not introduced to service the needs of migrants but rather to ensure that the children of migrants did not interfere with the education of white pupils. The logic of bussing was similar to the logic of the immigration laws – as long as there were not too many, black people could be managed and 'assimilated' into the system. The recognition by the state of the inhumanity of shipping young children such large distances as well as the vulnerability that these children faced in terms of bullying and harassment as a result of their isolation was never considered. Noorzaman, who joined the Asian Youth Movement at 15 and acted as Chair of the organisation in the early 1980s, recalls the experience as a young child: 'I had a seven mile journey as a four and a half year old to school, which is unheard of today. You could go up Lumb Lane and find something like 15 buses that would bus literally hundreds of Asian children to all parts of Bradford.'

The focus on English language education for immigrant children through 'immigrant classes' at high school further segregated newly arrived migrants from their white counterparts and was invariably used as a system to ethnically divide pupils. Tariq Mehmood, a leading member of AYM (Bradford) and later a member of United Black Youth League and Pakistani Workers' Association, recalls the struggle to be permitted into mainstream education: 'I still remember very clearly I learnt to speak English and I was left still learning English... I had to get one of my uncles to come in, and he said to the teacher, I could speak English now, I could read it... why do I still have to remain in the stream learning English?' Even children of South Asian origin who were born in Britain were sometimes herded into the English classes as British-born Bhupinder Bassi, who helped organise Birmingham AYM, recalls:

> I remember when there was a sudden influx of lads from India. Up to that point no teacher had ever decided that my English was significantly weak and that I needed any kind of extra tuition or remedial tuition. Suddenly all these Indian kids arrived and I was told, 'Oh, you have to go with them.' ... 'But I speak English', 'No, no, you have to go with them' ... Amongst these children I learned how to play *gulli-danda*, to play *korada kabaddi* (which is *kabaddi* without the wrestling ... And I learned to play marbles and so on with Indian rules, you know. [Laughs].

Tariq's and Bhupinder's memories are just two of many that highlight the struggle that South Asian children encountered in trying to access education in a system that was structured to segregate them on the grounds of culture and ethnicity. Ironically, for Bhupinder the experience enabled him as a British-born South Asian to learn more about Punjabi culture and establish a strong sense of identity with newer Punjabi migrants. These experiences highlight the establishment's construction of South Asian culture and language as a source of problems for young people from the 1970s onwards (Benson 1996).

Racist white parents also campaigned in some localities for the removal of black kids from their children's schools as Balraj Purewal, a leading member of Southall Youth Movement, recalls: 'I never connected it at the time, but when I went to primary school there were lots of white parents outside the school shouting every time we would go in and it was because of that shouting I think I got sent to another school' (Purewal 2006). Walker has commented on the racist aggression of National Front (NF) members who handed out leaflets attributing mugging to black people and the presence of black students as having a detrimental effect on the level of education (Walker 1977:155). Some teachers also made racist assumptions about the ability of Asian pupils. There are many tales amongst pupils from this generation who were often forced to sit CSE exams rather than O-levels which prevented them from furthering academic studies (AYM Sheffield 1983:7).

Many teachers also showed a general hostility towards migrant children by making jokes about their origins and crushing their identity. Re-naming was a common experience. Jani Rashid, from

Bradford AYM, was renamed 'Johnny' and Suresh Grover, who helped set up the Southall Defence Campaign in 1979, was given the name 'Billy' by a teacher. There was no attempt to understand basic cultural or religious practises and on some occasions an outward hostility towards this was also manifest, as Jani recalls:

> my main recollection of (my first) school was that having told the school that I was a Muslim and I couldn't eat meat, because they didn't provide halal meat at the time, that on one particular occasion a teacher took sympathy with me, because I was purely eating vegetables. ... She took pity on the diet that I was on and decided to force feed me a sausage. So that was, that was [laughs], quite a traumatic experience really ... I was force fed a sausage at the age of six in infant school.

The curriculum was also Eurocentric and racist, which inevitably alienated black children. Anwar Qadir, from AYM (Bradford), comments on his attempt to negotiate between the colonial perspective taught to him in school and the Indian nationalist perspective that his father had raised him with.

> I remember coming home one day after a history lesson at school and sharing the information with my father about what I'd just been taught that day and my father, sort of, corrected me, not because he was that educated in historical facts of India but – his own experiences. And I was taught in my history lesson how good the Empire was for India, and 'we built the roads for the uncivilised people out there' etc. When I came and shared that with my father, my father says, 'well most of the roads were already there', right, 'some roads were built by the Raj, but they weren't built for the benefit of the Indians, they were built so that they could get the stuff out of India a lot quicker and more conveniently, and as far as civilisation is concerned, we were running around in silks when this lot was still in animal skins! So, I went back and shared that information with my school history teacher. I wasn't very popular with the teacher after that.

Anwar was in fact from Indian occupied Kashmir and he was acutely aware of his family being divided as a result of the occupation of Kashmir by India and Pakistan. In this recollection it is significant that Anwar highlights the main contradiction for him in Britain, which was a colonial one.

South Asian children experienced racism both in the classroom and the playground. School also became a physically violent experience for many Asian children and a place where they had to learn to defend themselves. Almost everyone I spoke to who went to school in the late 1960s and early 1970s recall incidents of racist violence. Suresh Grover, who was to become an anti-racist activist, went to school in Nelson in the late 1960s and remembers his fear of violence which he tried to combat by calling himself Gandhi. It did not stop the fights, however (Grover 2006). Saeed Hussain, a member of United Black Youth League and a defendant in the Bradford 12 case describes how school life was 'a bit of a prison, 'cos most of us would not actually venture into surrounding areas. If you went to the local shops you'd be constantly getting chased. Money got taken off you or you got beaten up'. Tariq recalls:

> ...we were attacked as we were going on buses, we were attacked when we got off buses. And the only way we could survive was to meet lots of friends from other schools. Perhaps that's why so many of us are still in contact till this day.

Tariq's recollection highlights the way in which organisation for many young Asians at the time was not a luxury which they elected into but a necessity born of circumstance.

One important point that was noted by a number of activists was that the attitudes of teachers and pupils was not homogenous and a few did stand up against racism. Shannaz Ali, a member of the United Black Youth League recalls:

> I remember it was near Christmas and we were doing stuff in the class to make things for Christmas. One of the kids said to me, 'Oh, go back to the jungle', or something like that. And there was this teacher, and it was interesting, I don't remember any of the names of all the other teachers but I always remember him. On one level I was quite frightened of him 'cos he was always quite strict and red-faced, Mr Wilkinson, and I remember him, kind of making a really big issue of it. He stopped the class and he said that, 'I'm not having any of that'... And I suppose that stuck with me because it was somebody standing up for me.

Shanaaz's memory and recollection of Mr Wilkinson's name is not by chance, but a powerful statement of the impact of solidarity. These experiences were to teach the youth the most effective ways to organise. Tariq also recalls white kids who did not want to take part in the violence:

> not all white children were rogues... I think that many many white kids were forced into fighting their own friends. I mean that happened with a very very close friend of mine who really didn't want to join the white kids when we had a fully fledged battle in the school.

The role that progressive teachers played in encouraging Asian kids to stand up against racism is also present in Saeed's recollections:

> most Friday afternoons, but particularly end of term or the last day before the holidays, were the very common Paki-bashing days. I think what maybe inspired us to change a little bit was that there was a particular English teacher ... and he was saying he would be giving out certain things, you know, results. And we said, 'Well, can't you give them out today? We might not be here on Friday'. And people were a little bit more open with him I think. And he took three or four of us to the side and said, 'I know exactly what's going on, you know. And I know why you won't be here, but you could ask why school doesn't do anything about it ... But I'm more interested in you, what can you do about it?' And I think that really kind of inspired us. Do we need to take a different approach? And we did. ... And I think that Friday afternoon we did go back to school... and there was about four of us who went to the local shop and there was this bully, he was on his own actually walking towards the shop. .... We kind of reached a point where we're literally a yard away from him and he stopped. And we stopped. And he did say, you know. 'Get out me way you fucking Pakis'. And we looked at each other and said, 'We're not going anywhere. If you want you can walk either through us or you can walk round us. It's your choice today.' And after about a minute's stare, he did walk around us... head down and just walked off. That was the most liberating experience I think. Something I will never ever forget.

Saeed's account gives testament to the emotional impact of learning the value of self-organisation and self-defence. This was to stay with him as he became involved in politics. The incident also highlights the way in which racist violence impacted on regular school attendance. The fact that no action was taken by the school authorities indicates how complicit many schools were with racism. The support of sympathetic teachers was not an isolated experience. Jani Rashid was also encouraged by a teacher to defend himself against a racist bully. Other young people were also forced independently to defend each other themselves. Anwar first organised in order to defend his brother, that was maybe the beginning of the journey.

GROWTH OF RACIAL VIOLENCE AND FASCIST MOBILISATION

In promoting their racist agenda, the NF fostered a surge in support by exploiting situations such as the expulsion of South Asians from Uganda by Idi Amin in the summer of 1972. They created a climate of fear and mistrust of the new migrants with support from the mainstream media. They deliberately targeted areas where Ugandan Asians were expected to settle in the 1973 local government elections (Husbands 1983:8–11). By the General Election campaign of 1974 the NF were fielding 54 candidates across England and had organised marches and pickets, causing controversy and making themselves into a household name. While they did gain 77,000 votes across the country, they did not retain their deposits in any of the constituencies. By fielding this number of candidates however, they were given access to airwaves like any major political party.' (Walker 1977:195). In 1976 this meant whipping up resentment already fuelled by press reports in the *Sun* which created a racist hysteria over 20,000 exiled Malawian Asians arriving in Britain. The NF picketed Heathrow and Gatwick along with provocative demonstrations in cities with large migrant populations like Bradford. The strategy of marching through black areas by the NF was a deliberate attempt by fascists to declare the streets as theirs, to mark black people as not belonging to Britain and target them as the cause of the 1970s economic crisis. The NF believed that street marches and street action would enable them to 'march and grow' through the media profile that they would initiate (Hayes & Aylward 2000). In the face of such aggression, for the young South Asians that had settled in Britain, there was no choice but to defend their homes and their communities.

Bradford

The establishment of the Yorkshire Campaign against Immigration in 1969 in Bradford, which eventually became the British Campaign against Immigration may explain why one of the first inflammatory marches through black areas by the NF took place in Bradford.

In local political circles, as Dave Stark, an anti-fascist campaigner and member of the Trades Council, mentions, 'Race was always on the agenda in Bradford from the early 1960s onwards. And there were disputes between Councillors, between political parties about immigration and about race' (Stark 2007). The NF had already marched on St George's Day in Bradford in 1975, which had caused debate and controversy (as shown in Bradford's local newspaper, *Telegraph & Argus* 22 April 1975, 26 April 1975, 28 April 1975). However, while they had marched down Lumb Lane in Manningham that year, they had not attempted to hold their meeting at a school in that area. Instead, they had marched to St George's Hall in the city centre. In 1976 they chose to hold a march and election meeting in a school in Manningham – the heart of the South Asian area. The BBC's decision to screen an anti-immigrant message from the British Campaign to Stop Immigration on its public access programme at this time also swelled the wave of racial tension sweeping Britain in 1976 (Walker 1977:195).

The prospect that fascists were going to march through Manningham meant the left and the South Asian youth of Bradford had no choice but to challenge the NF in as public and vocal a way as possible. The trades council and anti-racist groups along with black youth protested the NF march and meeting, demanding that 'They Shall not Pass'. They argued that the NF meeting had nothing to do with electioneering for the forthcoming elections but was simply provocative and that fascists did not have the right to a platform. Articles in the *Telegraph & Argus* after the event highlight the fact that the meeting mainly contained people from outside of Bradford rather than Bradford constituents (*Telegraph & Argus* 23 April 1976). On April 23 1976, young people in Bradford attacked and stoned police vans that were defending the NF march leading to a running battle between the youth and the police on Lumb Lane, with youth even freeing friends from police custody.

A number of former Asian Youth Movement members comment on fascist activity as a clear impetus to the development of an Asian Youth Movement:

> I think there was a feeling that there was a need for an organisation to come together to fight against the injustices that young Asians and the young Asian community were facing at the time. We'd picked up on the activity of the National Front and how they were mobilising and wanting to essentially repatriate the Asian community – all this talk about the Asian community stealing our

jobs, stealing our homes, stealing our women, that kind of stuff... and in fact, you know, in 1976 the National Front decided to hold a meeting in a school in the heart of where we lived and... that was my first recollection of a riot in Bradford basically, ... where police cars were turned over, paint was thrown at them, and being chased by police on horseback, And that was basically because they'd allowed the National Front, I think it was Martin Webster at the time, to come to Bradford and hold a meeting in a school in Manningham. So that was, I suppose, the first real campaign that I can recollect of any kind which was about defending our homes and our community basically, because that was where most of us lived. I lived on Lumb Lane.

For the Asian youth of Bradford, Manningham was their home and they were determined to defend it.

The key concern to defend their community can be seen by the differing positions taken by the Trades Council and 'community leaders' and the youth during the anti-fascist march and protests on 23 April 1976. As Race Today commented, 'for the organisers, Bradford Trades Council, the issue was mobilisation of massive opposition to the Front. The black community, on the other hand, incensed at the fascist invasion, were concerned with defending their home territory. As the counter demo moved out of the immigrant area, many black demonstrators stayed put. Those blacks who continued with the march into the city centre soon returned when they heard that violence had broken out at home.' (Race Today 1976). Manningham was a predominantly working class community with relatively cheap terraced housing, mills and factories and by the mid 1970s it saw the settlement of a sizeable Asian community. Most of those who were to become the key AYM organisers in Bradford had attended school in the area and had defended each other at school and outside from racism before they formed the youth movement. Out of 14 key activists whom I interviewed in Bradford, 10 lived in Bradford 8, the Manningham area, 2 were from Bradford 3 where the IWA were influential and 2 were from Bradford 7. The concentration of individuals from one specific community explains their focus on defending the community. The importance of defending Manningham was further highlighted by the NF announcement following the street violence on 23 April to hold a propaganda motor cavalcade through Bradford on 1 May. The left of Bradford answered this threat by establishing the Manningham Defence Committee. A sit down across Mannigham

Lane was organised and the National Front were forced to call off their demonstration.

The left's lack of action on 24 April, however, had disillusioned the youth. Tariq Mehmood's recollections emphasise the feelings that the young people had at the time:

> We saw them [the fascists] as coming to wipe us out, kick us out of our streets... or start the process and we weren't going to have it and there was a very big march against the fascists. And the march, the big anti-fascist march led by the leaders of that time ended in the city centre. Now we lived in Manningham, or lots of us lived in Manningham, we marched to Manningham... sneaked past police lines because Manningham was ours and we had to protect it. It was there that we really started thinking that we've got to get our own house in order, we can't have this, we can't leave our future in the hands of people like the community leaders or the Labour Party types who would try to take control of our future. We believed, we can fight and we can win. I think that would have been the seeds of where the Asian Youth Movements began to be formed.

The need to organise was further intensified by events in the following months.

Southall

The Race Relations Act of 1976, which proposed a tightening of the laws against racial hatred and forbade discrimination in housing, education, employment and private clubs, was exploited by the National Front as a reason to continue their attacks on black communities which continued in May and June of 1976. Media coverage in the *Daily Mail*, *The Sun*, *The Mirror*, *The Telegraph* and *The Express* regarding the arrival of 20,000 South Asians expelled from Malawi also fuelled a climate of racism and intolerance which went beyond the National Front. *The Sun* is thought to have started the press reaction with the headline; 'Scandal of £600 a week immigrant', followed by *The Mirror's* 'New Flood of Asians to Britain' and *The Telegraph's* sensational 'Invasion of Asians forces borough to call for help'. On analysis *The Telegraph* was actually referring to 525 individual nights' accommodation spent by Asian migrants in a year, but the small print was irrelevant in the hype that the headlines created. *The Express* added to the tirade with their headline: 'The passport to plenty – more Asians on the way to join 4 star immigrants'. The NF were quick to exploit the situation with pickets at Heathrow and electioneering activities in many urban areas that played on unsubstantiated fears. The impact of all this was to create the climate of racism which led to the fatal stabbing of Gurdip Singh Chaggar in Southall on 4 June 1976. As Kuldeep Mann, a resident of Southall, who later became a member of Manchester AYM, recalls, the murder had a profound impact on the community.

> I remember his death. I remember the shock in the community. It was a very vivid personal experience for me. We went to the Dominion Centre, which was a big cinema in those days, and his body was laid out there and we all went to look at it. Marched passed it and the community was very united in its grief and people were feeling very angry. Young people particularly were. That was a turning point I think in my memory and for a lot of people in Southall as well.

Like Bradford, youth in Southall saw no alternative but to organise. Chaggar's death on a main thoroughfare in Southall and outside the Indian Workers Association's Dominion Centre, a symbol of self-help, was seen as a direct attack on the South Asian community. While the first response was undirected violence and the stoning of cars by gangs of Asian youth (Grover 2006) as well as attacks on several whites including a Communist Party member and a Newsline photographer, by the next morning, the situation changed (Rose 1976). Asian Socialist Forum printed a leaflet declaring 'Racial Murder' and IWA (Southall) organised a public meeting to demand an enquiry and also suggested organising a march. Young people who were at the forefront in experiencing street violence however, wanted immediate action and thousands blocked the street the following day and marched on the police station demanding justice. The first response of the police was to arrest two of the demonstrators, including a young man who had been with Chaggar on the night of the stabbing. The youth staged a sit in to demand their release, which they achieved after hours of refusing to move. The following day the Southall Youth Movement (SYM) was formed (CARF 1981). The movement did not have a political agenda beyond protesting against the killing of Chaggar, 'but the imagination of developing a young people's movement spread like wildfire' and had a profound effect on young Asians up and down the country (Grover 2006). Jamal Hassan from the Bangladesh Welfare Association recalls the time when the Asian youth in Southall, 'took charge'. 'That was a turning point for Asians in the whole country' (Jamal Hassan in Eade et al. 2006). For Mohsin Zulfiqar, the protests in Southall 'really gave us the basis that direct action [does bring] positive results, hence our own ability to challenge the National Front by saying that we're prepared to fight against you physically, not just have demonstrations and pickets and so on.'

The authority of individuals in SYM was accepted 'because some of them already had reputations as good fighters and organisers against racism in the schools – particularly in the fights with skinhead gangs several years ago,' (Rose 1976:5–6) indicating the close link between school experience and the formation of the youth movements. SYM immediately acted to warn off self-styled anti-white gangs that were beginning to form and urged the youth to organise in self-defence against racism. As Balraj Purwal, a founding member of SYM recalls:

> we went round kind of giving support. ... trying to make these areas that were no-go open for all... and to make Southall a no-go zone for racists and that was pretty effective, just so many people, you know. We used to find out something about the racist parties, get a list of who the people are and then go and find them ... and we had a white colleague who we recruited to the National Front and he would get the leaflets and we would know which pubs they're meeting in. I remember going to one in Isleworth. They used to meet there and plan which estate to attack. There used to be 80–90 of us, you have to imagine the scale of numbers.

The legitimacy of SYM as a representative force for the youth was proved by their ability to mobilise in large numbers. In July 1976, they organised a mass sit-down in Piccadilly Circus when two of their number were arrested for chasing racists on the pavements and refused to budge until their comrades were released.

The direct action methods by the Southall youth were inspiring for South Asian youth nationally. The British left, as Rose notes, were confused by their approach because while organising against racism they declared a desire for 'no politics'. This was in response to financial corruption and undemocratic practices within IWA (Southall). It was also an approach to try to prevent the British left from controlling their organisation. Trotskyite groups in particular were always quick to try to recruit new members. Soon after the formation of Southall Youth Movement, Trotskyite groups went 'down to Southall on a recruitment raid.' The two crudest British based organisations, the Labour Party Young Socialists (Militant) and the Liberals with Peter Hain, failing to understand the conflict between the youth and the IWA, 'actually put Southall IWA speakers on their platform thinking this was the way to credibility – much to the mirth of the youth.' (Rose 1976).

Although SYM was never an elected body, and there were influences of street gang culture in the organisation, they represented Indian youth in schools, colleges, factories, temples and sports teams. The youth challenged the stereotype of the meek South Asian that was held by many in Britain. Even *Race Today* absorbed this stereotype, by titling an article: 'Are Asian Youth breaking the mould?' The Asian youth themselves 'took objection to that' as Mohsin Zulfiqar from Manchester recalls 'it was not a question of us breaking the mould, we had always said there have been two kinds of movements within the South Asian community in this country, one is revolutionary, one is compromising and moderate and so on.' The inspiration of Southall encouraged youth in Bradford to consolidate their nascent organisation and by the 1980s groups began to form in a variety of towns and cities.

AYM (Bradford), in contrast to Southall while coming out of the same experience of needing to defend their community against the fascists, was never primarily a self-defence force, but a well-organised group that campaigned and struggled for black rights on a variety of levels, from campaigning against the immigration laws as well as racism in housing and education to engaging with an anti-imperialist understanding of global politics. As Marsha Singh, a founding member of AYM (Bradford) noted, 'we wanted to be disciplined about what we did ... we didn't want to be a rabble, and I don't think we ever really were.' Bradford's approach to political action in turn influenced SYM. By 1979, their activities varied from self-defence work to pickets of meetings by Enoch Powell in Hounslow and social/welfare activities such as actions on homelessness, sports activities and the organisation of a youth club that was particularly well used by African Caribbean youth (Peggie 1979:175).

A belief in the validity of self-defence and direct action against racism and fascism encouraged youth from a variety of towns and cities to organise and work together over the following years.

This commitment to direct action was a defining feature of the youth organisations. In this they contrasted with for example the moderate, Labour Party focused approach of IWA (Southall) and the more trade union centred approach of IWA in Bradford. The IWA in Bradford however was to support the youth in the development of their organisation, indicating a complex relationship of influence and conflict between the new youth movements and the IWAs. AYM (Bradford), while inspired by SYM's street defence action, was to influence the development of AYM politics in other towns and cities to reflect an anti-imperialist and Marxist political identity.

3
The Movement Spreads

'Black people must unite, Here to Stay, Here to Fight!'
(slogan of the Asian Youth Movements)

During the late 1970s and early 1980s, youth movements developed in a significant number of towns and cities with South Asian populations. The emergence of these movements was often a response to local events but the national media coverage of resistance by Southall and Bradford youth in 1976 was to play a crucial role in inspiring others. Bradford in particular was central in the development of the youth movements across the country. Its significance lies in the evidence it provides of an organisation which was not simply a spontaneous response to fascist violence but an organised one that developed a disciplined cadre to promulgate their anti-racist and anti-imperialist ideology. It was the largest of the youth movements and while they recognised their strength in mobilising locally, they also saw themselves as facilitators for the development of youth movements in other towns and cities.

> Right from our first inception ... we wanted to build a national organisation... we had a lot of connections with each other anyway. A lot of youth were connected either through families, temples, mosques or Gurdwaras ... there were various connections. (Mehmood 2006)

In investigating the development of the youth movements, therefore, the specific context of Bradford will be explored in detail as an example of how one of the youth movements developed and networked nationally while operating in a localised setting and responding to Bradford's 'structure of feeling' (Williams 2001). Despite its size, the history of Asian Youth Movement (Bradford) has been less documented than the movements in Southall and East London. The latter movements found a voice in magazines such as *Race Today*, *Mukhti* and *Race & Class* that were all published from London. The history and development of AYM (Bradford) will act as an example to explore in detail the way in which the youth movements were influenced by the migratory experiences of a town, British left organisations, migrant organisations as well as the specific geographies and spaces of a town.

BRADFORD ASIAN YOUTH MOVEMENT

Migratory Experiences in Bradford and Their Influence on the Asian Youth Movement

Northern towns and cities in Yorkshire and Lancashire such as Bradford saw the migration of a large number of migrants primarily from rural areas of Azad Kashmir and Indian and Pakistani Northern Punjab (Cohen 2004). Asian workers came to Britain because colonialism had left the former colonies with labour, but the capital lay in the industrial metropolis. Bradford had the highest concentration of Asians in comparison with any other northern town. In 1964 there were approximately 12,000 Pakistanis in Bradford. By 1970 the approximate figure was 21,000 (Dahya 1974:83). These migrants were mainly employed in the wool and engineering industries. Of the ten members of Bradford AYM who I interviewed, (who were aged between 13 and 22 in 1976), all of their parents were employed in the mills and factories of Bradford, although some parents quickly moved on after saving enough money to establish their own businesses or took up jobs as bus drivers and shop keepers (Ramamurthy 2011a).

The migratory experience involved declassing for most Indian and Pakistani families, who before migrating had been involved in a variety of lower middle class professions but now had to turn to factory work. A significant proportion of the group included aspiring families and individuals. Anwar recalls: 'my father was a business man before he left Pakistan, and when he came here he started working in a foundry in the steel works. But he was there for a very short time, because he quickly got into his own business.' Two key AYM members in Bradford were grammar school boys, showing the commitment to social progress that their families held. The declassing experience and the desire to better themselves was an experience that Bradford Asians shared with Asians in other towns and cities.

This experience can be seen as a contributory factor in why young people organised and their need to establish a sense of self-worth.

The burning desire for self-betterment and to demand equal opportunities is also articulated by Anwar Qadir:

> it was almost a magnet pulling us all together, ... we were a generation who were expected to go in and do all the jobs where our parents had left off – but we were a generation that was saying we're not going to be doing that. Life has a lot more to offer to us than working in the foundries and the mills, and driving the buses and cleaning hospitals, so we were a generation that was saying 'no'. We were not the generation that was thinking about, well we've got family back home and we need to look after them etc., etc. Because our parents had done that. We were a generation that was saying 'no we won't take it lying down, no we won't do these jobs, yes we will want to have white collar jobs, yes, yes we want to be in management, yes we want to be in your colleges and teach, yes, we want to be in your schools and teach, and your banks'.

Bradford was the largest South Asian community in the north of England. By 1970 there were 260 immigrant owned and operated businesses in Bradford (Dahya 1974:90). The majority of these shops and businesses were in Manningham. The development of a significant number of shops and businesses signified a community sense of self-consciousness that established a space in Manningham that enabled South Asian migrants to support each other and survive, despite an environment where racism was endemic. The youth movement in their street patrols and campaigns to defend their community were involved in defending shops from racist attacks, especially those on Carlisle Road and Lumb Lane. Unfortunately the shopkeepers did not return this solidarity when the youth were arrested in the case of the Bradford 12, arguing that their business would be adversely affected if they did.

A Second Generation Organisation

The sense of home being in Britain, on the streets in which they lived rather than in the villages of Kashmir or Indo–Pak Punjab which were becoming distant memories was a key factor in the impetus to organise in Bradford and across the UK. A number of members commented on the feeling of being here to stay. As Tariq mentions:

> I/we were becoming conscious of the fact that whatever was going on has become our life, I wasn't going back that easily... We were

meeting lots of people and women were coming in as well, so it was a bit more of a family life developing at the time.

The arrival of women into the migrant community was an important shift in the way in which the community thought about itself. During the early 1960s, men outnumbered women by 40 to one. Many of the key members of the youth movements came to Bradford in the 1960s, when the number of families began to increase but the Asian population was still predominantly male. Many of the fathers of these young people had come to work first. Those who did bring children when they first came brought their eldest sons so that they would eventually be able to contribute to the family income and send money back home as soon as they came of age. An increasing number of families began to come to Britain in the mid 1960s.

As the children of migrants, the youth of different sub-continental communities were brought together. 'The interesting vivid memories', for Gurnam Singh, a member of AYM (Bradford), 'were how much the community were integrated in terms of different religious groups. People saw themselves as Sikhs or as coming from Africa or from the Punjab, but there was lots of intimacy amongst Muslims and Sikhs and Hindus... there was a sense of togetherness that really did inform my politics at a later time.' For some, like Anwar, this appeared as a continuity of experience:

> I grew up with my father talking to me about his youthful days, about how Diwali or Basant or the Eids were celebrated together in the community with genuine love for each other and my schooling was in such a community. So, when I joined the AYM this was a continuation of where I was coming from, attending meetings where people from all walks of life were coming together to campaign on issues around injustice to people. I felt that we were also celebrating our coming together.

Although the memory is a rather nostalgic one of a pre-partition past, Anwar uses it to express the way in which the youth tried to foster a unity that did not in fact exist in contemporary India and Pakistan:

> Although the British Raj may have created the partition, we had brought ourselves back together by going to the immigration demos and mobilising the whole community to attend these events.

This experience of unity was one that was fostered to combat the racism of Britain, as Mukhtar Dar who was later to work in AYM (Sheffield) recalled:

> I was there in Pakistan when the war between India and Pakistan took place, ...our village was very close to an oil refinery, and the oil refinery got painted, so there was a lot of nationalism, patriotism, that I grew up in... All I knew was India was this horrible place, which denied our very existence as Pakistanis. So when I arrived in England I just couldn't understand why my father was staying with Indians and Sikhs.

Mukhtar ended up having a fight with a young Sikh boy before understanding the very different conditions of Britain that demanded new alliances.

Although there was a search for cultural unity, the migratory patterns pertaining to Bradford meant that the organisation was heavily Punjabi in its cultural and linguistic identity because of the number of members from both India and Pakistan that spoke (what were regarded at the time) as various forms of Punjabi. Many originated from East and West Punjab or from Azad Kashmir where the culture and language was similar to Northern Punjab. This cultural and linguistic coherence was influential on the strong sense of identity amongst the youth. While they may have been from a variety of religious communities they shared a common culture. The organisation however was open to other cultural or religious outlooks and included Gujarati and South Indian members as well as young people from Malaysia. The movement had members from all the major faiths in South Asia.

The Influence of the IWA and the British Left on the Formation of AYM (Bradford)

The first organisation to be formed in Bradford in 1977 was the Indian Progressive Youth Association (IPYA) with support from one of the IWAs in Bradford. Socialist and trade union organisations as well as the Indian Workers Association (Bradford), which was deeply integrated within the trade union movement in the UK and had links with the Communist Party of India (Marxist–Leninist), were influential on the development of the movement. The nature of one of the IWAs in Bradford contrasted with that of IWA (Southall) where greater conflict and friction emerged between the elders and the youth. IWA (Southall) was much more pro-establishment, and had a history of supporting the Labour Party as highlighted by DeWitt (1969:158–9). Bradford had two IWAs reflecting the split in the Indian Communist Party first into CPI (Marxist) and then CPI (Marxist–Leninist). One of the two IWAs in Bradford was Marxist–Leninist influenced and linked to IWA (Jagmohan Joshi) in Birmingham which had condemned the Labour Party's immigration strategies in the 1960s and had been instrumental in the development of the Coordinating Committee Against Racial Discrimination. Supportive of militant activity against fascists as well as strike action in the workplace against discrimination, this IWA influenced the youth. The predominantly Azad Kashmiri and Pakistani population did not have large workers' organisations (supported by communist party's in South Asia) that could support the development of a youth organisation.

In providing guidance for the youth as they began to organise, IWA (Bradford) first encouraged the formation of the Indian Progressive Youth Association. This influenced the youth in the structure of their organisation with the development of an executive committee as well as ordinary membership. The Indian Progressive Youth Organisation ran for one year from 29 May 1977. The organisation tried to participate in council politics through affiliation with the Bradford Community Relations Council and also raised awareness about the increase in violence against youth by organising a public meeting on Youth against Racialism on 12 August 1977. The meeting had speakers from IPYA, Bradford CRC and the Grunwick Strike Committee. They also provided transport for young people caught in violent racial harassment at Rawson's Hotel, Bradford and the Duchess of Kent when the NF and Teddy Boys confronted black youth in those establishments (IPYA 1977). The IPYA also realised the importance of data collection and tried to monitor racial harassment through collecting press coverage from the local and national press.

The need for a youth organisation which was Left and 'black' led however, could not be fulfilled by the IWA in Bradford because the community was mainly Pakistani and Kashmiri. As Jani Rashid commented: 'we were going around knocking on people's doors and asking them to join the Indian Progressive Youth Association... the feedback we were getting was... "well, you know, we're not Indian, were Pakistanis" ... So we very quickly within a year I think.... changed it from Indian Progressive Youth Association to the Asian Youth Movement.' There was a consciousness within the youth of the need for an independent organisation. IPYA was more like a youth wing of the IWA and for some former members like Marsha were an attempt to try to control the movement, 'so at the first AGM we made sure they (IWA) couldn't hijack it and we changed the name to the Asian Youth Movement'.

The Asian identity in the development of Bradford therefore rather than being a term of exclusivity was a term selected for inclusivity since it arose out of the dysfunctional nature of the term Indian in the context of Bradford. Calling themselves Asian defined what they were trying to do and that was to organise the Asian youth of Bradford. They worked with other anti-racist organisations in Bradford such as Bradford Black who were mainly active in organising the African Caribbean community. Bradford was the first town to use the term 'Asian'. Southall had identified themselves with their locality. As Balraj Purewal recalled: 'We called ourselves Southall Youth Movement because we were not a minority in Southall. Saying "Asian" made it sound like we were a special thing but we were the youth of Southall'. By identifying with their locality they were also able to invite African Caribbeans to work with them although in reality they organised amongst South Asians.

The influence of communist organisation had a profound influence on AYM Bradford and the way in which it developed and ran itself. This can be seen as a continuation of IWA influence. The IWA's influence on the youth is recalled in Tariq Mehmood's novel *Hand on the Sun*, where the young man Jalib clearly values the advice of the old comrade Dalair Singh: 'we must make our history into a weapon. We must learn from each defeat' (Mehmood 1983:88). The close links can also be seen in *Kala Tara*, where AYM published an interview with Jagtor Singh Sahota, when he became the regional secretary of TGWU in 1979 (AYM Bradford 1979:12). Strategies of direct action that the youth employed were supported by the IWAs and sections of the left. Dave Stark, a local trade unionist and anti-racist campaigner in Bradford, has remarked on the way in which the left and IWA worked together to support the fight against fascists through the strategy of direct action:

When the National Front began to move into Bradford, they held meetings, they held marches, it would have been a mix of trade unionists including members of IWA, Asian, black and white students, ... it was always direct action... there was a tacit agreement that you should confront the National Front and not just talk about it... any time they appeared.

The influence of the left can also be seen through the previous political experiences of three key members of AYM (Bradford), who were formerly members of white left, Trotskyite organisations before developing the AYM. Marsha worked in Militant, Tarlochan Gata Aura, a member of AYM and later UBYL, was a member of the Workers Revolutionary Party and Tariq was a member of International Socialists before establishing the Asian Youth Movement. Two of these individuals related tales of being used as the token Asian and their frustration with the privileging of class politics at the expense of issues of race. This was the experience of many black activists during the 1970s and earlier. It was recognised by CPGB's Trevor Carter as a failure of the left to make adequate links with Black workers (Alleyne 2002, Smith 2010). Tariq Mehmood recalls his experience in International Socialists (IS), which he felt a lot of affinity towards partly because they seemed to have a lot more Asian people with them, but he quickly felt used as the 'token' black.

> once they asked me to speak on racism. I must have been one of the few non-whites in Bradford in the organisation at that time. ... I just had no idea how to articulate what racism was, I knew how to fight it because I didn't have a choice, I couldn't articulate the theoretical concepts.

For Marsha Singh who had been involved in Militant as well as Labour Party Young Socialists, the experience was similar.

> I thought, 'what were they doing to me anyway?' Were they just using me as: 'we've got a black activist here!' ... They put me on platforms and things like this, and then it sort of dawned on me that I was a tool for them in one way or another... and I thought ... we haven't got a body which is organising around issues [of racism] for us and by us.

This opportunism led to Tariq questioning the basis of Trotskyism's idea of 'world revolution'. It was obvious to him as it was to all those that had seen and experienced the poverty of their countries of origin, that socialism in one country would bring tremendous benefit to workers and peasants living there:

> I just couldn't get answers from the theoreticians within IS... I wanted a socialist world because I felt, 'that's our only future'.

And by socialism I understood things differently to my white colleagues. I believed we could build socialism in one country. For me the idea of socialism means that somebody didn't have to leave their mother and go thousands of miles away, to have electricity, to have water, to go to school near where you lived and for all of you to have work, but we had all that in England... (with struggles)... but I was thinking of back home in my village and I said 'no', my concept would be to get what we've got here. It didn't make sense to say no, the revolution has to be global.

The lack of attention which large sections of the trade union movement and the British left gave to the issue of racism, along with the lack of a migrant workers organisation which truly represented the population in Bradford influenced the kind of organisation that these young people developed. In this they were supported and influenced by groups and individuals that had begun to see the secondary contradictions of racism in the working class movement as important.

The conflict between the white left and the AYMs was not simply related to the left's sidelining of the struggle against racism, but also related to how that struggle should be pursued. The left's lack of strategic interest in preventing fascists from marching through Manningham had already created a conflict over the importance of direct action. While the left slogans against the National Front proclaimed 'They Shall not Pass', they had let this happen in 1976. 'I couldn't live with that then. I just thought it was a betrayal of everything they were supposed to have taught me...' (M. Singh 2006). The same conflict was to become apparent again in the actions of the Anti-Nazi League and their failure to defend Brick Lane in 1978.

Geographies and Spaces

While social and political influences were key factors in the way the youth organised, spaces in Bradford city centre such as the library and Fourth Idea Bookshop cannot be underestimated. The central library in Bradford had a café which became a focus for ad hoc meetings and educational discussions. It was accessible for young people all over the city and walking distance from Manningham. It was a public space that enabled the youth quite profoundly. Tariq, who was estranged from his family, practically lived in the library and he associates this with his growing class consciousness.

... I had the library to stay in, so I had the advantage over others in that sense. They were grounded in school and stuff... But I'd be in the library as soon as it opened. I'd be there until it closed. ... I just read a lot, I had nothing else to do during the day... didn't have family, didn't have a home, I just read as much as I could. I began to understand that the world I lived in was really fundamentally unfair. I began to understand that this country was rich because we were poor and I also began to understand that we were here because they were there and I really believed that.

The library for Tariq as a young man without a family life became a sanctuary and as a result the library became a space to meet and discuss. Outside the boundaries of state schooling, the youth were able to access resources to question the colonial histories and ideas they were fed in formal education. The value of this education is highlighted by Gurnam Singh:

Sometimes I'd go to the library in the evenings as well as after school. Or actually slam from school, miss classes and end up in the library. Which I mean, I think back to that, and I think that was something to do with developing a critical education.

...We used to kind of go in the library cafe when it opened in the morning, ... We didn't have much money so we'd all buy a cup of tea ... just to prove that we were bona fide. ... we used to share what we were reading and then it would get into disputes about certain politics, and I would say, 'Go and get the book'. And so the library was like our kind of reference. ... I can remember reading *Capital*, Marx's *Capital*, and discussing that and talking about Gramsci and all these other people and becoming politicised. And this was around the age of 16 to 17.

For Gurnam and others it was in the library where a real education was taking place.

Near the library, the Fourth Idea Bookshop, run by Reuben Goldberg of the International Marxist Group, also provided a space of inspiration. There was a printing facility and Tariq recalls 'that the place really provided us with a lot of support, ideological support, support with ideas...'. These memories indicate the importance that the youth placed in educating themselves about politics and injustice. Such an education and the influence of migrant workers organisations as well as other socialist groups gave AYM (Bradford) the ability to organise in a more sustained capacity than some of the other youth movements.

The Aims and Working Practices of AYM (Bradford)

From the start the AYM (Bradford) had a developed set of aims and objectives – partly a result of their initial ties to the IWA as well as their experience in left organisations, where despite differences key members learnt the power of discipline and organisation. AYM (Bradford) adopted the aims and objectives that had been drawn up by what was first called the Indian Progressive Youth Association: 'To promote the interests of young people from the countries of (or originating from) the Indian sub-continent, i.e. Bangladesh, India, Pakistan, and Sri Lanka, in the areas of political, cultural, social and sports activities.' They established the organisation from the start as an anti-racist, anti-sexist, anti-imperialist organisation opposing 'all forms of discrimination based on race, colour, sex, religion etc., and to promote the cause of equal rights and social and economic opportunities.' Despite the racism of the trade union movement the AYM recognised the importance of workers unity: and that 'the only real force in British society capable of fighting racialism and the growth of organised racism and fascism is the unity of the workers movement – Black and White'. At the same time they acknowledged the need to 'fight against racialist elements and influences within these organisations' (AYM Bradford 1979:13).

The contradictions that existed within the working class movement meant the AYM did not adopt the slogan: 'black and white, unite and fight'. Such a slogan suggested that both parties were equal and that both blacks and whites were equally responsible for racism and the divisions that were creating disunity. In establishing their own slogans they adopted the rhythm and tenor of the previous slogan but focused on their role in organising their own communities: 'black people must unite, here to stay here to fight!' The AYMs had a black fist set in a red ideology. They believed that they were the best suited to organise in their communities and wished the white left to support the struggle against racism by taking on the difficult task of organising against racism in white communities:

> an argument that we had with our white comrades was that they should go to white areas to organise. They wouldn't do that. We couldn't do that 'cos sometimes we'd get bricked and [the left] would come to try to organise us and we felt they'd got it

the wrong way round, they should go where the racists were. (Mehmood 2007)

The failure of the British left to take this task seriously was to leave white working class communities easy prey to racist and fascist mobilisation.

The aims of AYM (Bradford) also affirmed support for national liberation movements worldwide, particularly Ireland, Palestine and South Africa. They also strove 'to keep members informed of political, economic and social developments in the Indian sub-continent' and 'to encourage solidarity with and support for the struggles of the oppressed masses' in those states. The sophistication of their aims and objectives were in many ways different to the usual formation of a youth movement which often emerges at a moment of crisis, as Southall did and then formalises as it develops (Castells 1983).

The formality and discipline of AYM (Bradford) was commented on by more than one member. They talked of how they operated almost like a communist party and how individuals had to apply for full membership.

> the AYM recruited members a bit like a Communist organisation in the early days. They had to be nominated. You couldn't just turn up and say 'I want to join'. Someone had to propose you, you had to be on a probationary period, the Executive Committee had to discuss your membership, your membership would then have to be approved after your probationary period was over, if you misbehaved or didn't stand up to the aims and objectives, you were warned and brought in front of a disciplinary committee and you were disciplined and thrown out if need be. We were building a cadre based body and probably at our height, we might have had a couple of hundred members... we were also discussing whether we should take on the Indian Workers' Association type of a structure which had an inner body that were part of the Association of Indian Communists which was more of a Marxist Leninist body ... or whether we should have a mass body and just fight our corner on the executive committee. (Mehmood 2007)

Such developed procedures indicate the seriousness with which the youth in Bradford took their work. They were not a gang, responding at the heat of the moment, but an organised group with clear aims and working practices that had been agreed following

KALA TARA

PAPER OF ASIAN YOUTH MOVEMENT BRADFORD.   No. 1.   20p.

3.1   Cover of *Kala Tara* (*Black Star*) Magazine, 1979, Asian Youth
Movement (Bradford) (courtesy former members of AYM
Bradford), SC2.

discussion and debate. In order to maintain discipline, Bradford
(and later AYMs in Manchester and Birmingham) had very firm
rules and practises to avoid any activity that would bring the
organisation into disrepute. They were not allowed to drink, for
example, before meetings or during political activity and they were
not allowed to date girls from families with whom the AYM were
campaigning. The behaviour of members however was a recurrent
issue of concern and was debated in AYM meetings. This approach
was very different to Southall which was almost entirely based
around a street politics of self-defence and where there does not
appear to have been the formal discipline which you would find in
a communist party. There was however extreme loyalty between
members in Southall as was appropriate for an organisation that
was involved in street level defence.

In order to prevent white left organisations from infiltrating
the group, AYM rules asserted that no member was permitted to

join any political party while holding membership of the Youth Movement. This included the Labour Party. The reasons for this were clearly understood as Marsha Singh explained:

> we had a policy that another member of a political party including sects... couldn't join, and the reason for that ban was because then the AYM would become a factional dispute between somebody who joined from RCP [Revolutionary Communist Party], from Militant, somebody who joined from IS... it'd become a debating chamber for their activists who'd infiltrated us, not a body of equals with no other agenda... so it was banned. But we were quite willing to work closely with anybody so long as they didn't try to dictate the agenda, and I think a lot of them were quite opposed to us, because in their view we should have been with them... the Militant position was... race doesn't matter it's all about class, ... well of course class is a central determinant to everybody's life, but race is an added feature to class and it sometimes requires a different response.

It is ironic that while Marsha articulated this position so clearly in reflecting on the AYM experience, it was he who betrayed this position (unknown to his fellow comrades) by maintaining his membership of the Labour Party even while acting as chair of the AYM for three years (Marsha Singh 2006).

AYM (Bradford) had about 200 paid-up members working and organising, along with hundreds of supporters. They ran successful anti-deportation campaigns, campaigns against racism in the police, racism in education as well as struggling against street racism. Its size and influence was far larger than any other Asian youth organisation. The size and influence of AYM (Bradford) meant that they were able to sustain themselves as an organisation right until 1986/7, although the organisation changed in its nature as it grew older, establishing itself more as a community centre than as an agitating and campaigning body. Although politics was at the heart of their work, the youth movement also organised a Cricket club and had a pool table in their office on Lumb Lane to provide a forum for social activity through which to engage other young people. From its inception AYM (Bradford) worked to build links with emerging organisations in other towns and cities and although the AYMs never consolidated themselves into a national body, Bradford in particular worked to try to develop such an organisation. They named themselves Asian Youth Movement (Bradford), to identify themselves as part of a large whole, a concept that was taken up by Manchester and Sheffield, who also put the city name in brackets calling themselves Asian Youth Movement (Manchester) and Asian Youth Movement (Sheffield) in order to identify themselves as part of a larger whole. Bradford produced the magazine *Kala Tara* to disseminate their ideas and youth from Bradford travelled across the country to build support networks. They shared their experiences of struggle and their commitment to organise independently. In the months and years that followed organisations were formed in a variety of towns and cities including East London, Haringey, Bolton, Blackburn, Manchester, Sheffield, Birmingham and Luton.

BRICK LANE

In 1978, fatal racist attacks in the East End forced Bangladeshi youth on Brick Lane to organise. In May, Altab Ali, a young Bangladeshi factory worker, was stabbed by fascists while he was returning home from work. 'It was not just any night. It happened on local election night in May 1978, when the National Front politically... hardly existed but they were agitating and organising. They stood a National Front candidate in every single ward, so there were 50 candidates standing for the NF' (Dan Jones in Eade et al. 2006:65). A number of organisations emerged in the East End of London to organise the community, particularly the youth. These included the Anti-Racist Committee of Asians in East London, the Bengali Housing Action Group, the Bangladeshi Youth Front, the Bangladeshi Youth Movement, the Progressive Youth Organisation and the Bangladeshi Youth Association (Eade et al. 2006, Leech 1980). In the East End of London the majority of young Asians were Bangladeshi and organised around this identity, which was particularly strong because of the struggle for independence of Bangladesh in 1971.

There were a number of different organisations and schools of thought that vied for influence after Altab Ali's death, those that saw themselves as 'community-type welfare organisations' and those that saw themselves as 'socio-political organisations'. The Youth Front, for example, saw the need to challenge things politically and included a number of individuals who were quite experienced with politics and had been involved in politics in Bangladesh (Nooruddin Ahmed in Eade et al. 2006:59). 'There was a degree of competition about who [was] more authentic and who [was]the more politically aware', as John Eversley highlights, and 'there were certainly those who aligned themselves with progressive political movements and [those] who were backward and who were more self-interested' (in Eade et al. 2006:61).

Nooruddin Ahmed describes the formation of the youth movements as 'a spontaneous response of the Bangladeshi community with support from the host community and a number of other communities who felt threatened by racism at that time. So it was a movement rather than anything organised'. The response in the East End in 1978 was similar to the spontaneous response in Southall two years earlier and saw a similar conflict between the desire by many young people for direct action and the attempt by community leaders to cool the situation down. As Bradford's *Kala Tara* documented: 'the first ad hoc committee ... basically saw the fightback in terms of a mass demonstration that being the sum total of their political activity'. Racist attacks however they argued do not go away as a result of a demonstration. 'Racism has to be put in its historical context and an organisation born that can at least deal with some aspects of this monster' (AYM Bradford 1979:7).

Members of AYM (Bradford) supported Bengali youth in the East End in establishing the Bengali Youth Front (Testimony of Kenneth Leech in Bradford 12 Internal Bulletin 1982 9:4). They saw a similarity in patterns of second generation conflicts that they had experienced in Bradford, while also recognising the specificity of experience:

> We went over, we had the basic organisational skills, ... there were a number of murders in East London ... In those days Brick Lane wasn't buzzing, it was very run down, and there was a meeting following the murder... And the old man in Brick Lane was saying almost the same sort of stuff as the old men in Bradford, the only difference was that they were speaking Bengali in Brick Lane ... I was part of those people who said that what we need to do was not to listen to the police ... the youths are the only ones capable of defending Brick Lane and that's what they should do... we had lots of conflicts with elders, but really to the credit of the youth they organised and they had far greater mobilizing power than we did in Bradford really, because they lived much closer and they felt the injustice of what happened. (Mehmood 2006)

While young people took the lead in the organisation of what was to become a significant part of anti-racist history and the history of Tower Hamlets, they did not break entirely from the older generation as Nooruddin Ahmed recalls: 'people experienced in the organisation of a demonstration, lobbying MPs at the Houses of Parliament, giving petitions... the 1971 movement [for Bangladeshi independence] affected what happened in 1978 and subsequently as well. So those were transferable skills and young people... learned from [the elders]' (in Eade et al. 2006:64).

The youth organisations in the East End quickly realised the importance of unity and despite their differences worked to support the establishment of the Federation of Bangladesh Youth Organisations (FBYO), who jointly called a 7,000 strong march in protest at Altab Ali's death. They did not just liaise with organisations in Tower Hamlets but also nationally, particularly with youth organisations. This included Southall Youth Movement, Asian Youth Movement (Bradford) as well as Haringey Asian Action Group. As Nooruddin highlights: 'We thought "OK, we have got so many youth organisations, not only in Tower Hamlets but in other parts of London, as well as in other parts of the country. Therefore we need to provide a united platform."' Altab Ali's death was significant because it mobilised the community. Dan Jones recalls how 'about 7,000, mostly Bengali, carried the coffin to Downing Street as a protest'. Tariq remembers the atmosphere: 'it was very tense, very emotional because really that could have been any of us, he wasn't killed because he did something. He was killed simply because of the colour of his skin'.

Altab Ali's death and Ishaque Ali's death a few months later raised the importance of self-defence for young Asians at the time. The police indifference and inadequate response to racist attacks had been keenly felt for some years. As Aloke Biswas, a social worker in the East End during the 1970s recalls:

One of the things that comes to mind is the role of the police... people have been beaten up and murdered... we went to the police and the police took the attitude that, 'What can we do?' ... 'Do you know who has done it?' How could we know, because it happened at one o'clock in the morning? They said: 'Then what do you want us to do?'... and there was the time when we said 'Right if you can't defend us, then we will have to defend ourselves.' (in Eade et al. 2006:80).

Police indifference was an experience that was witnessed again and again.

While believing in the importance for self-defence, the vast array of organisations that emerged after Altab Ali's death indicate the attempts that were made by the state and various political authorities to channel and contain the discontent and anger felt by the Bengali community as well as a recognition that the status quo could not be maintained. As Terry Fitzpatrick, founder of the squatter's movement and campaigner for Bengali rights in the 1970s highlighted,

> One of the things that I remember about the 1970s was this huge violent confrontation on the street... the National Front could put thousands [of] people on the street for a march... They saw that the way to raise racial tension was activity on the street... what they did was they created an atmosphere, in which... [they would say about] families [who] moved in: 'Let's go and kick them out. Let's go and smash their windows', [so] apart from the homeless Bangladeshis that wanted to squat... people just had given up, saying kids couldn't go to school, women would have their saris pulled off in the streets. People were just abandoning the tenants. I lost count of the number of rent books I have taken back to the council and said, 'here is another one gone.' (in Eade et al. 2006:79)

The reaction of the GLC was mixed and ill thought through with ghetto housing policies initiated in an attempt to deal with the problem of violence through simplistic solutions of separation (Copsey 2000).

The failure of the British left to defend communities was again a reason for Bengalis to organise independently. In August 1977 anti-fascists including the Socialist Workers Party fought the National Front on the streets of Lewisham in what became known as the Battle for Lewisham. In November of that year, the Socialist Workers Party formed the Anti-Nazi League (ANL) with the aim of engaging as many people as possible in the politics of anti-fascism. Coupled with the highly successful Rock Against Racism (RAR) carnivals up and down the country they certainly achieved this objective, with thousands of young people attending carnivals organised by RAR and the newly formed ANL (Renton 2006). The engagement, however, was at a very limited level; 'we can't dance racism away', as one AYM activist highlighted. The ANL's attempt to disseminate anti-fascist propaganda while successful in the distribution of over 5 million leaflets in their first year was limited in its effect at tackling racism because of the focus on Nazism. In concentrating on comparing the NF with Nazi's and through using images of concentration camps and Nazi troops with the slogan 'Never Again' and 'the National Front is a Nazi Front!', they represented the NF as 'sham patriots' and therefore reinforced patriotism. Paul Gilroy argues that their tactics even shut down the broader space of RAR because it 'located the political problem posed by the growth of racism in Britain exclusively in the activities of a small and eccentric, though violent, band of neo-fascists' (Gilroy 1987a:133). RAR also failed to involve South Asian activists and South Asian music in its cultural repertoire, cancelling an event in Southall with Asian music on the bill (Street 1986). In this way, many organisations from the Revolutionary Communist Group to the Asian Youth Movement and the Institute of Race Relations saw the ANL tactic as supporting the British imperialist state and deflecting attention away from, for example, the racism of the immigration laws (Copsey 2000:135).

Through the ANL, as Yaffe argues, 'the SWP divert[ed] attention from the racism of the British state and the Labour Party by urging all to unite with Labour politicians and trade union leaders to crush the National Front' (Yaffe 2001). The ANL initiative also drew the energies of the left away from broad based initiatives such as the National Coordinating Committee of Anti-Fascist Organisations and the All London Anti-Racist Anti-Fascist Coordinating Committee. 'Just when the anti-racist movement was doing very well and developing', Tariq recalls,

> CARF had developed, lots of Asian Youth Movements were developing in many cities, there were joint anti-racist committees where white organisations, workers groups, women's groups, left groups, youth groups, IWAs, people like that were working together around broad anti-racist work and unity, SWP launched the Anti-Nazi League and it really divided us in many ways. We felt that what was important was to consolidate the broadest possible anti-racist movement in Britain, by definition it would be anti-fascist – we didn't have to play up to Dad's Armyism... British imperialism fought the Nazis, therefore the British people were naturally anti-Nazi, we thought they were playing up to British chauvinism.

The glamour events of the carnivals were to lead to a deflection which enabled the National Front, the very organisation that the

ANL were trying to combat to march almost unopposed on 30 April 1978 in the East End of London, a month before Altab Ali was killed. 80,000 anti-fascists gathered in Trafalgar Square and marched to Victoria Park in the East End of London. A day later the NF marched from the West End to Hoxton in the East End. The organisers had been aware of the planned National Front demonstration, since the International Marxist Group and the All London Coordinating Committee Against Racism and Fascism had informed SWP, ANL and *Searchlight* on Wednesday 26 April. *Searchlight* confirmed through other sources that the NF were planning a March on the Friday. Members of the Hackney Committee Against Racialism (HCAR) tried to get the organisations participating in the carnival to produce a leaflet for circulation at the march calling for a mass mobilisation on May Day against the NF march:

> We were met with virtually a blank wall. When we made approaches to get an announcement made from the platform at the Carnival the organisers refused to do so, on the grounds that there wasn't time to organise a counter-demonstration that they could effectively control. (HCAR 1978)

According to Graham Lock any calls that were made at the carnival elicited little response. 'People preferred to lie in the sun and listen to music' (Kalra et al. 1996:143). Opposition to fascist meetings and rallies in fact declined in 1978 according to HCAR. 'At the Ilford by-election the picket was about 2,500, at Bristol the opposition was less that 1,000, on May Day the opposition was nil' (HCAR 1978).

In the summer of 1978 the attacks reached a climax, as John Newbigin, a youth and community worker in the East End, recalls:

> There was a good deal of open intimidation on the street – women and children being shouted out, people having bricks put through their windows, shit put through their letter boxes, clothes drying on the line would be cut with razors, cars would be damaged. An incredible level of violence and the response of the police was absolutely pathetic. The police did virtually nothing. (In Eade et al. 2006:80)

The criticism of ANL was to prove well-founded when they organised the second carnival in London in September 1978. Once the carnival had been announced, the National Front publicised a march through Brick Lane on the same day. While some members of the ANL argued that more attention needed to be given to preventing the fascists from marching, the attitude of the carnival organisers was focused on their own activities. One of the organisers, Jerry Fitzpatrick argued, 'Even if we had sent more numbers to Brick Lane, it couldn't have been enough. The police always had it covered. The Front were contained. ... We had to keep our eyes on the prize which was the carnival' (in Renton 2006:133). It is ironic that he used a phrase that was so iconic for the civil rights movement to limit the dream to a carnival.

The ANL position was not possible for the youth of Brick Lane who were not trying to make a political gesture but had no choice but to defend their community. The police clearly did not always 'have it covered'. Altab Ali had been killed in May and Ishaq Ali a few weeks later. When the police did come they were known to often arrest the victims, as the case of the Virk brothers in 1977 had proved. Attacked by racists when they were trying to fix their car, the Virk brothers called the police to find that the attackers were freed and they were placed under arrest. Their conviction for GBH in 1978 gave further proof of the need for self-organisation. The attitude of carnival organisers left a bitter taste in the mouth of the youth, as Tariq Mehmood recalls:

> We found out that the fascists had planned to attack Brick Lane. ... They used to have paper sellers at the bottom of Brick Lane and they wanted to consolidate that area... They were going to gather around there and we felt that they would charge up the road and attack people in the streets. It was really terrible because it was also the same day as the ANL organised this Rock Against Racism concert. ... Really the Carnival should have diverted as a historic gesture and wiped out the fascists from the street but SWP didn't seem to work like that. The Carnival wasn't interested and they refused to let people go and we heard that they were saying that there was more than enough people already in Brick Lane. In fact, on Brick Lane we were worried in case we were overtaken by fascists. We had youths at different points of Brick Lane constantly keeping in touch with the telephone hub and we had runners as well, somebody would physically run and say they are not at the top they are coming down from the bottom... We did keep the fascists from attacking Brick Lane, but the terrible thing was that there were hundreds of people dancing against racism. It was a ridiculous state of affairs. I believed they endangered the black community of Brick Lane and did a terrible

disservice to the struggle against racism, but it was a harbinger of what was yet to come because they did that over and over again.

For the ANL to suggest that the police could be left to contain the fascists in the face of such a history of racism was absurd. Like the youth of Bradford and Southall in 1976, and the African Caribbean youth of Lewisham in 1977, the Bengali youth from the East End confronted the fascists themselves, with support from groups such as AYM (Bradford), SYM, Haringey Asian Action Group, CARF, HCAR and Institute of Race Relations. As HCAR noted, incidents such as 'Lewisham may not get positive publicity that the Carnival has received, but that in itself is a good reason for asking who benefits from diverting protest off the streets, into the parks and away from direct confrontation with racists and fascists?' (HCAR 1978).

LEICESTER

The conflict between tactics, strategies and ideologies did not only exist between the ANL and the Asian youth but also between different political interests amongst the Asian youth. While SYM and AYM (Bradford) mobilised and argued for grass roots activism which enabled them to fight racism on the streets, there were other organisations that worked through state structures and in this sense did not embody a belief in self-help and self-organisation. One such organisation was the National Association for Asian Youth under the leadership of Ravi Jain. They worked to mobilise youth within a youth and community framework in Southall and while they were supportive to SYM, permitting them to use their offices and resources, conflicts also existed between the two organisations. SYM maintained a commitment to direct action.

One clash between state sponsored youth organisations and the emerging independent youth movements occurred at a weekend conference organised by the National Association of Asian Youth in Leicester in April 1979. This was the year of the general election. Margaret Thatcher had mobilised racist support for the Conservative Party through her 'swamped' speech and fascists were still marching through towns and cities with an Asian presence. They chose to march in Leicester at the same time as the conference on racism organised by the National Association of Asian Youth. As Anwar from Bradford recalls,

I remember it was election time. We got there on Friday and on Saturday we said 'right, how can we run this conference and sit in here whilst the fascists are marching on the streets of Leicester?' ... Southall Youth Movement as well as ourselves and other contacts up and down the country... we went as a bloc to the conference and said 'right we need to bring this conference to a standstill, we all need to leave here and go down to Leicester Town Centre and oppose the fascists'... so off we went.

In making a stand in Leicester, anti-fascists including members of the youth movement were confronted with police violence while the state mobilised huge resources to protect insignificant numbers of fascists. 30 people were injured in Leicester that day.

SOUTHALL 1979

Two days after clashes in Leicester, events in Southall proved the need for black people to organise a united defence against attacks on their communities yet again and revealed the extent to which the police would go to defend fascists and criminalise black communities. On 23 April 1979, a broad coalition of anti-fascists protested in Southall against a National Front meeting at Southall Town Hall. The Front had decided to stand a candidate in the forthcoming general election in the town where they had no local branch. SYM and the charity Southall Rights took the position that the meeting was a 'well calculated assault' on the Asian community, who now made up 50 per cent of the population of Southall. 'Our priority', they argued, 'lay in not allowing the meeting to take place' (AYM Bradford 1979:4). Other organisations such as IWA (Southall), SWP and ANL decided to march in protest. The lack of coordination between the groups about the kind of action that should take place, left protestors vulnerable to aggressive and intimidatory policing which took place that day. SYM gathered its supporters to march to the town hall around 11.30 a.m., where they formed a picket of about 200 people. They were forcibly dispersed by the police with many young people arrested. The police then sealed off the town centre before protestors scheduled to arrive at 5.00 p.m. gathered. Four different protests took place at each of the main road blocks. Thousands took part. Police tactics were documented as intimidatory and aggressive with the Special Patrol Group called in and equipped with riot shields, dogs, truncheons, armoured cars, cavalry and helicopters (Dummett 1980, Renton 2006). 'It was an organised riot by the police' (Grover 2006).

The confrontation saw Blair Peach fatally wounded and dozens of protestors hurt by the police. 700 anti-fascists were arrested and 342 people faced criminal charges. Overwhelmingly, the press represented the police viewpoint and any opposing position was represented by the SWP and ANL, thus suggesting that the protest was organised by external forces rather than members of the communities living in Southall. Yet many of those arrested were members of Southall Youth Movement and other local organisations. As the local Punjabi Press at the time reported: 'Monday's police terrorism has convinced people that Southall has been reduced to the status of a British Imperial Colony, from that of a town of free citizens' (CARF 1981:58). The Southall Defence Committee (SDC) that was formed to defend those arrested on 23 April 1979 was supported by a host of organisations including SYM, People's Unite and the IWA. For SDC a united community response had a chance to create a powerful defence. Yet SWP set up the Friends of Blair Peach. 'It was difficult' as Suresh reflected, 'you'd think individual organisations... because of the severity of what had happened would come together to save a town. But actually self-interest still dictated on a large basis.' SDC mobilised support from a wide variety of organisations. For Suresh Grover and others who set up the defence committee, police intimidation that began on 23 April continued after the arrests and in the courts. On the evening of the arrests, defendants found that 'typewritten charge sheets were ready and waiting for any random name to be put on them.' The cases were also referred to a special stipendiary court in Barnet, 20 miles from Southall, which made organising support for those arrested more difficult (AYM Bradford 1979:4–5). Although the conviction rate was 52 per cent following the campaign, this was lower than the 79 per cent conviction rate prior to the campaign getting started. The experience of Southall in 1979 was to provide another lesson in the need for self-reliance and self-defence for black youth nationally. Groups such as AYM (Bradford) supported the defence campaign, screening and selling the film *Southall on Trial* to their members.

ASIAN YOUTH MOVEMENT (MANCHESTER)

While the majority of youth movements established themselves as a result of violent attacks, Manchester AYM was formed as a result of the wider climate of racism as well as a political consciousness amongst founding members. In 1979 a member of AYM (Bradford) started at the University of Manchester and made links with young Asians both at the university and outside in organisations such as the Asian Workers Forum. As Nilofer Shaikh, a founding member of AYM (Manchester) and a member of the Asian Workers Forum recalls:

> we had heard of the Bradford Asian Youth Movement and one of the people who was in the Asian Workers Association came up to me and said, 'do you think there is a need for an Asian Youth Movement in Manchester and would you consider being involved?' ... I remember there were about seven or eight of us in somebody's house having an initial discussion about what we wanted out of the group. ... Then I remember we invited Bradford AYM to a meeting. That was at Longsight Library and Tariq Mehmood came and spoke to us. I remember being fascinated to learn about some of the things they had been involved in, what they were doing, how they were operating. We took a lot of lessons from that.

The different beginnings of AYM (Manchester) may have been a result of the different 'structure of feeling' in the city, with a wider range of migrants including students, professionals and labourers. Manchester saw a wider diversity in the cultural and ethnic origin of South Asian migrants, although large numbers of migrants still tended to settle where they had familial or community contacts and support. The city itself, the institutions and businesses that migrants established, as well as the historic institutions such as the regional hospitals and universities within the city of Manchester that were already established impacted on how AYM (Manchester) operated.

Many of the key members of AYM Manchester, unlike Bradford, were not entirely disenfranchised and were employed in areas such as community development. They experienced racism as black workers and as students, and wished to make links with others that experienced discrimination and speak up against it. Of the eight initial members of Manchester AYM that I learned about, two were overseas students and three were students with families living in Britain. Being a student is primarily an activity that is associated with and enables self-betterment. The three remaining members were working people, one of whom was a surgeon. Only one of the eight initial Manchester AYM members had been to school in Manchester after migrating to Britain at the age of 13.

Apart from the three that were registered students, the others were all working by the time they set up the AYM, one in a women's refuge, another in the WEA and a third as an electronic engineer. In terms of the membership therefore, Manchester AYM had more formal education and included members that were substantially older. All these qualities impacted on how they mobilised and what they were able to achieve.

Two influential figures in the establishment and running of Manchester AYM were overseas students with a substantial involvement in communist and left organisations in their countries of origin – Pakistan and Bangladesh. The link between this international influence was different to Bradford's influence from the IWAs, because the IWAs were migrant organisations set up by first generation migrants with influence from the various Indian Communist Parties. The influence for Manchester was more direct since two of its members had been involved in communist organisations in Pakistan and Bangladesh themselves. Mohsin Zulfiqar had been involved with the National Student Federation in Pakistan as well as with the National Awami Party during the late 1960s, coming to Britain in 1971. Quamrul Kabir, from Bangladesh had also been involved with communist organisations in Bangladesh and with the movement for Bangladeshi independence before arriving in Britain as a student in 1971. Both individuals continued to organise within the left in Britain after their arrival here, but the influence of Trotskyism in the British left (and its often opportunist use of particular campaigns to promote their own organisations) meant both moved outside of the British left and began to involve themselves in anti-racist campaigns such as the Imperial Typewriters Strike in Leicester and the Overseas Students Strike in Manchester and Loughborough Universities. The crippling rise in fees for overseas students in the 1970s impacted directly on both Mohsin, Kabir and their friends. Both Quamrul Kabir and Mohsin Zulfiqar were active in the Overseas Student Strikes which employed direct action such as sit ins to protest against the draconian fee increases.

As experienced organisers that had been involved with anti-racist politics in Britain, members of what were to become AYM (Manchester) responded positively to approaches from AYM (Bradford) to help them set up an AYM in Manchester. AYM (Manchester) was always much smaller than AYM (Bradford) with about 15–20 activists, although their demonstrations always attracted hundreds of people in the city (Zulfiqar 2006). As a movement they included members that were slightly older than the majority of AYM (Bradford), Mohsin was 32, Kabir was 26 and Nilofer was 22 when AYM (Manchester) was established. Others such as Kuldeep and Nirmal were students but in general they were not teenagers although they attracted younger members to support their campaigns. Some Bradford members saw Manchester as 'more mature' and less angry. Asian Youth Movement (Manchester) was involved with a number of anti-deportation campaigns and divided family campaigns particularly the Anwar Ditta Defence Campaign and the Walait and Akhtar Defence Campaign. They also supported dozens of campaigns by Manchester Law Centre including Nasira Begum, Rosmina Defence Campaign, Nasreen Khan Defence campaign, and the Parveen Khan and Manjit Kaur Defence Campaigns. They supported the defence of a mosque that was attacked by racists and supported initiatives to stop fascists marching in Manchester and organised protests against Zionist aggression as well as raised awareness about the situation of Tamils in Sri Lanka (Ramamurthy 2011b).

Like all AYMs they were determined to build solidarity between Africans, Caribbeans and Asians. They described themselves as 'the fighting front of the Asian section of Black youth' working 'against government policy of deliberately whipping up national chauvinism, provoking violence and implementing a policy which oppresses and discriminates against national minorities' (ARAF 1981). In solidarity with Africans and Caribbeans they supported Cynthia Gordon's Defence Campaign which involved a woman from Jamaica who was threatened with deportation. The close ties between African and Caribbean groups can be seen by their relationship to the Abasindi Drumming Cooperative in Moss Side whose postal address they used. In 1981 AYM also acted as a force to try to counter divisive police tactics aimed at creating divisions between Asians and African/Caribbeans. AYM spoke out about the way in which police blocked Wilmslow Road on one of the nights of the riots 'so that a few Asian shops would be broken', a tactic adopted by the police to create division, and called for unity between all black people: 'The incident could have been avoided' they declared 'if Asian community leaders would have joined in with the progressive Black organisations to appeal to the youth why black people must be united and the need for organised protest' (AYM Manchester July 1981).

LOCAL MOVEMENTS FOR LOCAL PEOPLE

Experiences of racial violence and the frequent criminalisation of the victims of attacks by the police led youth in other areas to organise too. In Haringey, young people came together to form the Asian Action Group in the late 1970s. They had close links with Bradford and Southall Youth Movement and like Southall were a grass roots organisation started by young people who got involved in both political activity as well as searched for ways to provide youth with space and resources. Bharat Mehta recalls how 'there was an amazing amount of passion and a strong belief that we could change things and change the world. It was a real awakening for a lot of us. It was a formative time and incredibly grounding – it didn't narrow you to Wood Green or Turnpike Lane but linked you to what was going on throughout the world and some very good friendships were formed out of that' (Mehta 2012).

Dewsbury and Batley Asian Youth Movement was another smaller movement that formed during this period with the support of AYM (Bradford). The group organised meetings in support of the Anwar Ditta Defence Campaign (see Chapter 5), as well as socials to educate the youth and develop their ability to defend themselves. A small Asian Youth Movement also formed in Nottingham when a member of AYM (Bradford) became a student at the University of Nottingham. They also supported the Anwar Ditta Defence campaign.

Asian youth in Bolton and Blackburn also began to organise in the late 1970s. In 1978 the Bolton Asian Youth Organisation (AYO) was formed when a number of Asian youth that supported an anti-fascist protest were arrested and charged with public order offences. A broad based campaign in defence of the Bolton 7 that was supported by anti-racist and anti-fascist campaigners in Bolton led to the formation of Bolton AYO. Unlike Bradford and Manchester AYMs, Bolton AYO worked closely with the Socialist Workers Party and the Anti-Nazi League to mobilise against a fascist attempt to march through Rotherham in 1978 as well as in defence of the Bolton 7. Their close links with the SWP can be seen from the anti-fascist rather than anti-racist slogans that they adopted: 'No Nazi's on the streets'. They also supported the ANL's Rock Against Racism initiatives. Their close links with the ANL and the SWP meant that they were less connected to the other Asian Youth Movements who had taken the decision to organise independently.

3.2   Demonstration to defend the Bolton 7 with the Bolton Youth Organisation.
(courtesy Greg Dropkin), GD6.

Bradford was to inspire further political organisation in Sheffield, Birmingham and Luton following the case of the Bradford 12 that highlighted the right of a community to self-defence. Luton youth, for example, who had supported the Bradford 12 campaign, travelling to the court pickets with the London support group, set up the Luton Youth Movement after a pig's head was placed on the Mosque in 1981. Luton Youth Movement was a wider coalition of anti-racists rather than just Asians, but it remained inspired by both the black and socialist politics of the AYMs. In organising within their communities it is clear that Asian youth made links nationally but also responded to local environments to mobilise effectively and organise against racism and within this process youth in Bradford played a pivotal role.

CONSOLIDATION AND EMERGING CONFLICTS IN THE YOUTH MOVEMENTS

During the early years of the AYMs, the organisations relied primarily on resources and funds that they mobilised themselves and most organisations remained independent of state institutions. As these organisations began to consolidate, differences of opinion emerged about the type of activities that they should prioritise.

3.3   Picket outside Luton Town Hall in protest at the attack on Luton Mosque which led to the establishment of Luton Youth Movement, 1981 (courtesy Fahim Qureshi), FQ1.

The AYM's deliberate disruption of the National Association of Asian Youth Conference in Leicester in May 1979 to encourage delegates to leave the conference and confront the fascists on the street shows the contrasting position that existed between groups operating under state patronage and those that were established as a result of self-help. Bradford's experience provides an example of the impact of state funds which some members believed would destroy the autonomy of their organisation. This eventually proved to be correct.

In the early phase of AYM (Bradford), the youth pooled resources that they collected for themselves. This did not mean that they had no formal organisation or offices. Both Southall and Bradford for example found empty spaces to occupy and used these offices for their organisations. In Southall, the youth movement squatted in offices belonging to the National Association of Asian Youth before formally renting their own when they applied to the Commission for Racial Equality for funding in 1978 (Purewal 2006). In Bradford, the youth made use of a building on Lumb Lane that had been a compulsory purchase by the council and was targeted for demolition.

As Tariq Mehmood recalls, the group paid no rent and ran the place through donations:

> we had a run-down office. It was on the corner of Lumb Lane... we had a room downstairs which we sort of cleaned out and we had an office upstairs, with a typewriter and a telephone. These were big facilities you know, we assume computers, but we were Letrasetting and its very important to realise that we were the literate children of very often illiterate workers. So these facilities were enormous for us at the time... a little while later we managed to get a table tennis table and put that downstairs.

Tariq was in fact appointed as the first employee of AYM (Bradford). Members paid him the average factory wage through membership contributions. Tariq recalls the sense of accountability that existed because of the collective donations that paid his wage:

> we were acting almost like a communist party, not a youth movement really, we had executive committees, we were able to organise a much more effective structure. We had records, we could keep minutes but it was not like working in projects now. I was very proud of the fact that everybody was paying money out of their own pocket and they were questioning me and what I did at the end of the week. And our facilities could not be abused because we were raising the money ourselves, but I think it allowed us to have a much more organised structure and it was very difficult to organise without having full-time organisers.

Around 1980 however, the youth movement decided to apply for funds from the Commission for Racial Equality (CRE). Tariq's reflections provide an account of the way corruption and divisions slowly crept in:

> I think we applied for £3,000... I started to get a lot more money, we had a telephone we could use, we had all the basic facilities. But I felt I was becoming corrupted by the money that had come in. And two or three things happened. Before the money was there, it was always the 25ps that were coming in. People were connected directly, putting in money, it was not deducted through a bank account, they came in and gave me the 25 pence, that got put into a pot. I was paid out of the pot. When we had money in our bank account from a CRE grant... I could make a phone

call, any executive member could make a phone call, but ordinary members couldn't make phone calls, the bill would have got too high, a division was coming between us. And why take the 25p from members now? We had £3,000 in our account and I felt that by people not giving money they were losing contact with the very process that we built. And when we were sending coaches to London for example, we raised the money, we didn't have to give an answer to anybody, we could spend our money on whatever we wanted. But the money from the CRE had to be audited, we were accountable for it. And one day I was thinking about how things changed. I felt that the AYM initially was a people's organisation and once we received funding we were answerable to an institution; the very same institution that we were fighting – the British state. A people's organisation should only be responsible to the people, not to the funders.... And I took a very strong exception as time went on believing that we shouldn't apply for the money.

Tariq was not the only member who could see state funds bringing in the onset of corruption, others such as Tarlochan Gata Aura shared these views. Marsha Singh, who eventually became MP for Bradford West asserted a different position, arguing that these funds were part of black people's rights and black people should access such funds. While all citizens did have a right to access Council services, this did not address the impact of funds on a people's organisation formed to raise the political concerns of a community. At their annual conference in early 1981, Tariq and Tarlochan argued that the non acceptance of state funding should be part of the AYMs aims and objectives since 'a people's organisation should only be accountable to the people'. Youth centres they argued were in any case not what youth needed. Youth needed work, not youth workers. Saeed Hussain, a member of the Workers Revolutionary Party in early 1981 recalls the debates of the time: 'I think the AYM (Bradford) ... at that point... was struggling to make that decision as to whether it wanted to become part of the institutions or whether it wanted to actually remain independent.' The final vote was tight, but Marsha's position won the day by one or two votes and the AYM split from this moment onwards. In following the path of funding AYM (Bradford) were similar to Southall and other youth movements in the East End and Haringey who were eventually absorbed into state structures.

The split in AYM (Bradford) was representative of two trends that were to exist in many anti-racist organisations at this time – one that increasingly sought respectability and the other that wished to maintain their external pressure group status. Marsha Singh's personal career interests and actions can be seen as representing the trend that sought respectability and a space within local government. From 1981 onwards AYM activity became increasingly revolved around the youth centre rather than the radical agitational politics of previous years.

THE UNITED BLACK YOUTH LEAGUE

The members who left AYM (Bradford) following the split set up the United Black Youth League (UBYL). In forming their new organisation activists recognised the contradiction that existed between their political identity as black and AYM as an organisation which defined itself along ethnic or geographic grounds. As Tariq reflected, 'it was a logical progression from Indian, to Asian to Black'. For Saeed Hussain

> The UBYL was very clear that we were a Black organisation ... we were a part of Black communities and we would work together with all other organisations as equal partners on issues such as anti-fascism, immigration, as well as anti imperialist issues, building links nationally and locally.

> We never actually formulated or formalised policies. The whole idea was for the youth to formalise it although the basic aims and objectives were understood, which were to unify the black community, i.e. Asians and Afro–Caribbeans. We had about one general meeting per week and then some of us spent quite a lot of time as well on other campaigns. The numbers varied. There were more or less 10 people permanently every week and others alternating. The numbers gradually increased. There could be 25 people. (Bradford 12 Internal Bulletin 12:7)

The fact that a predominantly Asian organisation called itself black was significant at the time. The other key organisation to have done so in 1979 was Southall Black Sisters. The commitment of UBYL to joint action and solidarity between black communities was consolidated by their defence of an African Caribbean security guard who was charged with assaulting a police officer. In early

1981 after an incident at a bar in Queens Hall, Gary Pemberton, who worked at Bradford College was accused of assaulting a police officer and found guilty at the magistrates court. Student members of the UBYL knew Gary and as Shanaaz recalls he was well liked by students: 'He was a fantastic person, we used to go in and chat to him and he used to advise us about boys and all sorts! He was a really great guy'. Following his conviction, the UBYL set up the Gary Pemberton Defence Campaign. They exposed the case as yet another example of police criminalisation of black people. It eventually became clear in his appeal that it was the police who had attacked him. Through active mobilisation for his appeal at Bradford Crown court UBYL helped win Gary's case. In the spirit of the Panthers, who took it upon themselves to watch police on the beat, UBYL exposed the name and number of the police officer who had assaulted Gary as Colin Malcolm Mackenzie, Police Officer 399 (tandana.org SC186). The tactic won Gary his case, although it was to antagonise the police who in the long run appear to have been determined to destroy the organisation.

The success in establishing UBYL created a substantial degree of animosity between AYM and UBYL although they continued to work together on immigration and self-defence campaigns, including the Anwar Ditta Defence Campaign and Jaswinder Kaur's Defence

3.4.   United Black Youth League members with Anwar Ditta and her children at a demonstration in support of Jaswinder Kaur, 1981 (courtesy Anwar Ditta), AD6.

campaign (see Chapter 5). The AYM took a firm decision not to support the activities of UBYL. In the minutes of an AYM meeting from 24 January 1981 the AYM declared that while they supported Gary Pemberton, they would not support his Defence Committee. The arrest of 12 leading members of UBYL in the Bradford 12 case meant that the existence of UBYL was to be short lived. The differences between those that wished to organise independently and those that sought to integrate with the state was to increase following the summer of 1981.

4
A Heterogeneous Collectivity

The Asian Youth Movements that sprang up across Britain and worked together to create progressive change did not always adopt the same approach to collective action or to their vision of the future. However, one thing that all the youth shared was a belief in a black political identity that was forged as a result of British racism. While the youth adopted the term Asian in the title of their organisation, they saw themselves as blacks in a white society. Black was not simply a skin colour but a political position, and this was a standpoint reflected nationally, not only across the Asian Youth Movements, but across the whole gambit of Asian organisations such as Mukhti, Awaz, the Indian Workers Associations, the Pakistani Workers Association (PWA) and the Kashmiri Workers Association (KWA). The term 'black' enabled a collective identity and solidarity with Africans and African Caribbeans in the struggle against racism. For AYM members, a black political identity did not exclude other identities, such as being Punjabi or Bengali. As Anwar Qadir put it, 'I am and will always be a Kashmiri but, when you have a common enemy at the door, then people have to unite to deal with the beast'. Adopting a black political identity was to recognise the link in experiences between Rastafarians turned away from school because of their locks or Sikhs refused work in bakeries because of their turbans. It was an identity that was inclusive rather than exclusive and drew on a desire to create both local collectivities and global ones.

BLACK POWER AND BLACK CONSCIOUSNESS

In forging this political black identity the AYMs were influenced by the American Black Power movement and the Black Panthers. By 1970 the concept of Black Power was gaining strength in Britain. The Black Panther Movement had begun to organise, holding a conference in Wood Green in May 1971 on the Rights of Black People in Britain (Black Panther Movement 1971). In contrast to America, the Black Panther movement in Britain articulated the links between the struggles of Asians, Africans and Caribbeans in their conflict with the state over immigration laws, police victimisation and racism in the courts, arguing that the way forward was to agitate and organise rather than seeing the ballot box as a solution. This approach was similar to the one that the AYMs would adopt in their early phase although the US Panther's saw themselves as literally 'at war' with the American police, while British groups adopted a belief in self-defence. Links between South Asian activists were also established prior to the formation of the AYMs when members of the US Panthers met Jagmohan Joshi and members of IWA (GB) in 1971 at a meeting in Wolverhampton.

The influence of the Panthers on second generation Black British youth was articulated by Sivanandan in his 1971 article 'Black Power: The Politics of Existence'. Siva compares the militancy of the first generation organisations such as the Universal Coloured People's Association and the Black Unity and Freedom party with the 'revolutionary Black Panther oriented struggles' that will be taken up by the second generation. 'For these are youngsters', Siva argues, 'who will not have known any experience but with the British, and it threatens to be an experience akin to that of the blacks in America. It is they who will more closely approximate 'the colony within the mother country' status of their American counterparts. And it is they who will take up the same solutions. They will have no country of the mind to return to. They are here and now and will take what British society owes them – as fully fledged British citizens – and will not give up' (Sivanandan 1982:63). Sivanandan more than any other intellectual, acknowledged second generation Asians as part of the black experience: 'for he too is no less a product of this society and his experience of second class citizenship is no different from that of the West Indian's. His language, his customs, his social orientation which once were Indian or Pakistani are now as wholly British as those of his Caribbean neighbour. Black to him is no less the colour of oppression than to the West Indian – and black power is no less the answer to his ills' (Sivanandan 1982:63). Black power, with its focus on self-help, pride and an indigenous culture, offered a metaphoric 'home' to the youth and AYM's identification with black power was articulated in the magazines that they produced, with titles such as *Kala Tara* (Black Star), *Kala Mazdoor* (Black Worker) and *Kala Shoor* (Black Consciousness).

The youth adopted the iconography of black power in their leaflets and posters. Badges, membership cards, banners, magazines and leaflets were marked with the symbol of the black power fist (tandana.org SC1, MN152, MH2, MH27). Bhupinder Bassi (2006) from Birmingham recalls the influence of both Black Power and the Panthers on the development of the Asian Youth Movement in Birmingham and their attitude to discipline:

> If you consider how the Black Panther Party emerges, AYM was very similar. It wasn't formalised to begin with but emerged slowly. We also adopted many of the rules from the Panthers. We would not criticise another black person in public for example. But the AYM, like the Panthers, had firm rules and if you infringed them you were taken to task. Once the AYM took me to task because of being drunk on AYM business.

Bhupinder had been active in student politics in Canada before getting involved with the Asian Youth Movement in Birmingham and brought the experience of black power and feminist politics that permeated most campuses in North America during this period with him. Like the Panthers, AYMs in Manchester, Birmingham, East London and Southall also supported youth involvement in self-defence training. Even the Dewsbury and Batley AYM encouraged young men to take up self-defence and included a display of Karate in a social that they organised (tandana.org AD68). Bradford AYM, never took any formal part in organising such training since they took the position that the political struggle should be primary.

A belief in the importance of black unity is apparent in dozens of posters and leaflets that were produced by the movement. A benefit organised at Sheffield University in support of the campaigns to defend the Newham 8 and win justice for Colin Roach represents this visually. The slogan 'Black Community on Trial' encircles the image of both an Asian and African/Caribbean protestor. In another leaflet in support of the Newham 7 and the Pryce family, the slogan 'One struggle, one fight' borders the pages (tandana.org MH152, MH156).

The urgency and need to organise for black rights was also ripe in an international context. In June 1976, six weeks after Bradford youth had been forced to defend their community against the NF and eleven days after the death of Gurdip Singh Chaggar in Southall, 23 school children in Soweto were gunned down as they protested against the government decision that all classes should be conducted in Afrikaans, the language of white South Africans. A year later, in September 1977, as the Asian youth were consolidating their

Brixton, Southall, Belfast, Orgreave

IT'S NO COINCIDENCE!

Public Meeting
Burngreave Vestry Hall
3·00pm
Sunday 31 March

Speakers

Newham 7	Umesh Desi
NUM Branch Secretary	Bernard Jackson
Campaign Against P.T.A.	Deidre O'Shea

4.1   Leaflet for a public meeting organised by AYM (Sheffield) linking the experiences of police repression felt by Asians, Africans, Irish and Miners, 1985 (courtesy Matloub Hussayn Ali Khan), MH197.

organisations, the Black Consciousness Movement leader Steve Biko was murdered by the South African state. While the gravity of oppression between South Africa and Britain was clearly different, young South Asian Britons understood the experience of police violence, murder and criminalisation and learnt from the South African experience. Newham Youth Movement adopted the slogan pronounced by the children of Soweto: 'Don't mourn, organise', after the death of Akhtar Ali Beg in 1980. South Africa, as Noorzaman reflected, 'made our blood boil'. For Noorzaman, South Africa 'probably dominated my thinking more than anything, because of the social injustice of what can happen in a country where there is apartheid'. Such global struggles provided the 'drivers' for many individuals that organised on local issues. They 'actually made me think about social justice where I lived and where I worked'. In trying to explain to his mother why he went on demonstrations Noorzaman drew on the international context:

> I related to her what happens in South Africa, that was my relation point, because she could see what was happening ... with Margaret Thatcher coming into office in 1979 and a few statements on immigration that were made ... I didn't say to my mother this woman can be like that [apartheid South Africa], I said she *will* be like that ... and that's why you must let me go on these demonstrations. [laughs] And she did. (N. Rashid 2006).

In Haringey, identification with the struggle in South Africa was keenly felt because one member of Asian Action Group was from Zimbabwe. The AYMs supported local branches of the Anti-Apartheid Movement in the cities in which they worked. The importance of the Black Consciousness Movement is also acknowledged through the name of Sheffield Asian Youth Movement's magazine, *Kala Shoor*, the title of which literally translates as 'black outcry', although AYM chose to translate it as 'black consciousness'.

BLACKNESS AS ANTI-IMPERIALIST CULTURE

This broad-based, inclusive political blackness was not unique to the AYMs. Aneez who was involved with student politics in Sheffield during the mid 1970s argued: 'we had a very very outgoing view of what blackness meant. We just said that "We're all oppressed" and that was how we defined it'. For the AYMs and others, who adopted an anti-imperialist black identity, the Iranians, the Chileans and any other group struggling against colonial oppression could be included in their blackness. It was a heterogenous collectivity. The spirit with which these young Asians embraced blackness as a political identity was important to the feasibility of such a concept, which could not have existed if simply embraced by people of African origin.

   This black political identity forged in a British context which built links between those whose families had experienced slavery and those who experienced colonialism was not simply a negative identity of rejection. The identity provided a framework through which the majority of the AYMs searched out the progressive aspects of the cultures of the subcontinent and elsewhere. This marrying of blackness with anti-imperialist and Marxist analysis was significant within the AYMs. It meant that they did not have a romantic vision of their countries as holding a pre-colonial idyllic past. In the AYMs the principles of class liberation, the critique of colonialism and imperialism along with a belief in the possibility of socialism in one country (including agrarian economies) that the IWA (M) and IWA (ML) pronounced, were linked to the politics of black liberation. As Anwar Qadir of Bradford AYM recalls:

> We had education programmes that looked at where we came from over the last 3,000 years – what happened in India over these periods. It was important to know where we were coming from before we started to challenge others ... Travelling to [demonstrations] was great because we heard some old songs by the people in the coaches; some of these people were involved in the Indian liberation movement. The Indian Workers' Association, along with the Kashmiri workers and the Pakistani Workers' Association, all came ... together in this struggle; ... it could be seen as a celebration, once again, of the unity. (Qadir 2006)

While Anwar's recollection of unity is quite romantic, it highlights the attempt by the youth to draw on the histories of an anti-colonial struggle, in which all those oppressed by colonialism came together in the subcontinent to resist against it, despite the later divisions created by the partition of colonial India which divided the regions of Punjab, Bengal and Kashmir. In drawing out the connections between their own struggles and those of the past, the youth revered the martyrs of the anti-colonial struggles of India, including Bhagat Singh, Udham Singh, Tipu Sultan and the Rani of Jhansi who were introduced to them by older comrades in the Indian Workers Associations. These links can be seen in AYM (Birmingham)'s calendar from 1986, which juxtaposed a photograph of the Bradford 12 campaign for self-defence with a photograph of the anti-colonial martyr Udham Singh, who shot and killed Michael O'Dwyer, the Lieutenant General of Punjab responsible for the massacre at Jallianwala Bagh in which 379 people were killed by British troops. Udham Singh adopted the name Ram Mohammad Singh Azad as a statement of unity between the religious communities of India before he shot O'Dwyer in 1940. His status as a symbolic figure of resistance can be seen by the number of songs dedicated to him in all genres of Punjabi music, from traditional folk to Asian Dub (Kalra 2000:90). The Bradford 12 case which involved the defence of Hindu, Muslim, Sikh and Christian South Asian youth who had defended their communities in 1981 were seen as belonging to the same tradition of self-defence.

The unity-in-diversity in which different religious identities did not create fragmentation but operated within a unifying framework was reflected on by Matloub Hussayn Ali Khan, who recalled how 'At the time of my involvement in the AYM there was no conflict between my religious identity and my affiliation with the term 'black' – everybody's religion was personal'. This broad-based unity meant that members united to defend temples, mosques and gurdwaras. At times this created conflicts with conservative elements in the community, which were resisted. As Mohsin Zulfiqar recalls:

> Attacks on Mosques were taking place and one of the mosques near Longsight was attacked by KKK type of hooded people who came and smashed windows and so on. In that particular incident we gave a call for a meeting in the Mosque and ... of course the majority of people who turned up were Muslims, but others, especially the Asian Youth Movement contingent came in to support Muslims. I was chairing the meeting and there were a number of speakers and of course you had sections within the Muslim community like Jamat-e-Islami, Muslim Brotherhood

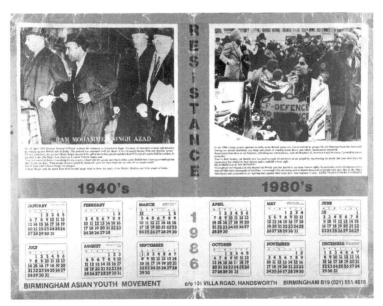

4.2   Calendar produced by Birmingham AYM connecting anti-colonial and black struggles in Britain, 1986 (courtesy Matloub Hussayn Ali Khan), MH98.

who objected when I introduced one of the speakers by name who was a Sikh. They said you can't have a Sikh speaker in a Mosque... I had to intervene... and there was a passionate plea that racists do not see whether you're Muslim, Sikh or Hindu when they're going to beat you up or kill you and it went to a vote... and everyone said 'yeah yeah let him speak'. (Zulfiqar 2006).

Such secularism was never a badge that was flaunted, but was just an inevitable part of an identity that aimed to build alliances between the oppressed. Balraj Purewal, of Southall Youth Movement spoke of how he had grown up in a 'profoundly secular environment... as a Punjabi, I did not think about Muslim or Sikh. At school, the person next to me was never a Muslim or Hindu. It never occurred to me to think like that'. It should however be noted that caste conflict was less effectively addressed by the youth movements and Southall Youth Movement was 'Jat' dominated.

The importance of building unity and an awareness that religion had been used divisively in anti-colonial struggles in South Asia also influenced the youth's approach to their understanding of contemporary anti-colonial struggles in Palestine and Ireland. Both situations provide a context in which religion had been used to confuse settler colonial conflicts. The youth believed it was imperative to support the Irish cause, because as England's oldest colony they were struggling against the same colonial oppressor. The attempt by the state to construct Irish Republicans as terrorists was understood by the youth in the context of their own experiences of criminalisation in Britain as well as within anti-colonial history. In supporting the right to self-determination for Ireland, AYM (Bradford) sent two delegates to the North of England Irish Prisoner's Committee. The solidarity was reciprocal. Bobby Sands who was to eventually die on hunger strike wrote a poem in support of Anwar Ditta (Chapter 5) which addressed the value of such solidarity:

> Alone I am without strength
> United there <u>are</u> chances and hope
> Solidarity wins wars. We're in this <u>together</u>
> There's love, for humanity, a prize
> We <u>shall</u> win.
> ...

(Poem from Bobby Sands to Anwar Ditta, 11 August 1980)

The following year, in 1981, AYM (Bradford) were actively involved in supporting the Irish Republican Hunger Strikers including Bobby Sands. The solidarity links between the two groups continued following the acquittal of the Bradford 12 in 1982, when members of the Bradford 12 were invited to join the Easter Commemoration in Belfast. Two years later, Birmingham AYM also organised a delegation of 34 Asian youth from Birmingham, Sheffield, Manchester and London to the North of Ireland for the Easter 1916 commemoration in Belfast. *The Asian Times* recorded how 'The Asian Youth were accorded a warm welcome by the nationalist people of Belfast when they joined the march to the republican graves in Milltown Cemetery'. Sheera who spoke on behalf of the youth highlighted the links between Irish and Black experiences in Britain, both in terms of racism and police victimisation as well as in relation to the experience of labour. 'We built Britain', he declared to applause, adding 'a freedom movement with the support of the people is something that can never be defeated no matter how powerful the enemy' (*The Asian Times* 1984).

Understanding the struggle for Palestine as a settler colonial rather than a religious conflict was an important part of political development for many of the youth. Tariq remembers when he learned as a school child that George Habash, the leader of the PFLP (Popular Front for the Liberation of Palestine) was not Muslim but Christian and how this changed his whole perception of the struggle. In analysing Zionism as a form of racism, AYM (Manchester) interrogated the internal conflicts within Zionism including its racism towards non-European Jews in Israel (Arab, North African and Indian), arguing that their immigration had been encouraged when Israel was first established because of the need for a cheap labour force. An article in *Liberation* was carefully researched making use of Middle East Research and Information Project Reports to highlight the fact that 92 per cent of Israel's official poor in the 1980s were 'Orientals' and noted their vulnerability after immigration: 'Oriental Jews, once having immigrated to Israel had nowhere else to go whereas European Jews could return to Western countries. This particular vulnerable position made it easier to turn them into a sub-proletariat' (AYM Manchester 1981c:11).

The massacre of thousands of Palestinians in Sabra and Shatila refugee camps in Lebanon in 1982 which was supported by the Israeli Defence Forces also brought the issue of Palestine to the fore. AYM (Bradford) supported the Ad-hoc Committee Against Israeli Genocide in Lebanon (tandana.org SC170). In Sheffield the youth

4.3   'Death to Zionism', poster produced by AYM (Manchester) for a demonstration in Manchester protesting at the massacre of Palestinians in Lebanon, 1982 (courtesy Tariq Mehmood), TM20.

mobilised to put pressure on members of the Trade Union Friends of Palestine Committee who had agreed to meet the Israeli Trade Union Federation, by circulating a message from the children of Palestine and Lebanon about the complicity of the Histadrut in the oppression of Palestinians (tandana.org MD33). Manchester Asian Youth Movement helped organise a demonstration to protest at the massacre, supporting the 1980s Palestine Liberation Organization call for 'Death to Zionism'. Bradford and Sheffield AYM also mobilised for the march. Their posters and leaflets affirmed the belief in the legitimacy of armed struggle in Palestine when confronted with such extreme state violence (tandana.org TM20). In the Palestinian cause, the AYMs saw those that resisted imperialism and colonialism called terrorists yet again.

Anti-colonial leaders from Zimbabwe were to interrogate the term terrorism around this time, as Tariq Mehmood remembers when the AYMs supported a meeting about Zimbabwe at which Edison Zovobgo spoke. Zovobgo had acted as Zimbabwe African National Union – Patriotic Front's (ZANU-PF) representative at the Lancaster House talks which brought independence to Zimbabwe:

> There was a meeting in Manchester and we mobilized to come to the meeting... and Edison Zovobgo spoke. Some white people had been killed in Zimbabwe... and all that time Zimbabweans, particularly ZANU-PF were projected as terrorists – always referred to as terrorists. It was a packed hall ... and I remember he said, 'They call us terrorists. If fighting for my people's liberation means I am a terrorist, so be it. I'm proud of it.' And he listed a whole series of injustices that were taking place to Africa and against Africans in Zimbabwe, about the denial of land and the usurpation by white people of Zimbabwe and if trying to get those back through the use of arms meant that he was being called a terrorist then he was proud of it. And I remember the room was electric and every time he said I'm proud to be a terrorist, we were shouting we are all terrorists... (Mehmood 2007)

Later, in the case of the Bradford 12, former members of the AYM were to find themselves charged with terrorist offences when they attempted to defend themselves and their community against racist attacks and were forced to challenge such labelling in their own defence. This anti-imperialist blackness could not be absorbed by state led anti-racist initiatives that were to influence the anti-racist movement in the late 1980s.

TRADE UNIONISM AND THE AYMS

Embedded in a Marxist philosophy that maintained a belief in the need for all exploited groups to unite, the AYMs recognised the need to support workers' struggles in all communities. The aims and objectives of AYM (Bradford) argued 'that the only real force in British society capable of fighting racialism and the growth of organised racism and fascism is the unity of the workers' movement – Black and White'. It offered commitment 'to encourage youth to integrate themselves into the organisations – trade unions and political parties – of the British working class', while recognising 'that the same organisations ... are not themselves free of racialist influences, and that in encouraging our members and sympathisers to join these organisations, it would be necessary for them to fight racialist elements and influences within these organisations' (AYM Bradford 1979:13). This approach highlights the influence of the IWAs in both theory and practise and the AYMs worked in conjunction with the IWAs in many of the strikes that they were to support. AYM (Manchester) educated younger members about strikes such as that of Imperial Typewriters to highlight the contradictory relationship of black workers to British trade unions in their journal *Liberation,* summed up by the statement from TGWU founder Ben Tillet: 'You are our brothers and we will do our duty by you but we wish you had not come' (AYM Manchester 1981a:8).

There were times when the struggle against racism and support for trade unionism worked together as in the case of the arrest and attempted deportation of Saeed Rahmon, a trade union activist who was arrested and imprisoned on suspicion of being an illegal immigrant, but the AYMs also gave support to trade union and workers struggles more broadly. Their main focus was to support black workers that were being treated unfairly. IPYA and members of AYM (Manchester) had supported both Imperial Typewriters and the Grunwick strike in the 1970s. In the 1980s Asian Youth Movements in Bradford, Birmingham and Sheffield supported non-unionised workers at Aire Valley Yarns in Bradford and Kewal Brothers in Birmingham (tandana.org JR1)

These strikes were not always about the racism of employers or trade unions. The strike at Kewal Brothers in Birmingham in 1984 and at Warrington Messenger in 1983 were examples of the youth challenging exploitative Asian businessmen. In Birmingham, the Asian Youth Movement and the IWA supported what were mainly Asian women workers in their rights to join a trade union, in a clothing firm where women workers were being paid as little as £1 per hour. In Bradford, Jani Rashid, a member of the National Graphical Association remembered the strike in Warrington as a key point in his trade union activity. The youth movement supported the strike against Eddie Shah, a black businessman who moved employees from Scotland to Warrington and tried to change their working conditions. In doing so they had to confront the racism of workers and activists on the picket line:

> The main campaign I remember that was of any use was not really in defence of black or Asian workers but in fact against a black employer. I used to organise pickets from Bradford to Warrington.

Eddie Shah basically tried to change the working conditions of printers who he'd moved from Scotland to Warrington under the pretext of giving them better livelihoods, but it turned out it was an opportunity for him to introduce new technology without fully consulting the workers. That turned out to be quite a massive campaign, supported by the Trades Council and trade unions. It sort of felt uncomfortable to me but in principle it was the right thing to do. There were racist comments that were made on the picket line every so often and we had to get on the megaphone and tell people that this was not a race issue and that the sort of comments that they were making were racist and shouldn't be made against anyone even if he was a bad employer... (J. Rashid 2007)

The complicated position of dealing with racism in the trade unions as well as building solidarity was also clear in the experiences of AYM (Sheffield) during the miners' strike. The AYM produced posters to mobilise South Asians in support of the miners and took minibuses to the picket line where they experienced both racism and solidarity. As Mukhtar Dar recalls:

we would go and wake up our members early in the mornings, throw stones at the windows so that mums and dads wouldn't wake up, get them out, get them in the back of the minibus, drive to Orgreave... I remember on one occasion this disgruntled young lad that I had woken at six in the morning. When we arrived one of the miners – not all of them – said 'what the hell are these Pakis doing here?' So this young lad turned round to him and said, 'thank you very much for waking me up at six in the morning only to get racist abuse'. To which my response was, 'brothers you've got to recognise that, we can see the bars and some of them can't'. (Dar 2006)

Others in the mining communities however welcomed and embraced the need for solidarity, as Mukhtar remembers:

... some of the mining communities that we went and stayed with, the way that we were treated, the humility, the humbleness of the miners, the hatred that we had for the police and the siege that we experienced in our communities, and the way we were being treated by the police, I saw that echoed by the mining families and the anger, the passion and the way they were seeking to organise... there were lots of parallels. (Dar 2006)

It was not just the youth, but the IWAs also supported the miners' cause. Jim Denham has noted how 'street collections on the Soho Road (a very poor black and Asian area) were known to be amongst the best supported in Birmingham and miners squabbled over who should get that "patch"' (Denham 2004). The solidarity offered by AYMs and IWAs was to have a lasting impression on those active in the miners' strike, as the committee minutes document: 'Brother

4.4 'Solidarity with the Miners', agitational leaflet produced by AYM (Sheffield) in 1984. The image depicted Asian youth protesting in Brick Lane after the death of Altab Ali that was first used in AYM Bradford's magazine *Kala Tara* (courtesy Mukhtar Dar), SC128.

from Lea Hall reported that they had a greater understanding of police harassment themselves now and would always support ethnic minority groups coming up against it in future especially as they were supporting the NUM so solidly now' (in Denham 2004). The miners returned the support during the Kewal Brothers strike, as Denham documents: 'Cannock miners, with barely enough money to feed their own families, hired coaches to take 150 Lea Hall and Littelton miners to the Kewal picket line'.

While the AYMs retained a commitment to trade union organisation and workers struggles, the attitude of the left towards them was mixed. Some organisations such as the Socialist Workers Party labelled them as Black nationalists and viewed their belief in the need for independent black organisations as reactionary. The SWP attitude to the AYMs and later the UBYL meant that they only offered token support to activities that the Asian youth organised. As Ijaz commented, 'All the time in the Bradford 12, the role was they'll come, they'll send one or two, they will never mobilse, they won't give money, they won't give any support they will come to sell their papers' (Ahmed 1987). Aware of the rising attraction of 'black power' in the 1970s, SWP produced their own pamphlets on 'The Black Worker in Britain' as well as the magazine *Chingari* (Spark) but these initiatives were critical of the 'spontaneous rising of a black vanguard' which they argued 'lead only to established dead ends' (Singh 1974). To the Asian youth who saw autonomy as an attempt to unite as equal, organisations such as SWP only appeared to want to control them or use them. Other sections of the left, such as the CPGB, were simply too preoccupied and were mainly concerned to mobilise the black community, 'into *their* political battles. They never had time to look at *our* immediate problems, so it became futile to refer to them. So blacks ended up in total isolation within the broad left because of the left's basic dishonesty' (cited in Smith 2010:62). A few organisations from the revolutionary left such as Big Flame, that were active from 1974 to 1983 (a similar period to the AYMs most active period), supported the right of black people to organise independently, offered solidarity and promoted black led struggles in their newspaper. Max Farrar (a former member of Big Flame) has described the kind of independent organising that AYMs and the Race Today Collective were involved with as 'black self organisation for socialism which is autonomous of, but not cut off from, the white majority' (Farrar 2001).

LANGUAGE AND CULTURE

In their organisational practise and the ideas that they articulated, the AYMs wished to develop the liberation of their own intellectual thought. Sivanandan's essay on 'the Liberation of the Black Intellectual' offered a perspective that influenced the youth. As Bhupinder Bassi of Birmingham Asian Youth movement recalled, 'There is a part of that book [A Different Hunger] where he invites the black intellectual home. I only ever met him once or twice but we used the words of Siva at meetings'. AYM (Sheffield) reproduced some of his writings in their journal Kala Mazdoor. This invitation 'home' was an acknowledgement that the rejection of colonial culture is not enough for the black intellectual, because 'however positive that rejection, it does not by itself make for a positive identity... to "positivise" his identity, the black man must go back and rediscover himself – in Africa and Asia – not in a frenetic search for lost roots' that created ossified romanticised cultures, but in 'an attempt to discover living traditions and values' (Sivanandnan 1982:89). The articulation of intellectual thought for activists by the IRR was a conscious part of the Institute's re-definition of their journal Race to Race & Class in 1974 that aspired to be a 'campaigning journal, "a collective organizer", devoted not just to thinking... but to thinking in order to do', linking 'the situation of black workers in Britain and the liberation' struggles in the underdeveloped world' (Race & Class 1975). The writings of Siva were to inspire young Asians in the 1970s and 1980s who in essence adopted Fanon's definition of a national culture as 'not a folklore, nor an abstract populism that believes it can discover the people's true nature,' but,

> ... the whole body of efforts made by a people in the sphere of thought to describe, justify and praise the action through which that people has created itself and keeps itself in existence. ... [it] should therefore take its place at the very heart of the struggle for freedom which ... countries are carrying on. (Fanon 1990:188)

In developing their political consciousness the youth learned to take pride in their language and culture and were influenced by Fanon's belief that 'A man's whole world is expressed and implied by his language: it is a way of thinking, of feeling, of be-ing. It is identity' (Sivanandan 1982:86). Language was therefore an important signifier of resistance to British cultural domination. Some members in Bradford recall how in order to improve their language skills, they would have a tin as they sat amongst friends and if anyone used an English word they would have to put money in the tin. They produced leaflets in both English and in their own languages and adopted slogans and songs in Urdu and Punjabi that were used by workers in the subcontinent, the knowledge of which they learned from the IWAs (Kalra et al. 1996). The Punjabi slogan, 'Police tey nah ithbar karo, apni raki aap karo' (Don't rely on the police, defend yourself), for example, was used repeatedly on demonstrations in Britain in support of self-defence often accompanied by the Punjabi *dhol* (drum) on demonstrations. Although wishing to develop cultures of unity, the membership of many AYMs was heavily Punjabi because of the size of the Punjabi migrant communities, the fact that they were one of the earliest groups of migrants from South Asia in the post-war period and hence were more 'settled'. Punjabi, therefore, as a cultural influence was extremely strong within the AYMs. Punjabi folk music in particular became a marker of identity and cultural pride for many members of AYM Bradford, Southall, Sheffield and Birmingham. Nilofer from Manchester, who is not Punjabi, remembers how they often invited the local Bhangra group Ajnabee (Stranger) to play at their socials and Sheffield had a strong relationship with the group Raza and Party. While the dominance of Bhangra has been seen to have acted as an attempt to represent an Asian authenticity which was hegemonic in privileging a form of expression that was Punjabi and male and the cultural dominance of Punjabi was also apparent within AYMs, Bhangra in the 1980s, as an expression of 'Asianness' also enabled Asian youth both within and outside the Asian youth movements, both those who were Punjabi and not, 'to affirm their identities positively within a dominant cultural formation that 'offers' either an acculturating process of assimilation into the British nation, or exclusion from it' (Sharma 1996:36).

The use of Bhangra as a form of affirmation outside of a dominant culture can be understood in the context of the AYMs attempts to foster cultures and histories of resistance, and their embracing of both their own cultural and musical traditions as well of those of other oppressed groups. They wished to foster the development of a new revolutionary and anti-imperialist culture. As such their blackness was 'de-essentialised' (Hall 1991, Sharma 1996). At study days and cultural evenings the AYMs shared poetry and music that spoke of their experiences of racism and

4.5   A social evening featuring Baba Baktaura, Mahmood Jamal
      and Raza and Party, organised by AYM (Sheffield) and the
      Asian Welfare Association. The English language side of the
      leaflet bills it as 'Cultural resistance' (courtesy Mukhtar
      Dar), MD46.

colonialism. The youth wrote their own poems and published them
in their journals. Some of these poems represented experiences of
violence, such as 'Just Another Asian':

Watching were the stars that night
Watching was the moon
As Abdul left the bus stop whistling a tune

The street was still and quiet
And the street lamps they were bright
But something gleamed more brightly in the alleyway that night
...

They stabbed him in the face and chest
They stabbed him in the back
Then they kicked him as he lay there and told him to go back

In the stillness in the moonlight stands a woman by her gate
Waiting for her husband but tonight he will be late
The police stand by the body

Nothing much to say
Just another Asian
Has been killed today

(AYM Sheffield 1983)

Other poems and songs expressed their determination to struggle:

We will serve we will suffer we will sacrifice
We will fight for our people, We will fight for our rights

When they come to burn our houses...
We will arm ourselves and fight!

When they come to attack our people...
We will arm ourselves and fight!

The above poem/song was first heard by the youth on a coach
going to a demonstration sung by an old African man. It inspired
the youth who saw how the lyrics applied universally to those in
struggle. The AYMs identified with resistance poetry produced by
black British poets such as Linton Kwesi Johnson, who's poem
'Inglan is a Bitch' had a resonance that is highlighted in the opening
of Tariq Mehmood's novel *While there is Light*, which reflects back
on the 1981 period: 'Mother, I am now in jail, in this bitch of a
country called England' (Mehmood 2003). Anti-imperialist poetry
by Faiz Ahmed Faiz, (AYM Sheffield 1986) and Pablo Neruda, as
well as British based Urdu and Punjabi poets such as Mahmood
Jamal, Bedi and Mumtaz Awan were also performed at AYM events.
   Musical traditions of resistance including reggae, Chilean and
South African as well as South Asian folk music also featured in
AYM socials and events. A leaflet for the victory celebration for
Anwar Ditta lists an Asian band and a reggae group, along with an
international disco (tandana.org AD56). Roots reggae, with its links
to Rastafarianism, represented a culture of resistance that many
Jamaican Britons adopted as an oppositional culture of self-respect

and became an integral part of the culture of Asian youth in 1970s and 1980s Britain, with tracks such as Bob Marley's 'Get Up, Stand Up' encapsulating their aims and objectives:

> ... if you know what life is worth
> Then you would look for yours right here on earth
> And now we see the light
> We gonna stand up for our rights.

(Bob Marley & Peter Tosh 1973)

British reggae bands such as Steele Pulse and Misty in Roots, both of whom were part of the Rock Against Racism initiative, also formed part of the AYMs cultural scene. Misty in Roots' song 'Ghetto of the City' resonated with their own experiences of black migration:

> ...
> Dreams are just an illusion
> Pavements are not gold
> Hatred, hatred and oppression
> Down in the ghetto

(Misty in Roots 1978)

The political and cultural links and camaraderie between African Caribbean and Asian youth in Birmingham led to one Caribbean group producing a reggae/calypso tune in support of the Bradford 12 (Ahmed 1987). Such cross-cultural links were to influence the development of Asian Dub that maintained their commitment to anti-racism through groups such as Fun-Da-mental.

A number of musicians within the South Asian diasporic community also sang about the migratory experience. Shaukat Ali's '*Main Vilayet Kaanoon Aiyaa?*' (Why did I come to England?); Alam Lohar's '*England di Jugni*' (The firefly of England) and A. S. Kang's '*Mai thai Peeneya vilayti mai thai peeneyah*' (I want to drink British booze) were songs that both young and old connected with. These songs spoke of the contradictions inherent in the glitter of materialism that attracted migrants to the imperial heartland but with an awareness that behind this lay the pains and suffering of many. Such songs, as Kalra has discussed, were appreciated because they spoke through lyrics, symbolism and performance of the experiences of alienation, loss and generational conflict that many migrants felt, often employing humour to subvert the tensions of everyday life (Kalra 2000:87).

At times performance and political action became infused, as with the local Birmingham singer Baba Bakhtaura who faced deportation. Baba Bakhtaura sang songs composed by the AYMs to highlight the attempts by the state to keep black people out of Britain and the need of communities to resist. These songs often used the tunes of old Punjabi folk tunes or raags that audiences were familiar with. Through the IWA the AYMs also met singers from the Punjab who also composed tunes for Bakhtaura (see Chapter 5). Reworking popular songs was a tradition that continued amongst former members and future activists. In 1993 members of PWA and the Bursalls' Strike Support Group wrote a song for the strikers based on Noor Jahan's 'Kendhe ne nehna':

> Hartalian na kehna
> Usi hoon ni behna...
>
> The strikers say
> They will not now sit down...

While adapting their own traditional cultures to produce a culture of resistance, and identifying with reggae and other resistance cultures, the youth movements also made links with trade union resistance cultures. Birmingham AYM, for example, had close links to Banner Theatre. These connections inspired Dave Rogers to write a song on the immigrations laws in support of Mohammad Idris.

BLACK OR ASIAN POLITICAL IDENTITIES

The belief in a broad anti-imperialist black political identity led some individuals to question whether they should join an AYM since this political identity conflicted with the idea of an Asian political organisation. While this was a contradiction, many of those that established the AYMs felt that their organisations *had* to be Asian, because the communities they could organise in most effectively were their own. As AYMs they could then liaise with any number of other black and anti-racist organisations from a position of equality. Saeed Hussain however reflected on how he was not entirely happy with the Asian label and this stalled his membership of the Asian Youth Movement. Although he probably would have joined in the end, he never needed to once the United Black Youth

League was established in Bradford in 1981. Aneez also took the logic of blackness to mean that they should not organise as Asians because this was not a political identity. Aneez's conflict also raises the complex nature of cultural identities. For many Asians born in Africa, their cultural identity was also partly entwined with Africa. The all encompassing term 'Black' offered a sense of belonging for the colonial migrant of many locations. It broke the notion of hybridity as only flowing between India and Britain or Africa and Britain, to recognise cultural and political links and influences between the corners of the former empire. This blackness enabled hybridity and cultural change that was not mediated by colonial culture and could develop in opposition to it. It was an anti-imperialist blackness.

WOMEN AND THE ASIAN YOUTH MOVEMENTS

The strength of the black anti-imperialist political identity with which the AYMs identified was a powerful political marker and engaged both men and women, through both political action and cultural expression. For the most part the attitudes of the AYMs were outward looking, but, like the Panthers and the Black Power movement as a whole, machoism and forms of masculinity that were sexist also influenced the way in which they organised. The focus on race undoubtedly left women's issues as important but secondary, although it should be remembered that the youth movements varied between different towns and cities in their focus and priorities.

The male domination of the AYMs was influenced by the early phase of migration from the subcontinent where workers first brought their sons or nephews to Britain to work. Many of the members who I interviewed came to Britain in the mid 1960s when the number of families would have been extremely small. The difficulties for those women and girls who were present from these traditionally rural communities to gain access to independence that would enable them to participate in political activity along with the predominance of young men in the community meant that Bradford AYM, for example, began its development as entirely male and even later women were only ever involved in small numbers. As Jani Rashid commented:

> We didn't have many Asian women in the organisation, my sister was a member, she didn't always come to meetings 'cos we were a largely male group. We did increase our membership to more

than just my sister later on, ... but I have to say in terms of membership it was very very limited in terms of women... there were accusations from ... all sorts of groups that we were a sexist organisation... but I didn't feel it was... most young Asian women were still sort of... kept at home by their parents, and you know to be exposed to the likes of young men from the Asian Youth Movement wasn't the right thing to do... (J. Rashid 2007)

In character it is therefore not surprising that there were elements of machoism present in the behaviour of the young men and in their organisation. It was not only influenced by traditional forms of masculinity present within South Asian cultures but also by traditional forms of British masculinity that were present in northern mill towns, where young men had historically gained their place and purpose in society through hard physical labour (Winlow 2001, Russell 2004, Kirk 2000). In reflecting on their past behaviour, many of the men involved in the AYMs, now in their fifties, recognise the way dominant masculinities existed both in their language as well as in their behaviour. As Iqbal from AYM (Bradford) reflected, 'I left Bradford around 1980 and when I left there were hardly any women, and there used to be one woman in AYM ... and there would be a dozen of us that would hover around her. It was terrible [laughs]'. There are also visual indicators of machoism in some of the images repeatedly used in AYM literature, such as the image of an 'angry young man' with a raised fist, which appeared first in *Kala Tara* to represent the struggles in East London, then on an early bulletin of the Bradford 12 campaign and, later, in leaflets produced by Sheffield AYM in support of the Miners' Strike in 1985 (Ramamurthy 2006:53). Harwant Bains has commented on the 'machismo' of the Southall Youth Movement and its patriarchal attitudes towards women, which he describes as similar to those found amongst male elders of the community (Bains 1988).

Shanaaz Ali, who campaigned with the United Black Youth League, reflects on the difficulties for women being part of political action. This was not just from the point of view of the dominance of men in the organisation but also because of the wider community's attitudes:

I suppose one of the memories is the difficulty in going to the marches 'cos a lot of them were at the weekends and we couldn't skive off college [laughs] and go without your parents knowing. And the dilemma I had at home was my father (because I was a girl) just saying, 'What are people going to say?' It wasn't the done thing that you went and did that sort of thing as a girl. ... Sometimes I just lied and went, and said, 'I'm going to the library to do my work'. Or I'm going off to a friend's or whatever.

It is clear that many of the youth involved in the movements were not always conscious of the difficulties for women members. As Shanaaz recalls,

The political activity was all wrapped up into this sort of social thing as well... you were socialising and politicising and you were going on marches... but we'd have to go home after marches, because it was just not on to go out late or anything like that. (Ali 2006)

Members of Birmingham Black Sisters (BBS) also remembered the way that the AYMs did not enable women to participate equally, since meetings were often held in pubs and clubs that many women did not wish to visit. The personal behaviour of some of the men was also shameful at times. Shanaaz reflected on how difficult it was to even get her own sister involved never mind other girls. Despite these difficulties, the political activity that she got involved with gave Shanaaz a sense of identity, where she could 'channel the feelings of being different' and Shanaaz comments that some older comrades appreciated the difficulties. Shanaaz's involvement and feelings of camaraderie with the young men with which she campaigned, highlight the importance of looking beyond the youth movements as an expression of an essentialised black masculinity, reified as 'a certainty around which all else revolves' (Alexander 2000:135). Her experiences highlight the complexity of the AYM and UBYL identities that were influenced by a performance of masculinity that was macho, but was not exclusively so.

All Asian Youth Movements did not have the same character-istics and the clear organisational structures in AYM (Bradford), for example, enabled them to curb machoistic attitudes to some extent. The aims of AYM (Bradford) clearly listed opposition to discrimination on the basis of 'race, colour, sex, religion etc'. In their practise, AYM (Bradford) also established codes of conduct to prevent women that they were working with from being harassed or intimidated. One of these rules established that no member of the AYM could date a member of a family that the AYMs were working with on a campaign. The differences between AYMs

Southall, Manchester and Bradford are reflected on by Kuldeep who was well placed to compare the experience of all three youth movements, since while born in Southall, she studied in Manchester and had friends in Bradford:

> what I like about Manchester was it was quite formal, and I think this is something, that discipline ... I think Bradford AYM was an inspiration in the way they were structured and they were quite formal about things in a way I think Southall wouldn't have been, because Southall had a degree of familiarity and a bit of a macho culture. And I liked the formality of Bradford and Manchester; their structures, committees, Chairs, you know, appointments, all that kind of stuff ... it was not just about people's egos and about people who were popular being appointed to positions and it was more democratic and fair, and encouraged women to get involved as well as stand for positions... People were much more committed to the cause and it was less about egos. (Mann 2006).

While Bradford tried to establish codes of conduct and operated formal structures to curb the excesses of machoism, AYM (Manchester) made an even greater effort to address women's issues and the involvement of women. A section of their magazine *Liberation* articulated Manchester AYM's position:

> Asian women are the most oppressed section of our community, subjected to oppression at home in addition to the general exploitation as blacks. Although we are living in an industrialised society, most of our people retain feudal values and customs. AYM will struggle against these reactionary aspects of our culture. AYM believes that the emancipation of women is a pre-requisite for the liberation of society at large. (AYM Manchester 1981c:6)

For its size, Manchester AYM had proportionately more women involved and two key members of the movement were women.

Manchester adopted an image on their membership forms of three Asians, two of whom were women, shouting through prison bars as a gesture to acknowledge the centrality they viewed women's role within the struggle. This image was first created by the Mukhti collective in London in the 1970s. The magazine produced by Mukhti expressed a similar anti-imperialist and anti-racist perspective. Manchester as a much bigger, more affluent urban environment, attracted a more diverse group of people than Bradford and the women members in

ASIAN YOUTH MOVEMENT

WE WILL BREAK THIS PRISON !

Membership Form

I am (or originate),from Pakistan,Bangladesh,India or Srilanka,below 35 years
of age and have broad agreements with the AYM general principles and wish to
Join/know more about,the AYM.My particulars are given below:

PLEASE DELETE AS APPROPRIATE

I do not wish to join the AYM but would like to be in the mailing list and
participate in the various social activities the AYM organises.
My particulars are given below:

name _____ age _____

address_____

_____

_____

Please return completed forms to Asian Youth Movement,c/o Abasinda Co-operative,
Moss Side People's Centre,St . Mary's Street, Moss Side, Manchester 16

4.6   Membership form for AYM (Manchester). The image was
first produced by Mukhti, a London based collective, in 1980
(courtesy Jani Rashid), JR23.

Manchester came from families that were from urban areas in
the subcontinent or were women students, many of whom were
not living at home. The commitment in Manchester to women's
participation can be seen from educationals they organised to
discuss the classic text *The Social Basis of the Women's Question*
and their first public meeting, which also highlighted women's
issues and women's contributions to liberation struggles through an
invitation to Amrit Wilson to speak about Asian women in Britain
and a female member of the Tamil Tigers to speak about women's
involvement in the struggle for Tamil Eelam.

Manchester was also the only AYM in the country to establish a
women's wing. Nilofer recalls the experience of the women's wing:

We had a women's wing and had some separate meetings and discussions about how we were going to organise. A lot of time was taken trying to recruit other women. It was hard to get women involved. Having a women's wing enabled more women to get involved. We talked to the families to allow the women and girls to come on marches. We had a separate form for women to affiliate to the women's wing and got involved in organising an international women's day event. We showed a film with Smita Patil, an Indian actress known for her feminist roles, to discuss women's position and the role of women in society. We also offered personal support to women like Nasira Begum ... , which was obviously something which men couldn't do. (Shaikh 2006)

While the women's wing was small, its existence was important. Given that two of the campaigns with which they were involved were Nasira Begum's and Jaswinder Kaur's – women who were facing deportation as a result of domestic violence – and that a third campaign, the Anwar Ditta Defence Campaign (which was a key campaign that galvanised AYM Manchester as an organisation), involved a woman struggling for the right to bring her children to Britain, the personal support that women members were able to offer victims of immigration discrimination was invaluable, although it was easy for women to be left organising women or with social care roles.

For AYM, racism was always emphasised over issues of sexism. The fourth key immigration campaign with which Manchester were involved was that of Akhtar and Walait. This campaign challenged the primary purpose ruling which operated from 1983 to 1997, which argued that thousands of arranged marriages were not valid by suggesting that the principle reason for the marriage was to gain residence in the UK. In this campaign it would have been possible to expose the Home Office's racism and sexism by suggesting that Asian women should go to live with their husbands in the sub-continent if they married men from overseas, but the campaign focused primarily on the issue of Walait as black: 'the home office message to Walait, a black British citizen, is if you want to live in peace with your husband, leave this country'. This left the Home Office's sex discrimination poorly articulated, since the Home Office's position was only made in the context of inscribing traditional gender roles.

Although AYM (Manchester) engaged with issues pertaining to women's oppression they were keen to do this in a way that did not isolate male community members if at all possible. In 1983 when the City Council decided to close North Manchester School for Girls, many families were concerned about the lack of a girls-only school in north Manchester. Two men in the community decided to set up a Muslim Girls' Sixth Form College. The curriculum that they established was narrow focusing on English, mathematics, crafts and cookery, and excluded all science subjects. One women's group publically denounced the Muslim girls' college initiative in the press. This created antagonism and galvanised men in favour of the college. Nilofer and Rifat from AYM (Manchester)'s women's wing argued that while they were against any religious schools, they wanted the community to be involved in the decision making and to be properly informed about what this college was really offering. They put out loads of leaflets focusing on the second rate nature of the schooling offered by the college and called people to come and take part in a public meeting. At the meeting they publically asked the proposed director Mr Salaam if he was planning to send his own daughter there. He was not because she was studying the sciences. In the end, only one person signed up for the college and the initiative collapsed.

In reflecting on the AYMs and their political strategies as a whole, despite a theoretical belief in women's emancipation and the structures and policies that they wrote, it is clear that the AYMs did not forefront gender issues in the campaigns with which they were involved, nor did they take up issues that were specific to women. In the deportation case of Jaswinder Kaur who was threatened with deportation as a result of leaving her husband through domestic violence, the AYMs in Manchester and Bradford as well as UBYL stressed the racism of the immigration laws with the slogan 'The racism of the immigration laws are destroying black people's lives'. They did not highlight the right of women to challenge domestic violence. Gender issues were never a priority.

The need by Asian women to raise issues of concern to them and to challenge patriarchal oppression within their own communities led to women forming their own organisations, the most notable being Awaz, Southall Black Sisters (SBS), BBS, and Organisation of Women of African and Asian Descent (OWAAD). Amrit Wilson remembers 'always having to fight our corner' in the wider anti-racist movement, and explains why it was necessary to set up separate women's organisations.

Many of us had earlier belonged to the predominantly male black movement or the predominantly white women's movement. By forming Awaz in 1977 we had taken a stand against the sexism of the former and the racism of the latter. But these were not the reasons why we, a handful of mainly young Asian women, had set up the group. It was rather that we desperately needed a way of addressing our needs and those of other Asian women. (Wilson 2006:161).

Awaz, for example, were the first to campaign against the scandal of virginity testing in 1979 after a 35-year-old Indian woman spoke out about the test she had undergone at Heathrow when entering Britain as a fiancée. They also supported Asian women workers at Grunwick's and Futter's in North London. They demonstrated in alliance with other black groups against police racism and also did the political groundwork to set up one of the first Asian women refuges in the UK (Wilson 2006:162).

Gita Sahgal has commented on how 'it was partly because of [SYM's] lumpen posturing and sexual harassment that SBS had been formed' (Sahgal 1989:14). While issues of racism were being raised repeatedly in Southall, there was little mention of women's oppression, and so 'women felt they ought to come together and make their voice heard' (Hendessi 1989:10). In November 1979, Southall Black Sisters was formed to support campaigns against both racism and women's oppression. While mainly mobilising South Asian women they did make links with African and Caribbean women too. As Avtar Brah highlights,

Our aim was to devise effective strategies for working within our own communities – for challenging the specific configuration of patriarchal relations of these communities as well as in the society at large – while actively opposing the racism to which all Black people, men and women, are subjected. We had to make connections between our oppression in Britain and that of women in the Third World. (Brah 1989:13)

The group supported Southall Defence Committee that came together to support anti-racist campaigners charged with public order offences after the death of Blair Peach, as well as campaigns against racist attacks. They worked alongside other groups in Southall such as Southall Rights to provide advice on aspects relating to women's lives. Like the AYMs, they also supported trade union struggles in the black community such as the strike by women workers at the Chix factory in Slough. Tensions between SBS and other organisations did exist, as Mandana Hendessi recalls:

> Some organisations tried to trivialise our role within the community – referring to us as a small group of women or mocking the name. Why don't you call yourselves Southall Brown Sisters. There were a lot of struggles in trying to assert ourselves as an important political group in Southall. We had to cope with sexism from other organisations. (Hendessi 1989:11)

SBS, Awaz and BBS were very much part of the anti-racist movement during the 1970s and 1980s, and the Asian Youth Movements supported some of their initiatives. AYMs in Bradford, Manchester, Sheffield and Birmingham supported the campaign by SBS in support of Balwant Kaur, murdered as a result of domestic violence in 1985. They also supported BBS' campaign to free Iqbal Begum, jailed for killing her husband after suffering years of domestic violence. Iqbal Begum's case brought the issues of racism and gender oppression together since she received a life sentence after believing the term 'guilty' meant *gulti* (Punjabi for mistake) when no interpreter was present to translate for her in the court. There is no doubt that there was a genuine desire from AYM (Bradford) and AYM (Manchester) in particular to support struggles for women's liberation, and this desire can be seen in the support that they won from organisations such as SBS, Awaz, and the Wages for Housework and Black Wages for Housework campaigns during the campaign to free the Bradford 12.

While the AYMs worked with Asian women's groups, tensions did exist. AYM (Bradford)'s failure to contact black women's organisations at the conception of their idea of a black freedom march led to criticism and the eventual abandonment of the whole idea. Macho attitudes in AYM (Birmingham) and their lack of women members led BBS to dub the Birmingham Asian Youth Movement as 'the Asian Young Men's Association'. The AYM in its turn critiqued BBS, as Sheera Johal recounts,

> Birmingham Black Sisters always saw us men as at fault but there was a class issue. In the Kewal Brothers strike, BBS wanted to organise the women separately, which caused divisions. We felt that it was imperative that all the workers were together. We had

a committee with various organisations and we organised funds and meetings. (Johal 2006)

Surinder Guru however, has highlighted the key difficulties for some of the women strikers at the time with both the racism and sexism of the Union being manifest. The Union for example organised a meeting in a pub with no childcare, and the sexism of the IWA, in particular, impacted on the strike support group:

Inside the meetings the atmosphere was one of such total domination that we found it difficult to speak out. This was made worse by the fact that when we did speak the men did not debate with us or even openly disagree, they merely humoured us and carried on making decisions behind the scenes. (Outwrite 31 in Guru 1987:278).

When BBS critiqued IWA in the feminist magazine *Outwrite*, the women were accused of being middle class. The criticism of women being middle class was a retort that many black women were faced with when trying to put across their perspectives. While this may have sometimes been the case, and Guru recognises this in her reflections on the work of the Kewal Brothers Strike Support Group, such comments did not engage with the problems that BBS were raising, of men holding on to information and making decisions without consulting the women involved (Guru 1987:279).

Amrit Wilson has reflected on the way that in many campaigns 'any woman that became articulate was suddenly labelled middle class, no matter what her or her parents' background' (Wilson 2007). Many Asian women's organisations had a large proportion of female students, because as students they were often less bound by the patriarchal strictures of Asian communities. Also as students they tended to have more time and be more willing to take risks. These students could not simply be dubbed 'middle class', many of the Asian students in the late 1970s and early 1980s came from families that were relatively impoverished and while they may have come from lower middle class backgrounds, as teachers in village schools or low-paid clerical workers in the subcontinent, they were often from rural communities and their parents were declassed through migration so the class positions were complex and constantly changing. Sometimes when Amrit raised issues about gender, she would be accused of not being 'black' enough, or being middle class, yet so many of the men involved in making these accusations were middle class themselves. The AYMs also recruited students in Manchester, Sheffield and Birmingham. Yet the high number of students in Asian women's organisations were criticised. 'What should have been focused on were people's roles within the struggle, what matters is what they do and their view of the world' (Amrit Wilson 2012).

5
Campaigning Against the Immigration Laws

'Labour Tory both the same, both play the racist game!'
(Slogan of the Asian Youth Movements)

The surveillance of black communities by immigration officials was another form of the policing of black communities in the 1970s and 1980s. The Asian Youth Movement campaigns against the immigration laws can therefore be seen to be linked to their wider protests against the policing and disciplining of black communities. It enabled the youth to highlight the institutional racism of the state and the media, whose attitudes fostered an environment that scapegoated black people as the reason for the ills in British society. The 1971 Immigration Act gave police and immigration officials sweeping powers to stop and search blacks or their premises on suspicion of illegal entry. They also had the authority to impose surveillance over 'ghettos' and carry out raids on social centres (Waddington 1992:79). The memory and knowledge of the colonial past influenced the AYMs in their struggle against the immigration laws: 'We are here, because you were there' was a statement asserted repeatedly. Jani and Noorzaman Rashid's father had been in the Scottish Dragoon Guards in Malaysia. Tariq Mehmood's father and grandfather had both been members of the British Army. 'It was ridiculous, we were good enough to die for the country but not to live here' (Mehmood 2007).

In comparison to other black communities, the immigration laws had a particular impact on the Asian community because these laws were brought in deliberately to stem the flow of South Asian migrants. There were therefore both personal as well as political reasons for this focus. In challenging the immigration laws they took on a struggle that was inter-generational, affecting both young and old. Their youthful energy and belief in social justice led them to pursue cases even when there was no legal avenue left. Their passionate engagement and determination meant that they adopted creative strategies with which to profile their cause. The youth movements always emphasised the role of both the Labour and the Tory party in endorsing immigration restrictions, which put them in conflict with sections of the left. Their activity on the immigration laws also highlights the wide network of support they tried to foster, as well as their desire to spread their organisational skills and empower those that were the most oppressed.

CONTEXT

When Britain left the subcontinent, she had left a pool of labour with no capital to make this labour productive. There was no alternative but for labour to move to the source of capital, to move from the sub-continent to the UK (Sivanandan 1976). The youth had witnessed families move from their home countries over a period of years, to work in factories across the UK. In Yorkshire, Asian workers had entered the wool textile industry when employers had invested in new machinery during the post-war period to be able to compete effectively with new factories in Europe. To maintain profitability, employers sought to run the new machines continuously, moving from an eight-hour day shift and short evening shift to a twelve-hour day shift and a twelve-hour night shift. While women had previously comprised the largest percentage of textile workers because they would work for less than male workers, with the introduction of the night shift a larger pool of cheap labour was needed and employers looked to the colonies (Ahmat et al. 1983). As the *Wolverhampton Express and Star* concluded in 1956, 'If Britain's present boom is to be maintained, more workers must be found. Where? The new recruits to British industry must come it would seem, from abroad, from the colonies, Eire and the Continent' (Brown 1995:9). Textile employers also believed that South Asians would be a more docile workforce. They believed that Asians would work for less than white workers and held on to racist concepts of Asians being more 'nimble fingered' than their white counterparts (Jackson 1992:202–4). This led to the concentration of South Asian workers in mills across the north of England, including Bradford, usually working the unsociable night shift.

Despite the economic necessity of non-white labour, racist attitudes cultivated during the colonial period criticised black migrants as lazy, on the scrounge, prone to high birth rates and harbingers of crime and disease. Such attitudes were used to justify the need for immigration controls and to develop a link between immigration and welfare reform as early as the 1900s (Cohen

2003). As Carter and colleagues (1987) have highlighted, from 1945 onwards both the Labour and Conservative parties debated the impact of black immigration and the need for controls. As early as 1951, the Labour Party had already recommended that any future immigration controls would 'as a general rule, be more or less confined to coloured persons' (Miles & Phizacklea 1984:25–6). Building on such ideas, some back bench Tory MPs instigated the artificial link between immigration control and good race relations in the late 1950s, suggesting that a small number of immigrants could be absorbed into society but large numbers would cause problems. From this period on, 'the numbers game' began to be played in immigration politics by both the Labour and the Tory parties, framing the black presence in Britain as a problem that needed containment.

On a personal level nearly all the members of the Asian Youth Movements had experienced at first hand the exclusionary practices of the immigration laws. The 1962 Commonwealth Immigrants Act established quotas for entry from those in the British Commonwealth and the young people who came here were aware of their families' exclusion:

> We knew our families could not come here. I came with my grandfather and I knew my mother and father could not come here to live with me... I came as my uncle, because a visa had been sent for my uncle after he had died. We were very poor and my grandfather decided to take me to England as his son. I had been partly raised by my grandmother anyway... another Uncle used to beat me to try to make sure that I understood that my name would now be Tariq Mehmood Ali, that I had a date of birth, and I was forced to learn all these things... and they said that I would have to go back if I gave the wrong answers to the immigration man who would interview me when we got off at the airport... so that idea absolutely terrified me... the prospect of being taken away from my grandfather. (Mehmood 2007)

These personal memories and experiences are testament to the impact and pain that these laws caused in their lives.

Despite Labour's pledge in opposition to repeal the 1962 Act, in 1968 they brought in measures to curb Commonwealth immigration further to prevent East African Asians with UK passports moving to Britain. The act removed the right of all UK passport holders to live in Britain. The only ones that would be free from immigration control were those that could prove they had a parent or grandparent that had been born, adopted, registered, or naturalized in the UK. These were largely white people. For those with passports and no naturalised parent or grandparent in the UK, a quota system was established to restrict entry. The act was a clear attempt to further control non-white immigration to Britain. Jayesh Amin came from Nairobi in Kenya:

> we came to Britain because my family were all British passport holders and during the 1960s the political situation changed. In 1966 Kenya introduced a Kenyanisation policy which meant a British passport holder couldn't work, that meant that there was nowhere else to go … we finally got our visas in 1971, that's me and my mother, 'cos my father died in 1967 so that was more difficult, (pause) to earn a living really in that sense of the word. (Amin 2006)

Their own personal lives therefore documented the brutality of the immigration laws that dehumanised their existence in the eyes of the wider public and presented them as unwanted 'problems'.

The 1971 Immigration Act cemented the divisions that the quota system had introduced by constructing two types of citizens. This division also impacted on people already living in Britain. Whereas UK law had previously divided the world into British subjects and aliens, this act changed that division into patrials and non-patrials. It was only patrials that had the right to live in the UK. To be a patrial you had to have a parent or grandparent born in the UK, been naturalised or registered in the UK, or have lived in the UK for five years previously. All the categories ensured that fewer black citizens than whites would have 'the right of abode'. By creating criteria for the right of abode, the act removed the rights of some British subjects to the point where nationality became practically worthless (Clayton 2010). The Act also gave the state the right to imprison those that could not prove their citizenship, in so doing as AYM (Bradford) wrote in *Kala Tara*,

> the act… has institutionalised one law for the whites and one law for the blacks. It has institutionalised racism. Since this act came into effect on the 1st of January 1973 over 6,000 blacks have been imprisoned under its powers. … police can enter any black person's home without warrant on suspicion that an illegal immigrant lives there. … This act gives … powers to: throw us

into prison, separate our families, carry out virginity tests on our mothers, sisters and daughters, give X-rays which would not be allowed here and which can cause cancer to pregnant women and children. (AYM Bradford 1979:9).

The idea of suggesting that a person could be illegal for nothing more than their desire to work and feed their families and categorised as criminal, rather than referring to actions that someone had taken as illegal was challenged through the dozens of campaigns that the youth supported.

Campaigning against the immigration laws enabled the AYMs and others to expose the racism of the state and its intrinsic violence, rather than simply focusing on the violence of right-wing extremists on the street. The first campaign that AYM (Bradford) led was the anti-deportation case of Saeed Rahman, a trade unionist who was arrested and imprisoned on suspicion of being an illegal immigrant. In October 1978, with the support of the Campaign against Deportations and Racist Immigration Laws (CADRIL), AYM organised a picket outside Armley Jail to protest against Rahman's arrest. The picket secured his release. AYM (Bradford) along with other campaigners used the case to push forward the campaign against the immigration laws nationally. On 21 October 1978 a demonstration was called by CADRIL. It aimed to be 'the START of a campaign against the immigration laws – not a one off event... to unite all the organisations and individuals black and white, anti-racist and in the Labour Movement... into an effective campaign' (Leamington ARAF 1978:12).

Over the next few years, AYM worked tirelessly to campaign against the immigration laws to expose the inherent racism of the state. They worked within broad umbrella organisations such as Campaign against Racist Laws (CARL), CADRIL and Campaign Against Immigration Laws (CAIL) as well as in individual case campaigns. A number of key organisers in the movements in both Manchester and Bradford comment on how the campaign against the immigration laws took up the majority of their time. The AYMs worked particularly closely with CARL under the chairmanship of Jagmohan Joshi, leader of the IWA. A host of black organisations supported the establishment of CARL such as the IWAs, the KWAs, the West Indian Standing Committee, along with the Communist Party and the Anti-Nazi League. This organisation focused on the racist nature of the laws and galvanised a broad front to protest against existing immigration legislation as well as against the Conservative Party's forthcoming Nationality Bill. The new legislation aimed to further limit the black presence in Britain. It would remove a right that had existed since medieval times – that children born in Britain had the right to citizenship. As a CARL newsletter outlined:

> racial discrimination is fundamental to the division into categories of citizenship which is the very core of the Bill. The Government and its supporters talk of 'close connections' as the basis for full British citizenship; when examined these turn out most often to be connections of ancestry. A third generation settler in Argentina or South Africa whose grandfather was the last to set foot in Britain and who has the nationality of the country he lives in as well as UK citizenship has 'close connections'. An Asian with only UK citizenship who was recruited into British Government service in East Africa, has lived in Britain but not for five continuous years and has all the rest of his family here does not have 'close connections'. (CARL 1981:2–3).

In CARL, AYM along with the Indian Workers Association and other anti-racist organisations helped to mobilise a march of 20,000 people against the Nationality Bill in London. They coined the

5.1   AYM (Bradford) at Trafalgar Square for the national demonstration against the Nationality Bill, 1979 (courtesy Mohsin Zulfiqar).

slogan 'End Racist Immigration laws, All immigration laws are racist', as well as: 'Labour, Tory both the same, both play the racist game' to highlight the drive by both parties since 1962 to curtail non-white immigration. While the first slogan was cumbersome and some activists on the left argued that it should simply be 'End all immigration controls' (which would eventually be the slogan of the 'No one is illegal' campaign established in 1997), the AYMs along with other organisations in CARL felt that the longer slogan was the only way to emphasise the issue of racism. Because racism was the central reason for the existence of the laws and why they should be combated, they believed it needed to be reflected in campaign slogans.

CASES INTO ISSUES

One of the key strategies that the AYMs adopted in struggling against the immigration laws was the development of individual immigration campaigns. They believed that it would enable them to humanise an issue that could seem distant and dry, embedded in migration statistics and policy arguments. The turning of cases into issues is a strategy for political mobilisation and education which Sivanandan has pointed out was frequently used by black communities as an organisational strategy during the 1970s and 1980s:

> Cases are one off, local, disconnected; issues are national and anti-state. The trial of the Bradford twelve, for instance, brought to national prominence the issues of self defence and conspiracy law; the murder of Blair Peach at the Southall demonstration brought into question the role of the Special Patrol Group and the validity of internal police investigations; the New Cross Massacre and the case of Colin Roach showed, among other things, the bias and inadequacies of the coroners court. (Sivanandan 1990:74)

We could continue this list by highlighting the individual immigration cases that the Asian Youth Movements took up to present the human impact of these racist laws. As time went on the difficulties of such a strategy became apparent. Firstly it was not possible to create individual campaigns for everybody and this meant that those that were selected could appear more 'worthy' than others. Secondly, when the state began to fund anti-deportation campaigns in the mid 1980s the youth ended up feeling like social workers and sometimes were even identified as such. In the late 1970s however, the cases acted to expose the inhumanity of the state.

Of the dozens of immigration campaigns that the AYMs were involved with, the Anwar Ditta case stands out. It was a campaign that won national support and coverage, created a forum through which youth in Manchester, Bradford, Dewsbury and Batley, Nottingham and Sheffield worked together. It was a heartbreaking story. The campaign highlights the way in which the youth movements worked to put the families at the centre of campaigns to promote the issues rather than their organisation. It reveals their tireless determination to struggle for justice. For the young people in the AYMs if the law was wrong, it should be changed. With the support of the youth movements and her own resolute determination, Anwar Ditta spoke at about 400 public meetings in less than 18 months. Her case made clear that the racism of the immigration laws was not an issue of Conservative Party discrimination versus Labour Party acceptance of migration. Anwar's children were first refused entry under a Labour Party authority. The Tories continued the injustice. In their leaflets the AYMs even highlighted that the party most responsible for perpetrating racist immigration laws were the Labour party. Finally, Anwar's case exposed the ludicrous judgements that the immigration service would go to keep black people out of the country. It exposed their racism.

THE CASE OF ANWAR DITTA

Anwar Ditta was born in Birmingham in 1953. Her parents separated when she was nine years old. Her father was given custody of the children, and she and her sister were sent to Pakistan. She was married in 1967 although below the age of consent and had three children, Kamran, Imran and Saima, while living in Pakistan. In 1975 she and her husband decided to return to England. They left the three children in Pakistan while they found work and a place to live, intending to send for the children as soon as they were settled.

On returning to Britain, Anwar Ditta and her husband remarried believing that their Islamic marriage would not be recognised under English law. Since they believed that their previous marriage was not recognised, they gave their status as bachelor and spinster. This was to prove a costly mistake. They applied for their children to join them in England in September 1976. After two and a half years of waiting, in May 1979, the Home Office declared that they were 'not satisfied that Kamran, Imran and Saima were related to Anwar

Sultana Ditta and Shuja ud Din as stated'. The Entry Clearance officer even came up with the absurd idea that,

> no clear evidence of Anwar Sultana Ditta ever having been in Pakistan had been produced... . It appeared that there might be two Anwar Ditta's, i.e. one who married Shuja-u-din in Pakistan in 1968 and the other who Shuja-u-din married in the United Kingdom in 1975. (Anwar Ditta Defence Committee, 1980)

The Home Office also suggested that Anwar's children actually belonged to her sister-in-law: 'there is a similarity in ages and even in names between the children and Jamila and the three applicants'.

Anwar had photographs of herself in Pakistan with her husband, her family and with her children. She had birth certificates for all her children and, despite having asthma in England as a child and needing frequent medical attention, there were no medical records for her in Britain for 13 years until she re-registered in 1975. When Anwar's fourth child was born in Rochdale, the hospital also confirmed that this was her fourth child. None of this evidence was adequate to accept the children as hers.

In November 1979, Anwar attended a meeting at Longsight Library in Manchester about the deportation cases of Nasira Begum and Nasreen Akhtar to find out more about what she could do.

> I went down to that public meeting. ... Everybody spoke there about Nasreen's case and there was a question at the end of the meeting, 'Has anybody else got a problem?' And I just stood up and told what I was going through. (crying) I says, 'Yes I have got a problem and this is what we're going through. I've got three children that were born there and they're not allowed. And I've given all the birth certificates, the documents, everything, photographs...' People were shocked and I was shocked myself because I couldn't control myself... And people said 'We'll come to Rochdale' and that's where the struggle started. And after that it was non stop. (Ditta 2006)

Anwar Ditta's case like so many cases before and after, are testament to the possibilities of joint action. Manchester Law Centre, Friends of Nasira Begum, the Revolutionary Communist Group and Chez Dolan from the CRE were all involved in the initial meeting in Rochdale. Asian Youth Movement (Bradford) and the Asian Youth Movement (Manchester) also got involved in supporting the establishment of Anwar Ditta Defence Campaign in November 1979. As Steve Cohen recalled, it 'was an AYM campaign, that's where the main energy was coming from'. The campaign however was supported by a wide variety of organisations apart from the AYMs of Manchester and Bradford, including the Indian Workers Association, Rochdale Trades Council, Rochdale Labour Party, members of the Conservative and Liberal Parties, National Union of Public Employees, Rochdale CRE, Rochdale Asian Women's Movement and individuals such as the MP Joel Barnett and Vanessa Redgrave.

The first picket as Anwar recalls was in front of the Conservative Party offices on Drake Street, in Rochdale. From then,

> the campaign just grew and grew... I wouldn't have done it without the support of people outside the house. I was just an ordinary housewife. Didn't know anything from outside or what was going on or how to do things. But it was all the support from everybody. (Ditta 2006)

The campaign organised pickets and demonstrations in Rochdale and Manchester, with 'energetic petitioning' particularly in Rochdale where they collected thousands of signatures for a petition to Timothy Raison, the Home Office minister, to demand an appeal hearing as soon as possible since her children were growing up all the time (CAIL 1980:1).

Anwar was granted an appeal date on 28 April 1980 and with the help of supporters and legal advice from South Manchester Law Centre she built her case. The legal support from the law centre, however, was hindered by the inexperience of the solicitor assigned to the case. On 30 July 1980, Anwar lost her appeal, despite the provision of more evidence in the form of affidavits from family as well as documentation from Rochdale hospital that she had had four children.

The Home Office upheld the adjudicator's decision on the basis that Anwar and Shuja had lied to the authorities when they got married in the UK since they had registered themselves as bachelor and spinster. Second, when marrying for the first time in Pakistan, a family member had recorded Anwar's date of birth as 20, since as a minor at 14 she was under the legal age of consent, this was also presented as Anwar's own lies. Third, they suggested that Shuja had entered the UK by deception, and fourth, that Anwar had deceived the authorities by applying for a UK passport in 1975

5.2   Photograph of a march in support of Anwar Ditta's case in Rochdale, showing the mobilisation of the community in support of the campaign and not just the production of a media campaign (courtesy of Anwar Ditta, 1980), AD 35.

(before her UK marriage) in her maiden name. The fact that there were understandable reasons for each of these issues were ignored and the couple were presented as having deliberately deceived the state.

Steve Cohen recalls the politics that the state played at that time. The other key immigration case in Manchester was that of Nasira Begum who had been forced to leave her husband as a result of domestic violence was also under appeal at this time: 'The verdicts in both Anwar and Nasira's case were given by the same adjudicator ... on the same day in Manchester, Nasira wins, Anwar loses' (Cohen 2003:217). It was like 'the numbers game' being applied to appeals.

Losing the appeal left no legal avenue open to Anwar. It inevitably caused conflict in the committee and the Law Centre were expelled from the Defence Committee because of their failure to represent Anwar effectively, although individuals such as Steve Cohen continued to support the campaign. The youth movements found a new solicitor and continued to mobilise in support of Anwar. The strength of the campaign along with the determination of Anwar Ditta herself led World in Action to commission a documentary to look into the case, which was screened in March 1981. The documentary led to Anwar's new solicitor Ruth Bundey, a politically committed solicitor travelling with a Granada Television camera crew to Pakistan to collect evidence from teachers, religious figures and the local community that Anwar and her children were who they said they were. They found Anwar's Pakistani identity card with her thumb print on it, and took all the evidence and witnesses – including a goat – to the British High Commission. Finally blood tests from her children and Anwar were analysed in London to prove that the children were undoubtedly hers – an examination which she had always offered to undertake. Following the screening of the documentary on national television, the Home Office refusal was overturned. Anwar's children arrived in Britain in April 1981. The tireless and selfless work that so many individuals did for her led to Anwar giving support to others struggling for justice in the years to follow.

THE SIGNIFICANCE OF THE ANWAR DITTA DEFENCE CAMPAIGN

The success of Anwar Ditta's campaign should not be seen as simply the result of media coverage but lay instead in the community support that was established without which World in Action would never have been interested in the case. The Anwar Ditta campaign represents the strength of the AYMs to organise and build solidarity as well as their ability to empower the victims – in this case, Anwar Ditta. Short in stature, and wearing traditional *salwar kameez*, but with her broad and distinctive northern accent, she was a striking figure. She spoke with a passion and emotion that could only come from a mother who wanted to see her children:

> I am willing to give a medical test. I am willing to give a skin test. I am willing to go on a lie detector to prove that they are my children. I am not telling them any lies, why should I tell them lies? Why should I claim other people's children?... People think why did I leave the children? This is not a crime. I didn't know English law. I didn't know I could bring my children straight away and that the home office would have provided them with accommodation, money and everything. ... I thought if I go to England and get a job and buy a house and we have got settled, then I'll call the children. I didn't want my children to suffer. ... We never even have a decent day, we are never happy. ... Why? Because they are our children. There is no one in the world who

can prove that they are not our children. (Friends of Anwar Ditta AD240:2).

Such speeches, as Tariq Mehmood remembers, had an emotional and powerful impact: 'There are many grown men whom she reduced to tears'. The support which she garnered along with her own energy encouraged Anwar to believe in her right to justice and drove her campaign:

> I went everywhere really, you name it. Universities, colleges, law centres, law society meetings, public meetings, demonstrations, student union meetings. There were support groups... and I used to go everywhere. ... I can remember when I went down to see Ian [Macdonald] the first time in the London chamber. We set off from Rochdale, we went to Nottingham, there was a law society meeting there. We went to the meeting and we weren't allowed to speak. And you know, we literally forced ourselves in and said 'I want to speak at the meeting', so we did. I did speak. From there we went to Birmingham, talked at a meeting there. We ended up in London. And we used to do meetings like that... my husband used to come back from work, I'd make dinner, go in the car, feed him while he's driving, going down to Liverpool, speak at the meeting there...

The memories of the hundreds of meetings at which she spoke can be felt in the catalogue of events that she lists in the account above, which are still powerfully remembered after 25 years. The Asian Youth Movement's empowerment of victims can also be seen in Anwar's speeches from the time. She learnt to highlight the way in which her own case reflected the injustice of a system that appeared to criminalise and victimise her for being black.

> When a person commits a crime, for example murder, they only need one or two witnesses to convict him. I've got more than ten or twenty witnesses who can prove they are my children, but the Home Office doesn't bother to ask them. ... Why am I going to these meetings? Why am I getting people to help me? Because they are my children. Do you think it's easy to campaign? Do you think it's easy to go out in all weathers to petition? Do you think it's easy doing all these things? It's really ridiculous making black people suffer and destroying their families. What kind of a

law is this? God knows what hell we are going through. (Friends of Anwar Ditta AD240:3)

In building solidarity, the campaign liaised with trade unions, left organisations, religious organisations and celebrities. Anwar learned to speak in front of hundreds of people to publicise her plight. The youth movements through their prolific campaigning and networking, as well as their unqualified support for justice against racist and imperialist systems enabled them to not only nationalise, but internationalise the struggle of Anwar Ditta. Irish Republican Prisoner Bobby Sands declared:

> Unity is <u>stronger</u> than courts.
> A building will <u>crumble</u>.
> Through <u>your</u> life and <u>your</u> children,
> You are <u>eternal</u>.
> Laws can <u>NEVER</u> weaken that ever

> (Poem from Bobby Sands to Anwar Ditta,
> 11 August 1980)

The success of Anwar Ditta's campaign, as well as that of Nasira Begum, was to motivate others to struggle for justice.

CREATIVITY AND PARTY POLITICAL CHALLENGES

An important quality in many of the immigration campaigns that the AYMs were involved with was their lack of any secondary political agenda as well as their constant creativity in finding new ways to challenge state racism. They exposed the often contradictory rules that existed within British law. This was a key factor in their success, as was their belief in self-reliance. The cases of Baba Bakhtaura and Mohammad Idrish from Birmingham highlight the AYMs commitment to keeping the family's interest at the centre of campaigns. In the process they exposed the opportunism of the local Labour Party.

Baba Bakhtaura was a Punjabi folk singer living in Birmingham who was charged with overstaying in 1982 after he had served as a musician for religious ceremonies and marriages in temples and elsewhere. He was initially imprisoned with a magistrate's recommendation that he be deported.

He was a singer and entertainer as well as an occasional contributor to gurdwaras in the form of religious hymns and so on. And we … felt that he had some value to our community and even though he originally arrived as a visitor, his own brother and most of his family were settled here. He also had an existing disability, which meant to some degree that he was dependent on his father and his mother and his brother and sister who were all here. (Bassi 2006)

The campaign led by Asian Youth Movement (Birmingham) raised funds within the community to support the defence of Bakhtaura who eventually won a High Court ruling that the interests of the community had not been taken in to consideration when the decision was taken to deport him. The Home Office, however, then appealed the decision and the Court of Appeal ruled in the Home Office's favour.

The AYM took up the case, as with the case of Anwar Ditta, when legal avenues for the campaign were running out. The youth looked for new ways to gain publicity and attention to Bakhtaura's plight. They found this in a loophole that existed in the law in 1983, which permitted any Commonwealth citizen to stand in a general election in the UK. The contradiction of being permitted to stand for election as a member of parliament in the UK but not being permitted to reside in the UK amused members of the youth movement and they decided to exploit it. While the local Labour party and the IWA in Birmingham had supported the case of Bakhtaura to begin with, the minute the case could interfere with the interests of a local Labour Party election they withdrew all support, despite the fact that the tactic of standing was never intended as an attempt to win, but rather to raise awareness and support for Bakhtaura. The Labour party not only withdrew support but actively campaigned against Baba Bakhtaura, opening up offices on Soho Road in Handsworth directly opposite the office of the Bakhtaura campaign. As Bhupinder reflected on the way they viewed the struggle at the time:

the only way for Black people to fight was through a process of dignity and self-reliance through our own communities … ultimately our white comrades would leave. … like when Baba Bakhtaura … stood against Claire Short… I remember me and Tariq walking into the *Ivy Bush* one day and Claire Short walking in… 'Everyone can have a drink except that bastard' and she pointed at Tariq… And here she is, this great leftist, has no possibility whatsoever of actually losing the election ... she could have shown some humility of knowing that that was actually the case. I mean Baba Bakhtaura must have picked up all of 300 votes and she must have had a majority of 36,000 or something stupid. And she still felt the pain of the 300 votes that she'd lost. Not recognising that because of that process the AYM had used whatever means necessary to highlight the case of Baba Bakhtaura and the effect on our community and the effect on his family and the effect on other families.

Through the perseverance of the youth, Baba Bakhtaura eventually won his right to remain after seven years.

As with the Anwar Ditta Campaign, the Asian Youth Movement used music and culture to develop and consolidate the campaign within the community. As a local singer, the use of music was an organic part of the campaign. Influenced by the traditions of the IWAs where music was integral to political events, Bakhtaura not only sang at AYM socials and fundraisers but also wrote a song with the AYM to represent the attitudes to immigration controls that the AYMs and IWAs expressed:

> *labouraan vi ayaan, ithay torian vi ayaan*
> *Phar kay kanoonaan dihaan boreeyaan layayaan*
> *Sanoo sooth payaa ay kanoon saraay*
> *Ni ki ba noo kalyaan dha*
> *Inaan khadnain valait vichoon saray*
> *Varoo vareen saryaan te time aoo ga*
> *Khatay ho ka jay ajh nahinay larnaan*

> Labour and Tory have ruled here
> They bring sackfuls of laws
> None of these laws suit us
> What will happen to (us) blacks
> They will kick us all out of Britain
> Turn by turn your time will come
> Unless you unite and fight today

A visiting Punjabi musician also wrote a song about the immigration laws to support Baba Bakhtaura's case. The links with progressive musicians from the subcontinent were supported through contacts with the IWA.

Torian da dekho jalva
Millaan Khali payaan daindian dohayaan
Ni laralapa lai rakhday
Te reportaan pichay parolan raziaan

Look at the deafness of the Tories
Empty mills are crying out
They keep dangling enticement
And they search our bed sheets on the words of informers.

The songs brought to life the experiences of South Asians in Britain, highlighting the experience of migration, the decline of the textile industry as well as the surveillance of South Asian communities through the primary purpose rule established in 1983 to cast doubt on marriages, using the opinions of informers to police communities.

The campaign against the deportation of Mohammad Idrish was another example of the Labour Party's qualified support for anti-deportation campaigns. Mohammad Idrish, a founder member of the Dr Barnardo's National Association of Local Government Officers (NALGO) branch in Birmingham, was charged with deportation after he separated from his wife despite the fact that he had lived with his wife for five years and was formally married for two and a half years. At his appeal, the adjudicator dismissed Mohammad's case because of his focus on the validity of the marriage due to the growing government suspicion over marriages and the constant assertion that many marriages were simply 'marriages of convenience'. Because of his work for NALGO, the union supported his campaign politically and through funds, and as a result of union support, the local Labour Party also offered support to the campaign. However, when Idrish lost his last legal appeal he had to search for support from the Asian Youth Movement in Birmingham to find a way forward:

The tactic was obvious to us. I remember clandestine meetings with Idrish in the Everest Social Club where the Idrish campaign used to meet. ... and we'd say 'Look, the only thing you can now do is that there's a local election around the corner and you know we could win a local election. We could win it, but you must stand against the Labour Party'... and Idrish: 'Oh, no, no, that's inconceivable. I'll talk to my committee and I'm sure that because I'm an upstanding member of NALGO now and NALGO's very supportive of me and is responsible for selecting

Labour candidates and so on, they will be giving me full backing and I could become the official Labour candidate.' And we said, 'well, if that happens, we'd say it was a minor miracle, but we won't stand against you.' Idrish's thought's were quite naive because the Labour Party made it clear to him that they thought he was a worthy victim but not a worthy candidate. (Bassi 2006)

Idrish's decision to stand against the Labour Party led to nearly all the white people on the committee, and one or two Asians leaving. The youth movement took control of the campaign which lost by a few votes, but achieved the intention of raising the profile of Idrish's case. Bassi's analysis of the defeat, however, exposes the way in which the Labour party exploited sub-continental conflicts to ensure that their candidate won:

And the basis of the defeat was most interesting because ... it signals the true intent of Labour in power. Idrish was winning this election before it even started. Initially it was a white candidate to stand against Idrish. Idrish would've won hands down. ... The first thing the Labour Party did to stop Idrish winning was to withdraw the white candidate two days before the deadline and replace him with a Pakistani. And literally the whole campaign after that was sloganed by the local Labour apparatchiks, Pakistani apparatchiks, who supported this Pakistani candidate with, 'this is a rematch war of the Bangladesh war of independence and the AYMs represented India'... and this time Pakistan would win. ... So the Ghoras (the whites) were quite prepared to draw a point where they knew black people would fight frantically to the end.

In the end Idrish won his campaign, which highlighted the value of AYMs commitment to self-reliance and solidarity. Both the Baba Bakhtaura Campaign and the Mohammad Idrish Campaign exposed the Labour and Conservative Party as responsible for the development of state racism. Self reliance proved important both in terms of financial independence but also in terms of understanding where unconditional support lay. This had been a reason for the establishment of the AYMs in the first place.

BLACK FREEDOM MARCH

While organising for individuals, the Asian Youth Movements never lost sight of their goal to challenge state racism. In 1980, during the height of the Anwar Ditta campaign, AYM (Bradford) decided to organise a Black Freedom march from Bradford to London. The driving force for the march was the forthcoming Nationality Bill. By focusing the march on the issue of immigration, the AYMs aimed to highlight the immigration laws as central to the struggle against racism. It enabled the youth to emphasise the role of the state in fostering and maintaining racism in Britain. For Anwar Qadir,

> the Black Freedom March is something that we talked about in the light of Martin Luther King's march in the South and we felt it would be a good idea if we could organise a demonstration which highlighted the plight of the Black community in this country. (Qadir 2006)

In highlighting the black communities' plight, they linked the struggle of the immigration laws with other issues such as police harassment, the events of Southall in 1979 and the death of Blair Peach, and an end to the bussing of black children to school. The campaign leaflet stated: 'We want: Freedom from racial harassment, freedom from police harassment; freedom from unemployment; freedom to organise independently and freedom to live with dignity' (tandana.org SC1).

Although the march never took place, the planning of such an event enabled AYM (Bradford) to network across the country. The youth wanted to use the event to build a national organisation between all those struggling against racism in Britain. As Tariq recalls,

> we felt that we could follow some sort of a long march as they used to do in China or in America and we thought that in that process we would be able to organise a national body. ...We had lots of contacts, we had enormous support right across little towns and you know we thought that we would take these issues of the immigration laws or racist violence to lots and lots of British working class communities who we felt were the most important ones who should fight racism... We organised the Black Freedom March to have a big event which we could be a part of. (Mehmood 2006)

The Black Freedom March was an idea that enabled them to link very local struggles such as the defence of an Asian father who was thrown out of a pub for speaking in Punjabi to national struggles against the immigration laws and access to opportunity for black people. As a concept it expressed the influence of international struggles on the youth. At the same time they attempted to build solidarity with white workers. As Anwar Qadir recalls:

> I'd never heard of Runcorn until the Black Freedom March, and now I'll never forget it because I went to a meeting there and it was fantastic!... seeing white working class men and women sitting in a room listening to what these young guys had to say, these young Asians who spoke fluent English in a northern accent, who were saying 'look, we're no different to you'... and drawing parallels, saying the issues of exploitation for Black people and working class people were the same... because people aren't stupid and when you raise their level of awareness and draw the parallel, when the thread goes right seamlessly... people can see 'yeah, we're all one'. (Qadir 2006)

Anwar's reflections articulate their desire to communicate their Britishness to wider communities – they were 'here to stay, here to fight'.

The march was organised meticulously and was to pass through Bradford, Huddersfield, Rochdale, Oldham, Manchester, Sheffield, Alfreton, Derby, Burton on Trent, Walsall, Birmingham, Coventry, Leicester, Market Harborough, Northampton, Bedford and Luton before moving on to London and its environs. Each of these areas were ones in which AYM (Bradford) had made political links or promoted organisation. It was advertised extensively through their own networks as well as through newsletters such as CAIL (1980:8). AYM (Bradford) hoped that the Black Freedom March would be a forum through which the youth could establish a National Asian Youth Movement and a powerful anti-racist network. As an organisational leaflet for the march indicated, 'the most important net result of the march is expected to be the formation of a national black organisation in Britain' (tandana.org SC1).

The march did not succeed because of conflicts between London-based organisations and those in Bradford. According to AYM members in Bradford, London-based organisations were unable to accept initiatives from the North. There were criticisms that women's organisations had not been involved at the inception, which Bradford members accepted, although there had been no deliberate attempt to exclude any organisations from involvement with the march. As a principle, AYM (Bradford) had profiled 'End all sexist and racist laws' in their leaflet for the march. Whatever the

5.3   Collage of immigration campaign posters (courtesy Anwar Ditta,
members of AYM Bradford and Matloub Hussayn Ali Khan).

conflicts over the organisation of the march, the inspiration taken
from both the civil rights movement and the Chinese revolution,
along with the experience of making links across all kinds of
communities struggling to make their voices heard was testament
to a commitment to a progressive broad-based unity where all those
struggling against oppression united as equals. The immigration
laws were a central part of this struggle.

JOINT COMMITTEES AND CAMPAIGNS

The AYMs initially spent considerable energy on individual
campaigns while also linking the struggle against the immigration

laws with wider struggles against racism. As time went on however, it was clear that there were so many individuals facing deportation that single case campaigns could not be the only strategy to make cases into issues. Following the success of Anwar's campaign, the Asian Youth Movements and other organisations that had supported Anwar such as CARF, Big Flame, Revolutionary Communist Group (RCG), South Manchester Law Centre and others tried to mobilise support for groups of families that were divided and facing deportation. In Oldham and Rochdale local anti-racist groups including Oldham CARF and South Manchester Law Centre set up the Bangladeshi Divided Families Campaign (BDFC) to try to raise awareness of the plight of Bangladeshi families split between Sylhet and the UK. The BDFC eventually had about 40 cases of families unjustly divided. Just as World in Action had collected evidence in Pakistan for Anwar Ditta from local teachers, religious figures and individuals, the BDFC sent a cameraman with the solicitor Sushma Lal to collect evidence from similar individuals in Sylhet to verify the relationships of individuals and prove their right to enter Britain (tandana.org ST34). The campaign however did not meet with the success of the Anwar Ditta case. The strategies used by the Anwar Ditta Defence Campaign had been new. The focus on a single human story had also helped mobilise the press effectively for their cause. The AYMs in Anwar's case had turned the human story into an issue.

Focusing on the individual human story was also problematic. It was easy for individual campaigns to focus on the hard luck story and sell such a story of exceptional circumstances to the press. The AYMs had gone to considerable lengths to link Anwar's situation to the broader context of the immigration laws to challenge the idea of the exceptional case while using her story to humanise the issue. They had educated Anwar Ditta on the politics of racism, which lead to her speaking at dozens of meetings and rallies, including the national protest against the Nationality Bill in London in 1981. As a result, following reunification with her children, Anwar offered her own solidarity to others. This broader context was not always so clearly established in future immigration campaigns. Paul Kelemen, an anti-racist campaigner living in Oldham at the time has reflected on the dilemmas over joint and single family campaigns:

> In the divided families campaign, people came forward who could not get family unification on all kinds of spurious grounds and they tried to get together to gather more information to support

their case. Anwar Ditta's case helped to bring this issue of divided families forward. ... But the divided families campaign fizzled out and I think we may have contributed to it fizzling out because we started taking up individual cases. It initially seemed like a good tactic because it got much more press sympathy, we could get a newspaper article on it – we could get the television station to come in on it. You could always mobilise sympathy on an individual case in a way that you couldn't generally. So I think we fell into this trap of taking up case after case of individual hard luck stories.

Perhaps the failure of the divided families campaign was not simply in the difficulty of linking the issue with the human story but also with the focus on families as victims without a powerful appeal to resist which is detectable in the campaign's publicity. The title of the poster makes a journalistic statement 'Families fight to be united' rather than making a clear demand from the government to unite the families involved.

Joint campaigns did meet with success in Bradford. In 1982 the Asian Youth Movement established the Joint Committee against Deportations with the slogan, 'Defend the Bradford 18' (tandana. org SC9). This campaign run by AYM (Bradford) was successful in winning the right of all the individuals to stay in the UK. The Bradford campaign, however, rather than focusing on a sympathy vote for social justice, focused on the racism that created government policy arguing:

> The government is following a policy of mass expulsions and mass repatriations by the back door. The home office will not listen to any argument about justice and humanity. The black community must stand up and support them because YOU MAY BE NEXT and there might be nobody left TO FIGHT FOR YOU.

Bradford AYMs strong community base may also have enabled them to run such a campaign and galvanise enough support to meet with success. By the mid 1980s, however, some members of the AYMs stepped back from organising on anti-deportation and divided family campaigns, because it prevented them from organising on other issues such as that of self-defence. As Labour-controlled councils began to fund immigration aid units some activists also felt they were positioned to play the role of unpaid social workers in such campaigns, especially as the issue of immigration restrictions was represented in such councils as a Tory initiative.

6
Bradford 12 – Self-Defence is No Offence

'People say it's victory for the Bradford 12. But it's not. Its freedom for us, but victory for black people generally: the right to defend ourselves. The end result will encourage black people to not simply lie down and be murdered, but to take actions to prevent it happening.' (Saeed Hussain)

The defence of their own communities was the impetus for the formation of the majority of the Asian Youth Movements and remained a central concern to all the youth movements. The lack of police response to racist attacks and the frequent criminalisation of victims led many young people to see self-defence as the only solution. The case of the Bradford 12 was pivotal in challenging the state's attempt to criminalise communities. On 11 July 1981, while unrest exploded across the country, members of the United Black Youth League made petrol bombs that were never used, in order 'to be prepared should the need arise, to protect themselves and their community against fascists'. Three weeks later on 28 July over a dozen members were arrested and twelve young men were charged with 'Making an explosive substance with intent to endanger life and property' as well as 'conspiracy to make explosives ... for unlawful purposes'. The Bradford 12 case and campaign acted as a national focal point against repressive policing policies and practices towards black people. It challenged both the Labour and Conservative party's representation of the police as victims of mob violence following the unrest of 1981 (Solomos 1989:107–10). It highlighted once again the police as a force of repression in their attempt to 'de-citizenise' black people by representing them as criminals and symbols of disorder (IRR 1987:vii). Its significance beyond those of other cases of self-defence such as the Newham 8 and Newham 7 lay in the example it provided of the state's direct attack on political activists with the attempt to represent them as aggressors and agitators, rather than as individuals who had been central to the struggle in defence of their communities over the previous five years (CARF 1991). It was a political trial that was to enshrine in law, the right of a community to self-defence. The significance of the case was summed up by Tariq after their acquittal: 'The police made a mountain out of a mole hill and in so doing made a monument to our beliefs: the right to self defence by a community under attack.' In current literature on the unrest of 1981, there has been very little reference to the case of the Bradford 12, because the focus has remained on a sociological analysis of the reasons for unrest rather than on the attempts by communities to organise in their defence. In assessing the significance of the case, this chapter will therefore provide a detailed account of the campaign and the trial.

THE 1981 REBELLIONS AND THE ARRESTS OF THE BRADFORD 12

The events of 11 July were foreshadowed by a year of increasing antagonism between the police and black communities. The police attack on the Black and White Café in St Paul's, Bristol, in 1980 had already highlighted increased hostility, especially within the media's constructed discourse of the unrest as exclusively between black youth and the police, despite the fact that 30% of the rioters were white (Rowe 1998:6–7, Joshua et al. 1983). In January 1981 the police's lack of response to the death of 13 young black people in New Cross, London, when racists firebombed a 16-year-old's birthday party further exacerbated the situation. With poor forensic investigations, the dismissal of evidence that the fire was started by racists and the hostile treatment of young black witnesses who survived the event, compounded by the coroner's ruling of an open verdict, left black communities in no doubt that they were on their own (tandana.org SC102). 'Thirteen dead; nothing said' went the slogan to emphasise the media's apathy on 2 March 1981 when 25,000 people marched in protest on the National Black People's Day of Action. Asian youth, including those who would later be among those arrested and charged as a part of the Bradford 12 joined the demonstration that saw confrontation with the police which was again racialised in the media as black aggression, with headlines such as 'Rampage of a Mob' in the *Daily Mail* (Solomos 1989:104). The attacks on black families continued with a mother and her four children burned to death when racists petrol-bombed their home in Walthamstow on 1 July 1981. At the same time, Thatcher rolled out 'Swamp 81', a police operation, which was used to stop and search thousands of black youth on the pretext that they may be doing something illegal. Saturation policing methods, endorsed by the state's premise of black criminality, fuelled unrest in Brixton in April 1981 that was to later spread to dozens of towns and cities. The media reports of the Brixton riots were to continue the representation of the rioters as criminals and also projected a police initiated discourse that was to continue throughout 1981 of the 'outside agitator' as responsible for the unrest (Joshua et al. 1983:183).

While small outbreaks of violence took place between April and July 1981, the next major conflict between black youth and the police took place in Southall when police failed to defend the community from fascist intimidation. On 3 July 1981 fascists attempted to stage a skinhead concert at the Hambrough Tavern in Southall (two days after the death of the Khan family). Prior to the event, fascists had handed out leaflets issued by Robert Relf, a former member of the Ku Klux Klan who called for right-wing groups to form a united front for a 'White Nationalist Crusade' on 18 July. They attacked an Asian shop and a woman in the Southall area (Page 1981, Silver 2001). Tensions were high and, as usual, the police arrived to defend the fascists. Asian youth gathered outside the pub, eventually breaking through police lines and burning the pub down. The unrest was again interpreted by the media as an expression of black violence and criminality: *The Daily Telegraph*, for example, declared '80 HURT IN RACE RIOT: Police become victims of clash in Southall' (4 July 1981). The *Daily Mail*'s banner headline of the same day read: 'Terror in Southall'. With headlines such as these, the representation of the police as victims and the age old image of black people as violent so prevalent during the colonial period and in struggles against colonialism was reiterated again (Carruthers 1995). Even the *Guardian*, which highlighted the struggle as one between skinheads and Asians, presented the police as innocent victims caught in the crossfire: 'police who tried to end the confrontation came under a hail of petrol bombs and stones'.

Subsequently, the heightened levels of antagonism between police and black communities led to four nights of unrest in Liverpool following the arrest of a black motorcyclist by police. The media coverage of Liverpool continued the image of black aggression and criminality. The *Daily Mail* reported the event as: 'BLACK WAR ON POLICE' in a headline that covered a third of the front page. The *Guardian* printed images of policemen hiding behind riot shields underneath the headline: 'Hand-to-hand fighting in streets marks Liverpool's second night of rioting: Police forced to retreat' (13 July 1981). This image visually encapsulated the state's position of the police as victims when it was published on the cover of the Scarman Report in the following year (Scarman 1986). The involvement of white youth in rioting and unrest was hardly mentioned in any coverage. Reporting of the unrest in Liverpool and later Manchester also continued to propel the notion of the agent provocateur as responsible for the riots (Joshua et al. 1983:195). The actions of the rioters were represented as that of crazed mobs, associating them with criminal activity such as looting and blaming parents for lack of control (Rodrigues 1981, Gilroy & Lawrence 1988).

30 years later the language of the press was similar in relation to the riots of 2011, with youth being described as 'feral' and parents again being blamed for lack of control (*Manchester Evening News* 16 August 2011, Alleyne & Ford Rojas 2011). The widespread condemnation of the riots by ordinary people at large in 2011, with the limited discussion on the social justifications for them, is testament to the resilience of Thatcherism as a doctrine that was intent on breaking resistance from communities. The trial of the Bradford 12 was a key moment in this struggle. The police's belief in the existence of instigators was to impact on the arrest of black activists in Bradford and the charges they faced.

It was in the wake of unrest in Brixton, Southall and Liverpool that Bradford youth from the United Black Youth League as well as members of the Asian Youth Movement decided to prepare to defend themselves when rumours began to circulate that fascists were coming to Bradford. 'Hundreds of people, black and white, were out on the streets that day to meet such a threat... Shops and market-stalls were ordered to close down by the police, and shutters began to be put up' (Bradford 12 Internal Bulletin 1). These youth, many of whom had defended the streets of Manningham in 1976, were determined to do so again. In the previous month the UBYL had received a threatening letter from J. F. Neil of the 'New National Front' claiming that they would be victorious over the league and arguing that their support was growing by the week. As Saeed Hussain recalls:

> we would not let fascists walk in and actually destroy a part of Bradford where Black communities lived. So we took a decision that we would actually find ways of defending the community ourselves. And that decision led to the fact that Molotov Cocktails were manufactured and they were hidden and as and when the need arose we would be prepared to use those. (Hussain 2006)

At the same time Tariq recalls,

> we met with the Indian Workers Association and AYMs and lots
> of people and we called people to come out and patrol the areas.
> The IWA took the Leeds Road area where they were particularly
> strong... I lived in Manningham and many of our members lived
> in Manningham, we took that area... we were going around areas
> and in some places women actually ... came out of their houses
> and gave us food because we were walking around protecting
> the streets, so people in the area knew what was going on and
> that we could not rely on the police... And that evening on July
> 11th there was a sort of minor altercation with the police. Many
> youth turned up in the city centre, white youths... who had not
> come to attack us but to support us and they were numerous. We
> must have been in dozens and they must have been in hundreds.
> (Mehmood 2006)

Some members of the Bradford 12 were first arrested on that day
in July.

> Nothing did happen, in a sense that the fascists didn't attack
> Bradford. ... And then the decision was taken that since no attack
> has taken place we would actually destroy the manufactured
> Molotov cocktails and as far as I was aware that was to be done
> and that was the end of the matter really. (Hussain 2006)

Rebellion on July 11 was witnessed across the country. Areas
with Asian communities such as Handsworth, Luton, Woolwich,
Camden, Kilburn, Hounslow and Southall all mobilised against
fascists. The same weekend also saw the dispossessed working-class
youth in areas as diverse as Manchester, Stoke, Blackburn, Blackpool,
Fleetwood, Kettering, the Wirral, Wallasey, Leeds, Leicester,
Nottingham, Preston, Bolton, Hackney, Cirencester, Wood Green
(London), Southampton, Halifax, Bedford, Gloucester, Derby,
Birkenhead, Hull, Walthamstow, Sheffield, Coventry, Portsmouth,
Bristol, Edinburgh, Maidstone and even Tunbridge Wells erupt
in anger with incidences of violence and looting in over 30 cities
(Harman 1981). The *Daily Star* noted how in the ten days from
3–12 July, 2,554 arrests had been made by the police (13 July 1981).
During the weekend of 11 July, 1,200 were arrested. The tensions
that were felt in Bradford were widespread. It was not just young
people who were discussing the 'disturbances' but academics and

professionals drinking in the beer garden of the Dubrovnik Hotel in Bradford whose only conversation that evening was about the disturbances (Harrison 2011). In contrast to many other towns and cities, despite the high feelings in Bradford there was very little unrest. 'It was about three weeks later' as Saeed recalls,

> that I got a phone call to say that comrades had been arrested. ... by this stage it was quite big headlines in the local newspaper, the T&A [*Telegraph & Argus*], 'Bomb Factory Discovered in Bradford:... a number of people are assisting police with the enquiries'... the two things didn't tally straight away,... bomb factory and half a crate of Molotov cocktails! But I think one thing it did highlight... it may have not seemed a big thing from our point of view but it certainly was going to be made into a big thing. (Hussain 2006)

The sensational headlines that had filled the papers earlier in July were repeated in relation to Bradford and the police were again represented as the victims of Black criminality and violence, except this time the media narrative constructed a story of successful police action and intervention. On 5 August 1981 *The Standard* announced: 'Black Gang "in plot to bomb police": A plot to petrol bomb a city's police, skinheads and large stores was foiled when its three ring leaders were arrested, a court was told today.' The following day the *Telegraph* declared 'Eleven Asians "in plot to bomb police"'. The *Sheffield Star* in its turn declared: 'Bomb "Factory" find in Yorks: Police smashed a huge petrol bomb "factory" in Yorkshire today ... taking charge of at least 100 bombs and holding four men for questioning' (30 July 1981), while the *Northern Echo* suggested, 'Petrol bombs "ready for riot"' (6 August 1981). The sensationalism of the press and the image of rampaging youth continued over the coming year with *Telegraph & Argus* describing 11 July, during which very little had actually taken place in Bradford, as 'Bradford's night of terror' the following May (8 May 1982). All these headlines used statements from the police and prosecution at Bradford Magistrates Court with none of the papers representing the position of the defence. It created a picture of police authority and measured control following what had been a period of media representation in which they appeared vulnerable. It was an image of successful coercive control that supported the Thatcher government's attitude to the rebellions summed up by William Whitelaw's assertion in the Civil Disturbances debate in

July 1981 of the need to 'remove the scourge of criminal violence from our streets' (quoted in Solomos 1989:107).

The state's attempt to charge defendants with the most serious offences in order for them to act as an example to others had already been witnessed with the charge of 16 random individuals from the St Paul's area of Bristol with 'riotous assembly' following the unrest in Bristol in April 1980. The charging of individuals with such serious offences were seen by the community of St Pauls as public punishment and an attempt to enforce coercion, especially since riot had been so rarely used in English law and only in prescribed circumstances (Joshua et al. 1983). The charging of the Bradford 12 with conspiracy – in other words, as terrorists – was another example of the state's attempt to use a trial to deter protest. The police were well aware that nothing had actually happened but by charging the defendants with conspiracy the police set the stage for a major trial, in which the circumstances that gave rise to the making of the petrol bombs by a political organisation were explored along with a debate as to whether organised and armed self-defence by a community was permissible by law.

The Arrests

The arrest and charging of the Bradford 12 sent shockwaves throughout the local community. Many of the younger members of the Bradford 12 were simply in the wrong place at the wrong time. About half of the final 12 met inside prison. The difficulties for the 12 began with Tarlochan Gata Aura's surprising crumbling under interrogation after only two hours. Although the right to remain silent was enshrined in law in 1981, most of the twelve defendants caved in under pressure signing statements, many of which the police wrote for them. The statements by leading defendants however affirmed the political consciousness with which members of the UBYL had acted. Tarlochan stated that they had 'made petrol bombs in defence of our community which has been consistently under attack by the National Front and the British Movement and also Columns 88' on 30 July 1981. The following day Tariq Mehmood reiterated their act of self-defence:

> In view of what had happened in Southall, London and other areas where black families had been petrol bombed and murdered, where black youth as in Deptford had been burned to death, we took the news that coach loads of skinhead thugs were coming to Bradford very seriously. Many people in Bradford, of all walks

of life were openly talking that this was so. On the morning of Saturday 11th July 1981 I went into the town centre, I met many people whom I had known for a long time and almost all were talking about skinheads invading Bradford. It is my belief that when a people are attacked it is their right to act in self defence. The nature of that defence depends upon the nature of attack and attackers. ... During the course of our stay in and around the centre of town and in view of what we saw and heard; we saw small groups of skinheads, about 3 to 4 strong, and heard that more were definitely on the way;... we decided... that an organised defence of our community was necessary. (Statement by Tariq Mehmood to West Yorkshire Police, 31 July 1981).

The political nature of the arrests was recognised from the outset by both the community and the solicitors involved in the case. It was to become 'the Trial of the Decade' (*Race Today* 1983) and the struggle in defence of the Bradford 12 became representative of the struggle between the black communities in Britain and the state. As Ruth Bundey stated at the bail hearings, 'it is the fear of the community that they [the 12] may be on trial for what amounts to their political beliefs and their previous lawful actions in fighting racialism' (*New Statesman* 4 September 1981).

Criminalisation of Political Activists

The police attempted to portray the case as a criminal one. Individuals who were involved in petty criminal activity such as joyriding were arrested alongside the key defendants. The intention was to associate such activity with senior members of the UBYL in order to discredit them. The police deliberately created situations after the arrests to exacerbate conflict and picture these men as common criminals. Tariq recalls how a skinhead was picked up and thrown in his cell when he was first charged.

The skinhead was just an ordinary lad who hadn't done anything. I don't know what they charged him with ... I just said to him, they've thrown you in here so that we have a fight, I am going to do life anyway, so you can either have a fight or there is one blanket and it is cold and we can share it. (Mehmood 2006)

The police also attempted to fragment the defendants by providing a wide variety of duty solicitors in the immediate aftermath of the arrests, some of whom publicly distanced themselves from any political connections in the case. As Ruth Bundey recalls:

> at the initial stages of that case, when we were time and time again applying for bail for the defendants who were remanded in custody, I would stand up and explain on my instructions what the case was about and the politics of the case as best I could ... and then local Bradford solicitors would stand up immediately after me and say they wished to disassociate themselves from my remarks and this was not a case of politics but simply a case of young men misled by others who were more sophisticated etc etc... that was not a very good basis for a united defence. (Bundey 2006)

Some of the younger UBYL members, however, had begun to attend UBYL educationals and were beginning to understand the social, economic and political conditions that had created them (Internal Bulletin 12:1–2). This politicisation enabled the 12 to ultimately stand together and create one voice that could not be divided by police tactics. This was not without a struggle however, as Ruth recalls, 'When the defendants asked for a transfer of solicitors, which is their absolute right, there were threats of cutting off legal aid. Gareth and I said we would represent them for free.'

Despite the attempts by the state to construct the case as a criminal one, it was clear from the outset that the police raids and arrests were an investigation into the political activities of some of the defendants. As Shanaaz Ali, recalls:

> I remember.... they asked me about the United Black Youth League and I was kind of vague about it ... And then they had all these pictures of us with the Gary Pemberton campaign,... pictures of us outside the magistrates court and a few other marches... (Ali 2006)

While Shanaaz was arrested, she was not charged. The image of a 19-year-old Asian girl wearing *shalwar kameez* and fasting during Ramadan would not have fitted with the image of the 12 that the police wished create. It would have been hard to create the label of 'yobbos' or 'fanatics' with her in the midst of them.

African Caribbean youth that were associated with the UBYL were also arrested. They were charged with other criminal offences, but in Tariq's view 'the state deliberately did not charge them (with us) to stop unity being built between Africans and Asians'. As more and more people got involved with the campaign, Tariq recalls how the way that the defendants were treated began to change:

> the regime relaxed inside. We got cigarettes and food, we were treated with some sense of dignity... when we went to prison ... it was very clear that some of the guards were actually very sympathetic, they didn't really think we deserved to be inside. (Mehmood 2006)

While trying to criminalise the young men, the involvement of Special Branch in the arrest and interrogation of the Bradford 12 indicates that the state viewed the case as political. The first question to Tarlochan when interviewed after his arrest related to his membership of UBYL (Internal Bulletin 3:1). For Tariq, too, the interrogation was mostly political, 'about Angola, Mozambique, South Africa and apartheid. And I was... asked if I thought that the police were instruments of oppression' (Internal Bulletin 3:3). The investigating officers tried to project the police's understanding of the 1981 riots on to the case, arguing that the defendants were linked to the unrest in other parts of the country on the days leading up to 11 July 1981. During the trial, DI Windle admitted that the Special Branch were part of the team that visited Tariq's house, 'to determine connections between disturbances in Bradford, Liverpool, Brixton ...' (Leeds Other Paper 1982). Yet as Tariq recalls,

> Everyone was aware of the riots taking place up and down the country. How could we not be aware of these. We did meet people from Liverpool a few days before July 11th. These were youth, like us, who told us what the police were doing in Toxteth. We were concerned but not connected in any way to Liverpool or other places, other than that it was in our belief that we opposed police brutality, our sympathies were with the youth and not the state. (Mehmood 2006)

The fact that the defendants were charged with conspiracy offences, was in itself an indication of the political nature of the trial. Conspiracy did not require evidence of any particular crime having been committed. Any meeting could be interpreted as a conspiracy – a point not lost on campaigners. The bail conditions for the 12 affirmed the political nature of the case since the conditions included a ban on attending any demonstrations, public meetings or

6.1 'Gagged' posters exposing the political nature of the bail conditions for the Bradford 12, 1981 (courtesy John Sturrock and *Socialist Worker*).

political rallies. For the leading defendants, for whom political activity had been their life and their family, this was a devastating and isolating requirement. In addition, one leading defendant's bail condition included living outside of Bradford. 'Gagged' was the slogan used by the campaign in response.

The UBYL were aware from the start that members of the police force were keen to attack the organisation, because they had exposed the violence and racism of individual police officers during the Gary

Pemberton Defence Campaign. They had ignored rules of sub-judice and named the officers who had attacked Gary in their leaflets. In 1981, the West Yorkshire police were also suffering from a dent to their reputation with their failure to have apprehended the Yorkshire Ripper earlier. Demands for a public inquiry were made by the public, by families and by MPs after his conviction (*Guardian* 28 May 1981) and criticism of the Ripper case came from as far as Atlanta (*Guardian* 6 June 1981). Having come under scrutiny and national criticism some senior officers may have hoped that the case of the Bradford 12 was a coup which could help them to heal their tarnished image.

The Campaign

From the beginning there was enormous support for the young men from both the community and local activists. As Dave Harrison, a journalist and anti-racist activist recalls, 'On Saturday, the court was full... the public galleries, the corridors and the steps of the magistrates court were full of people... and there was utter bewilderment as to how this could possibly happen in the name of justice'. Within days, a meeting attended by members of the AYM, Bradford Black, IWA, SWP, Fourth Idea Bookshop, Gay Liberation Front, Lesbian groups, RCG, Irish groups and concerned individuals established the July 11th Action Committee. Giving themselves this name linked the arrests and charging of the Bradford 12 with the unrest and rebellions across the UK.

The engagement and support of the local community was immediately visible with a meeting attended by 800 local people at the Arcadian cinema on 12 August 1981. As Dave Harrison recalls,

> the cinema was packed, and Amin Qureshi, journalist and later councillor for Bradford delivered what I think is 'the best political speech I have heard in my life'. He ignited feelings that you can get from listening to Rafi [Indian singer], and the mood was electric, the ferver was tangible and in the middle of the speech Qureshi declared: 'If they made them, why didn't they use them' and there was an uproar of support. (Harrison 2011)

As a report of the meeting in *A Report on Racist Violence in Bradford – 1981* stated, this support not only came from the youth but from all generations of the community: 'The speakers representing black groups in Bradford and most political views were unanimous and emphatic in interpreting the arrests as a direct threat to the security of their communities' (Stark 1982). A statement from the UBYL at the meeting argued:

> Our fathers and mothers, sisters and brothers are attacked and murdered in the streets. The police do nothing. Our homes and places of worship are burned to the ground. Nobody is arrested. Families are burned to death. The murderers and fire bombers speak openly of their organised violence against our communities. They are not charged with conspiracy. The politicians and police have failed us. Our youth are our only protection. These young men defended Anwar Ditta, Jaswinder Kaur, Gary Pemberton and many others. Now they have been taken away from us. We must not fail them. We must fight to bring them back. They have defended our community. We must now defend them. (July 11th Action Committee, tandana.org SC37)

The political nature of the case was highlighted in the first slogan of the campaign 'Whose Conspiracy, Police Conspiracy: Free the Bradford 12!' Early leaflets also highlighted the racism and corruption of the West Yorkshire Police who had fabricated statements to ensure convictions in cases that were eventually quashed when an officer was caught having constructed detailed confessions.

In the early stages the committee included members of the UBYL, Bradford Black, friends and family, local activists and a variety of left organisations. While many individuals talk about the widespread support that existed for the 12, the campaign encountered substantial conflicts and problems. The conflicts were partly a result of political rivalries, a jostling for positions as well as a result of the rifts that had already emerged with the split in the Asian Youth Movement over the acceptance of state funding. The difficulty in running a campaign along the principles with which the AYM and their supporters had always worked – the belief that defendants in a case should always be kept at the centre of a campaign and its decision making – was another problem. Difficulties arose because the defendants were incarcerated and contact with them was minimal so it was sometimes difficult to know what their opinion was. To begin with the only contact that campaigners had with the defendants was through their solicitors. As a result of an array of differences, a number of groups emerged in Bradford over the course of the months leading up to the trial. These included the United Black Youth Defence Committee, the July 11th

Action Committee and later the Bradford 12 Defence Campaign. For a short while it appeared that the campaign would splinter. Conflicts erupted between Courtney Hayes from Bradford Black and the July 11th Action Committee because the latter believed that Courtney had acted undemocratically in taking campaign decisions without wider agreement with the committee (July 11th Action Committee 4 October 1982). In order to maintain unity, the defendants dissolved the United Black Youth League, whose leading members were incarcerated and asked for the dissolution of the July 11th Action Committee and the building of a unified national campaign. The AYM decision not to support any UBYL campaign as an organisation was also maintained and a note was added onto AYM minutes for 31 January 1981 which states: 'The AYM will not participate in any meetings or involvement in any committees or talk at any meeting in defence of the Bradford 12.' Support for the 12, however, was widespread amongst individuals in the organisation and Marsha, despite his differences with Tariq, put up his bail costs and spoke in court in his defence. The lack of organisational support was a position never articulated by AYM members at the time or later, and dozens of leaflets in support of the Bradford 12 campaign are included in the AYM Saathi Centre files. The

6.2   Bradford 12 campaign posters (courtesy Matloub Hussayn Ali Khan and Tariq Mehmood), MH97, TM19.

AYM also supported a campaign for six individuals that had been arrested at Bradford 12 court appearances (AYM Bradford 2 May 1982). However, no Bradford 12 document lists AYM (Bradford) as affiliated to the Bradford 12 Campaign.

The conflicts in Bradford and the difficulties of organising a national campaign meant that for some months activists outside of Bradford ended up coordinating a Defence Campaign with two further organisations being established – the Bradford 12 National Mobilising Committee in Leeds, initiated by Big Flame, and the South London Bradford 12 Support Group in London, run by activists in Southall but supported by individuals across London. The fact that activists in a variety of locations and involved with different organisations took the reins to keep the campaign going indicates the significance of the case nationally. It was an attack on the right of political organisation. Amrit Wilson from the London Support Group recalls, 'I felt this is us, these are my friends and I can't let it happen'. Bradford 12 Support Groups eventually emerged across the country in London, Leicester, Sheffield, Birmingham, Manchester and elsewhere. These were places in which members of the AYMs and UBYL had built political links. As Suresh recalls:

> I saw them as colleagues and friends and comrades and one thing I have to say about Bradford AYM, whether its Tariq or Tarlochan ... they did make the effort of making huge amounts of contacts... so the first thing I did was to phone up all these contacts.

This network of contacts was pivotal in developing a strong base for a London support group.

While activists in Brixton and Liverpool organised the Brixton Defence Committee and the Liverpool 8 Defence Campaign, the Bradford 12 campaign was the only national campaign that developed as a result of the 1981 rebellions that was successful.

> There was no other defence campaign of a similar nature. A large number of people who came to the London group wanted to do something about the 1981 riots, not necessarily Bradford 12. They wanted to contribute to some kind of defence campaign because of policing issues and race issues. (Grover 2006)

The campaign therefore enabled people both within and outside of AYM networks to be mobilised. 'Until the 12 are free we are all imprisoned' was more than a slogan, it was a sentiment that was sharply felt by those involved in the campaign. As the South London Bradford 12 Support Group warned:

> The repressive arm of the state may first be used against minorities but it is always ultimately used against everyone: The black community recognises its need, its right and its ability to defend itself against state and police racism as well as against violent attacks. The state has reacted with ever greater repression, and in effect the trial of the Bradford 12 represents a trial of the entire community for its growing spirit of defiance – a show trial in every sense. The implications are serious not only for black people but for the Labour Movement as a whole... It is vital for all of us to support the Bradford 12, and unite in a solid, single, wall of resistance in solidarity with a just struggle.

There were intense discussions inside the committees on what the central slogan of the campaign should be. A number of the key organisers believed it should be 'Self Defence is No Offence' right from the start. This was opposed by the lawyers on the grounds that the defence does not need to tell the prosecution what its defence strategy will be. Tariq also recalls:

> What we felt was that we as defendants, those who would go down for life possibly, wanted to be the ones who decided what our defence, legal and political ought to be. In this there was no confusion about the right to self-defence, but there was for us the issue of some of our comrades, against whom the police had next to nothing, they could walk out by sticking to their guns, so to speak. This at least applied to Jayesh, who had not broken under police pressure and admitted to all sorts of ridiculous things. Whilst Jayesh clearly supported the principal of self defence, why did he have to say, I want to be a martyr, hang me as well? What was important was for us to be united, and this needed a defence where we were not blaming each other. Jayesh's defence in court did not incriminate anyone else and therefore he didn't need to say in court that 'I did what I said I didn't do because I did it for self-defence'. His case was that he did nothing other than watch cricket.

As Ruth Bundey observed,

> When we got to court the prosecution were totally caught off guard. I think they thought we would challenge the legitimacy

of the confessions and interviews, which indeed was done. But they did not suspect that the defence case would so clearly be based on self-defence, for this implied, organised and armed community self-defence and not individual acts of fighting on the street. (Bundey 2006)

During the ten months before the trial, the campaign groups organised pickets at every hearing and court appearance of the 12 first in Bradford and then in Leeds. Pickets were also organised at the Offices of the Director of Public Prosecutions in London, and public meetings at the London School of Economics. Three demonstrations were also organised in Bradford and Leeds. In order to maintain a constant presence during the trial, the campaign organised a rota for mass pickets at the court on a Wednesday. One week it would be the responsibility of trade unions and students to mobilise, another week IWA and AYM (Birmingham) would take the responsibility to mobilise, and another week it would be London. There was even a 'women's day of action' with a women only picket to encourage women to participate. Activists in Leeds and London produced campaign literature in collaboration with individuals in Bradford. Good contacts developed with *Leeds Other Paper* who later provided detailed coverage during the trial. As the campaign developed it garnered support from a formidable list of hundreds of local, national and international organisations. The commemorative booklet produced by *Leeds Other Paper* and the Bradford 12 campaign following their acquittal listed approximately 275 organisations and prominent individuals, these included workers organisations, black organisations, welfare organisations, trade unions, socialist organisations, communist parties, anti-deportation campaigns, temples, mosques, *gurdwaras*, national liberation organisations, women's groups, law centres, film cooperatives, feminist and socialist publishers, disabled groups and students organisations who in their turn raised the case of the 12 in their constituencies (*Leeds Other Paper* 1982:23).

While building solidarity links, community support was crucial in the success of the campaign since some organisations only offered token support. Trotskyite organisations, for example, viewed the Bradford 12 as black separatists and therefore did not prioritise support for the campaign. It was to cause conflict between SWP and some of their members. Following the Bradford 12 campaign SWP expelled two dedicated anti-racist organisers from their organisation. Geoff Robinson, for example, campaigned selflessly for the 12, who had become his comrades and friends. Rather than seeing the campaign as a struggle against state racism, SWP argued that such dedication to the campaign advocated support for black separatism, of which the party did not approve and expelled him from the organisation for being part of an 'unconscious faction' (M. Singh 2006).

The importance of solidarity in the campaign's success is reflected in a statement issued by the Free Bradford 12 National Mobilising Committee after the acquittal:

> The campaign had its problems and setbacks. But we emerged victorious and hopefully the problems will teach us a lesson for the future. ... People from all over the country came to the trial. Support groups had been set up in London, Birmingham, Leicester, Nottingham, Leeds, Coventry and Sheffield. Support came in other forms from most major cities including Liverpool, Manchester and Glasgow. Support continues to come in for the 12 both nationally and internationally. Most important abroad was the support from Ireland, from IRSP, Sinn Fein and Na Fianna Eireann, but also from North America, Sri Lanka, Guyana, Jamaica and other places.

One Bradford 12 leaflet even featured a picket organised by the Black Wages for Housework Campaign outside the British Consulate in Los Angeles on the day the trial started. This picket was supported by the Feminist Women's Health Centre, the Los Angeles Women's League and the Los Angeles Wages for Housework Campaign (*Leeds Other Paper* 1982). The speakers at campaign meetings and rallies also reflected local, national and international support. The three key speakers from the 20 March 1982 demonstration in Bradford reflect the array of support. Anwar Ditta from Rochdale spoke emotionally in support of the 12, representing their history of challenge to state racism. Pat Wall, president for Bradford Trades Council and later MP for Bradford North, also spoke representing the support from the left and trade union movement. Finally, Amandla Kitson, the anti-apartheid activist, spoke in their defence, representing international support (see tandana.org SC32).

Trial

Over 500 people protested outside the court at the start of the case on 26 April 1982. Pickets continued throughout the eight weeks of the trial. The protests outside the courts ensured prominent publicity for the case in the national media. All twelve of the defendants pleaded not guilty to conspiracy to cause explosives and endanger lives. The trial was to prove significant from a number of perspectives:

- The existence of a mass campaign to defend the 12.
- The challenge to the jury selection process to ensure 'a jury of your peers'.
- The decision by Tariq Mehmood to defend himself.
- The decision to argue the case of self-defence by a community.
- The decision by the young defendants to make statements read from the dock and not to be cross examined – a right that was later removed from defendants.
- The strong links between the campaign and the lawyers who defended the 12.

One of the cardinal principals of the British legal system is the trial by jury of one's peers. When an all-white jury was selected from areas of Leeds with no Asian presence, this was challenged by the defence team who argued that an all white jury would discriminate against their clients. The sustained challenge to the composition of the jury had a precedence in political black trials. In 1971 the jury selection had been challenged by counsel in the trial of the Mangrove 9. They had been charged with conspiracy to riot when they had marched to Notting Hill Police Station to protest against police brutality (Hassan 1982). The judge rejected the defence demands for the jury panel to stand down, but when a Bradford panel was selected it was found to have no Asians on it. 'The inescapable conclusion', argued by the Campaign, was that 'black people are being systematically excluded from the opportunity to serve on the jury'. The right to a representative jury and the right of black people to serve on a jury had taken on national significance in 1981 after Lord Denning, the Master of Rolls had been forced to resign following threats of libel action from African Caribbean and Asian jurors that had performed their civic duty in the case of the Bristol riots. Denning had argued in his memoirs that the jurors who acquitted the young men in Bristol charged with rioting against the police had done so because they came from countries where 'truth was not the norm' (Pierce 2011). Sigbat Kardri, representing Ahmed Mansoor argued 'if the defendants are convicted by a jury which did not even have a possibility of an Asian sitting on it, they will say that the defendants had "no chance" and that it was fixed' (Internal Bulletin 2). Tariq Mehmood representing himself asserted 'I think it would be impossible to tell a jury of what my experience and feelings are if there is not even one of my own people on it.' (*Leeds Other Paper* 1982:4). The jury panel was eventually expanded to include 100 jurors including two Asians. Jurors were questioned about their attitudes towards non-whites and whether any member of their family supported far right organisations. After a lengthy legal battle a jury was selected, which had Asian, African and white working people, one of the main requirements of the defendants.

The decision by Tariq Mehmood to defend himself was another significant factor in the way in which the trial resonated outside of the court room. This decision had been agreed by all the defendants and enabled the 12 to speak in a language that was not just rational but also passionate. It enabled the defence team to ask questions or make interventions that were not custom and practise. If he was going to go down for life, Tariq argued that at least he wanted to do it in his own words. It gave him the chance to cross examine the officers who had cross examined him and to challenge every line of their statements. The younger defendants who the lawyers felt would not be able to cope with the strain of cross examination offered statements that were read out from the dock. It is significant that this legal right to give a statement from the dock was withdrawn following the Bradford 12 case.

THE CASE OF SELF DEFENCE

While legal proceedings usually restrict debates on disturbances to concerns over violent and criminal behaviour, the case of self-defence demanded and permitted the defence to present the experience of racial violence by minorities in Bradford and more widely in Britain within the court. The prosecution tried to argue that 'there was no threat to the black community from fascists' and that the defendants had made the petrol bombs to use against police and large shops and 'generally use in a riot'. They tried to argue that these were criminal acts. The judge also asserted that the proceedings were criminal proceedings.

To prove the case of self-defence, the campaign supported the defence counsel in gathering evidence. From the start the July 11th Action Committee had asserted the importance of researching into racist attacks on people and property in the Bradford area and the response of the police to such incidents (Stark 1982:1). Dave Stark, a committed anti-racist and trade union activist in Bradford, coordinated the research and writing of a report which offered a systematic investigation of racist attacks in Bradford since the late 1970s, in order to prove why the 12 and the community as a whole had a right to defend themselves. The report documented the frequent police indifference and in some cases hostility to the victims of racial attacks. The report augmented the Home Office Report on Racial Attacks published in November 1981. The murder of the taxi driver Mohammed Sharif in Bradford in November also provoked a spontaneous reaction amongst Asian groups. The aim was to 'disprove the common sense view of "isolated" violent incidents', a conclusion which was consistent with the Home Office Report as well as the Joint Committee against Racialism's report on *Racialist Violence in the UK* (JCAR 1982, Home Office 1981). The report listed the dozens of violent attacks that had taken place in Bradford and its environs focusing on 1981 in particular. It asserted that the collection of data could not simply rely on police and official statistics since many racist attacks went unreported. It was therefore important to consider general impressions:

> It is apparent from other enquiries of this kind that the general impression is one of an increase in racist violence over the past 18 months or so. Official concern locally is reflected in the evidence which the West Yorkshire Labour Group submitted to Scarman. ... The extent or rate of increase is difficult to assess due to the lack of consistent monitoring over a period of years. (Stark 1982:4)

Through this process the report challenged the concept of 'good race relations' which Barry Thomas had referred to at a reception for the Race Relations Consultative Group and focused specifically on racist violence as opposed to other forms of discrimination in housing, education or leisure activities.

The police repeatedly argued that race relations were good in Bradford. Chief Inspector Ellis argued that he was proud of these 'good race relations'. Chief Inspector Sidebottom claimed to know nothing about the Home Office study that had been published in November 1981 about racist attacks and the fact that Bradford had been part of the study (Internal Bulletin 4:3). He declared he had no knowledge of most of the racist attacks that were mentioned to him, did not know of the local fascist paper *New Order* nor did he believe that the burning of the Hambrough Tavern in Southall had anything to do with fascists, nor did he keep a record of racist incidents. Every opportunity was taken to prove that their lack of knowledge was in fact a lie. Even the police review from 6 February 1981 had included an article on 'White Power and the Nazis' (Internal Bulletin 7:7). In questioning DI Holland, the inspector in charge of the investigation, Barrister Kadri reminded him of the time he had spoken to Pakistani community leaders in Halifax in 1975 declaring that there was no such thing as racial violence (Internal Bulletin 7:8). At one point Kadri declared that he was 'charging the police with criminal negligence' for being unaware of the fascist threat that was faced by the Asian Community in Bradford (Internal Bulletin 3:2).

In challenging the prosecution case the defence set about to prove that the police were not just negligent but racist, which left the community with no choice but to defend itself. The report on racist attacks in Bradford gave a damning image of police racism as not simply existing in the West Yorkshire police force, but as something that appeared to be positively encouraged. It quoted a statement used by counsel in court from DI Holland, Deputy Head of the Criminal Investigation Department in Bradford, who had overall charge of the criminal investigation of the Bradford 12 to highlight the extent of the force's racism:

> Police officers must be prejudiced and discriminatory to do their job. Prejudice is a state of mind drawn from experience. Searching long haired youths in bedraggled clothing produces drug seizures, and searching West Indian youth wearing tea cosy hats and loitering in city centres could detect mugging offences. ... Subordinate officers are expected to act in a discriminatory way; that is against those people who by their conduct, mode of life, dress, associates, transport, are most likely to be criminals. (in *Telegraph & Argus* 13 September 1981).

DS Huntingdon's suggestion in court, that Enoch Powell was not a racist and that to him left wing meant 'anyone against the police and the general running of the country', while right wing was 'anyone who conducts himself within the general running of the country', confirmed the extent of prejudice in police attitudes (Internal Bulletin 5:1).

The defence challenged all aspects of the prosecution case to highlight police corruption and the process of attempted criminalisation of activists. Many of the police statements had been made on 18 August, weeks after the initial arrests and the defence counsel argued that these were therefore not only inaccurate but that the officers had pooled information and fabricated the events

(Internal Bulletins 2 & 4). At one point even the judge commented on the fact that two of the officers, Sidebottom and DS Huntingdon, were sharing notebooks (Internal Bulletin 5:1). Two of the three statements signed by Tarlochan Gata Aura, for example, were not written by him, and Patrick O'Connor argued that Masood Malik's statement must have been fabricated because phrases such as 'Further to my previous statement' and 'I would like to clarify the point which I did not mention before' were not the words of an 18-year-old Yorkshire lad. Helena Kennedy and Paddy O'Connor both highlighted the violence that their clients Saeed Hussain and Ahmed Masoor had experienced because they had not given the police what they wanted (Internal Bulletin 6:1, Wilson 1982:10). There was evidence on Pravin Patel's detention sheet that 31 July had been changed to 1 August, and that, while Police Constable Windle's notes suggested that Parvin Patel had been asked 69 questions and given 69 answers, all notes on the interview were written from memory afterwards. Tarlochan Gata Aura, Saber Hussein, Masood Malik, Ahmed Mansoor and Giovanni Singh all maintained that their statements were constructed by the police through various forms of intimidation (Internal Bulletins 9–12). Tariq Mehmood argued that evidence from police notebooks was untrue because he would never say phrases such as; 'Coloured people who are less intelligent than police officers are intimidated...' (Internal Bulletin 7:3). A number of the lawyers also raised the fact that none of the defendants had been allowed a solicitor for 14 hours, despite the fact that they had asked and this had been to intimidate defendants and to question the younger defendants about Tariq and Tarlochan and their political activity (Internal Bulletins 5:3 & 7:1).

The political rather than criminal nature of the case was also asserted in court. E. Alexander and Sigbat Kadri both argued that Special Branch had controlled the case from the beginning. They had been responsible for searching Tariq and Tarlochan's house and interrogating them when arrested. The defence then used the history of political activity that Tariq and Tarlochan had been involved with from the 1976 fascist march in Manningham onwards to prove that both were not criminals out to smash or loot shops or the police station indiscriminately but that they had wanted to do what they said they did – to defend their community as they had been doing for the last five years through anti-fascist marches, the George Lindo case, the Anwar Ditta case, deportations cases and the Gary Pemberton campaign (Internal Bulletin 7:6). Dozens of witnesses were called to support the case of community self-defence.

Reverend Kenneth Leech, Race Relations Officer for the Church of England acted as a character witness for Tarlochan. Members of the Fourth Idea Bookshop including Reuben Goldberg as well as Jan Fielding from Dalys bookshop were called to confirm the knowledge of the rumours that fascists were coming to Bradford. Reuben Goldberg also catalogued the attacks that the Fourth Idea Bookshop had suffered and that the attacks had continued unabated in 1981. Anwar Ditta spoke to highlight Tarlochan Gata Aura's involvement in her campaign. She also highlighted the fact that herself and Tarlochan had received abusive letters from fascists after coming into the public eye when she won her case. She spoke of the threats of violence which she faced: 'At night ... we have to keep buckets under the front door in case petrol is poured through the door and set on fire..' (Internal Bulletin 9:6). Councillor Mohammed Ajeeb, chairperson of Bradford CRC recounted the report of racial violence in Bradford that he had given to the Home Office team in 1981 noting how there had been 'a marked increase in the number of racial attacks' and that there was 'a lack of confidence in the police force' (Internal Bulletin 10:2). Piara Singh Khabra of IWA, Southall and the Joint Committee Against Racism spoke of the impact of the events in Southall on the Asian community in Britain as a whole and the fact that the fascists had aimed to attack ordinary people (Internal Bulletin 10:5). Trevor Phillips, who was working for London Weekend Television also testified to the lack of police support in Southall when the community was attacked. The statements from younger members of the 12 including Masood Malik, Ahmed Mansoor, Vasant Patel and Pravin Patel corroborated the fear of attacks and the way events in Walthamstow, Deptford and Southall affected the decision to make petrol bombs (Internal Bulletin 10:4). Zikrullah Khan, editor of the *Daily Jang*, also spoke to highlight the catalogue of racist attacks that had been reported in the paper over the past year to prove that all those in the community would have had knowledge of such events. A member of the Walthamstow Fire Brigade was called to highlight that 13 arson attacks had taken place on Asian homes in the last two and a half years. Jim Thakoordan from Luton Community Defence Committee spoke of skinhead attacks in Luton and victims of racist attacks in Bradford were also called to testify to the violence they had suffered and the police inaction in their case (Internal Bulletin 10:6). The impact of events nationally was brought home in Saeed Hussain's statement when he described how the Walthamstow firebombing 'affected my mother so much that she got my brother to seal up the letter box' (Wilson 1982:10). Finally Marsha Singh from the Asian Youth Movement testified that AYM were also patrolling the streets on 11 July: 'We, the AYM, patrolled areas in Bradford on observation for skinhead invasion. ... Our members were in a state of preparedness... We would alert the members of the community – we have quite rapid communication.' Marsha affirmed that AYM too did not tell the police because 'the police have consistently harassed us.' And, like members of the UBYL, he affirmed 'I regard the police as an anti-black institution and in certain circumstances as an instrument of oppression' (Internal Bulletin 12:4). The case gave a national platform to both the experiences and political ideas of the youth.

The power of the self-defence case was made not simply in the court room but outside. On the first day of the defence case the mass picket called by the campaign included Jaswinder Kaur, Nasira Begum, Nasreen Akhtar, Cynthia Gordon, Najat Chafee, Pow Shein Leong and Pow Yean Leong – all individuals facing deportation whom the defendants had supported over the previous years. The mass support proved what the defendants said was true – they were defenders of their community. 'You could here the chants of "Free free free the 12", "Whose conspiracy, police conspiracy" and "self defence is no offence" in the courtroom on mass picket days' (Mehmood 2006).

The political nature of the trial was reasserted in the prosecution's appeal to the jury at the end of the trial. 'What sort of society are we going to live in if one side and then the other, feels justified in using such devices?' (Internal Bulletin 12). Helena Kennedy's reply was that 'if the trial wasn't political already such a question had made it so'. Each of the defence barristers in turn interrogated this idea of the society that we wish to live in, Paddy O'Connor asked: 'What kind of society is it which allows racist attacks, which tolerates and fosters that kind of hatred?' In his own defence, Tariq Mehmood Ali pleaded:

Everything you have heard so far about the charges against us is about a human reaction – our action in defence of our people was a natural reaction. I am not begging for mercy. I don't ask for forgiveness. I am asking for understanding... You are my protection because you are ordinary people. The threat of fascist terror affects every one of you and not just black people. ... The prosecution suggest that the UBYL broke from the AYM because we wanted violence. That is rubbish. It was to avoid the corruption that arises from state funds. We are not a violent organisation. Anwar Ditta was subjected to violence and in response we initiated a prolonged mass campaign – not violent – and it was the same with Gary Pemberton. ... The whole case against me amounts to nothing but a political prosecution. It is aimed at my political views. I am not a terrorist but a victim of terror. (Internal Bulletin 12, 4 June 1982)

Acquittal – and Aftermath

The acquittal of the 12 on all counts was to prove the right of a community to defend itself. As Gareth Peirce wrote in the *Guardian:* 'By its verdict, the jury accepted the proposition that a society should afford protection to all its citizens and that if it did not, as the evidence they heard showed clearly that it does not, then those unprotected can arm themselves.' (Peirce 1982). The sympathy with which the jury viewed the 12 is evidenced through their delight in celebrating victory with the lawyers and defendants after the acquittal. One juror even brought a rose, which she placed in a milk bottle to adorn the table around which they sat. It inspired the cover of *The Leveller* that month which declared 'Self Defence is no offence' and sported a graphic of a milk bottle with both a rose and red flames.

The campaign marked a high point in independent self-organisation amongst South Asian youth in Britain. It served as a symbol of victory and enshrined in law the right to self-defence. It was a campaign that was to influence others in its politics and slogans as can be seen through the repeated use of slogans and visual iconography from Bradford 12 campaign posters. In reflecting on the impact of the trial and campaign at a thirtieth anniversary commemoration of the Bradford 12, Gareth Peirce stated, 'The Bradford 12 were acquitted after telling the whole truth, it may be that they held the line on racist attacks... maybe they held the line on the NF growing and growing and becoming a monster. ... but whenever there is a victory it doesn't result in living happily ever after, it results in the state moving the goal posts yet again and so it's imperative to be as brave and as watchful and as intelligent and as imaginative as the twelve defendants were in their days in Bradford'. The goal posts were moving before the trial was even over.

The acquittal of the 12 was a powerful symbol of resistance to police and state oppression. At the same time the level of police harassment and victimisation appeared to continue, as the Newham

6.3 Later visual resonances of Bradford 12 campaign in leaflets produced by Newham Youth Movement in defence of Newham 7 defendants; Bangladeshi Workers Organisation for a campaign to 'Stop the Racist Health Service Bill'; Asian Youth Movement Sheffield for Ahmed Khan Defence Campaign. (courtesy Matloub Hussayn Ali Khan), MH58.1, MH6.

8 and Newham 7 trials are testament. While the state did not gain a victory in the Bradford 12 case, they smashed in its infancy a militant black organisation that had leaders with incredible energy who believed passionately in the unity of all black people, African

and Asian. The use of the conspiracy laws was a significant part in the state's strategy. The state's determination to crush independent and militant organisation led to the re-use of the conspiracy laws against the Newham 8, sometime after their first charges had been issued. The increase in repressive policing tactics was evident within weeks of the rebellions in July 1981: police were issued with extensive protective equipment, (including new types of riot shields, helmets, and armoured vehicles) as well as with CS gas, plastic bullets and increased capacity for water cannon. All these measures were endorsed by Lord Scarman who not only accepted the need for a whole array of offensive riot technology but also condoned the expansion of special patrol groups that had been used so extensively in Operation Swamp 81. These powers were further endorsed by the Police and Criminal Evidence Act which enshrined in law the power to arrest and detain suspects without charge in 1984 (tandana.org SC47). The act also removed the right to silence in the UK and the right to give a statement from the dock without being cross examined was also removed shortly after. In 1981, it was clear that the discontent amongst black communities could not simply be addressed by coercion. There was a need to manufacture consent. The acquittal of the 12 further confirmed the urgency for change. Lord Scarman's report was to advocate the development of consensus politics through the establishment of a whole array of community participation projects and systems which were eventually to buy many activists off the streets.

7
The Later Youth Movements and the Drive Towards State Funding

The split that had manifested itself in AYM (Bradford) in 1981 between those who wanted to work within state structures and those who believed that the state was fundamentally oppressive became more apparent in the development of AYMs and other organisations post-1981 as the state set out to marginalise those that demanded radical change. The state's agenda can be seen as early as August 1981 in Heseltine's cabinet report, 'It Took a Riot'. While Heseltine recognised inner-city depravation, and expressed concern to ameliorate conditions that were not compatible with 'traditions of social justice and national even-handedness', his report emphasised the government's need to act to prevent 'infiltration... which burnt the Liberal's fingers' and to control community organisations, because of the belief that 'if we do not, these groups will not disappear: they will be easy prey for those who seek to use them for other purposes' (Heseltine 1981:8). He argued that there was 'no effective leadership' in Liverpool and that this meant that 'the hard left – and more extreme forces are at work. They are now arguing: "All traditional methods have failed: It's time for more radical measures"'. While making no references to police racism, the report saw the need for better police and community relations and advocated the recruitment of black police officers for the purpose of aiding crime prevention and law and order policies.

Three months later the Scarman Report, while endorsing the reality of depravation, also failed to recognise institutional racism. Although Scarman challenged Margaret Thatcher's attitude that 'nothing that has happened to unemployment would justify these riots' (*Financial Times* 12 April 1981), and argued that the disturbances of 1981 arose from 'a complex social, political and economic situation... not special to Brixton', it did not call the police to account. It reproduced official accounts of the events in Brixton taking little evidence from the people of Brixton (Benyon 1984). Scarman took the official position that the police, in their efforts to maintain law and order in an area of a high incidence of crime had created suspicion amongst ethnic minorities (Scarman 1986). There was no acknowledgement of racism within the police force. This was a markedly different perspective to the one which the defence counsel for the Bradford 12 highlighted the following year. Scarman only highlighted racial discrimination in job opportunities and housing. As Devon Thomas from the Brixton Defence Committee argued, the Scarman report 'created a false sense of hope for many who thought that the Inquiry would investigate the *real* causes of the 1981 uprisings and make recommendations accordingly. It fooled many into thinking that the Government would then take substantive action...' (Thomas 1984:190). The report included recommendations to involve local communities in the planning, provision and management of services that they needed. Heseltine's recommendations to create what the state defined as 'effective leadership' were established. Yet police harassment of black youth, for example, did not shift dramatically and the 1980s saw some significant self-defence trials such as the Newham 8 and Newham 7 that, like the Bradford 12, developed national campaigns.

The impact of Scarman's social policy recommendations was to have a dramatic effect on the way in which organisations within the Asian communities and black communities generally were to develop. While Sheffield and Birmingham youth movements maintained the spirit of an independent, anti-imperialist force, AYM (Bradford) – that had been so inspirational to others – changed fundamentally. In Newham, when a youth movement emerged to challenge the police harassment and criminalisation of black people, a monitoring project emerged and absorbed a large amount of organisational energy. The process was filled with contradictions. The chapter will explore the work of Sheffield and Birmingham AYMs to highlight the continuing spirit of resistance that existed amongst some sections of the youth. It will also explore the changing face of AYM (Bradford) as an example of the trend to accept both the restraints and benefits of resources that state patronage could bring. The pursuit of state funds was to lead to the disintegration of the movement.

SHEFFIELD

With the formation of independent youth organisations in Bradford, Batley, Manchester, and other towns and cities, the council and youth organisations in Sheffield attempted to coordinate a Sheffield response as early as October 1980, when Mohammad Younis, 'a youth worker of Asian origin' set up a meeting at Attercliffe Youth Centre. The meeting involved young people from the Attercliffe area, some of whom, like Matloub Husayn-Ali-Khan (aka Matloob Hussain), were unpaid youth workers who were involved in the youth club. The aim was to form a group to discuss the 'situation regarding the Asian Youth in a multi-racial society'. The meeting focused on the establishment of a core group to discuss these issues with the offer of a residential weekend for the group. A large part of the meeting was then devoted to the establishment of an Inter-Asian Cricket Tournament. Along with these council controlled 'offers', Younis also invited Anwar Qadir from AYM (Bradford) to speak about the establishment of a communication network. Anwar suggested that 'a self-defence group of ethnic youth should be formed' for the youth of Sheffield and Rotherham. According to Younis' report of the meeting 'this did not meet with a good response from the local youth because they said the situation is not the same as it is in West Yorkshire' (tandana.org MH221). Yet it was clear that black communities in Sheffield were suffering police harassment in the 1970s, and campaigns in support of Caribbean and Yemeni workers took place during that period, particularly in Burngreave. Matloub, for example, who was at the meeting organised by Younis, was also a member of Sheffield Campaign Against Racism from 1977 because of his desire to combat such harassment. Matloub had also experienced racism in the work place. The Pakistani community, who were in fact mainly Kashmiri, were involved in manual trades in the steel industry, as Matloub remembers. Matloub was the only Asian to have an apprenticeship to become a trained mechanical engineer. All the other Asians were involved in manual jobs such as sweeping in the machine room or worked in the jobs that white workers did not want to do, such as working in the foundry room with molten metals. This hard and hot work was difficult but poorly paid since it was not classed as skilled work. In Matloub's memory the Amalgamated Union of Engineering Workers was riddled with racism and the union never challenged this.

> Some of the workers were paid for semi-skilled jobs when they should have been given skilled wages and Asian workers were always given the harder jobs that were regarded as either unskilled or semi skilled and were overlooked for the skilled jobs which were worth more money. (Husayn-Ali-Khan 2005)

The environment in Sheffield was relatively similar to elsewhere in the country. The conclusions of Younis' minutes show the way in which council-driven initiatives were about controlling youth organisation. The future meetings listed at the end of the minutes did not include any liason with AYM (Bradford) but were focused around literature produced by the Commission for Racial Equality (CRE), two meetings about the cricket tournament, one to be held with the Sheffield Friends Cricket Club. These attempts at control were later shattered by the youth when they finally established an Asian Youth Movement following their involvement in the Bradford 12 campaign in 1981/2.

Other anti-racist formations in Sheffield within the university also influenced the development of the AYM in Sheffield. These included the overseas students strike that was to develop across the university sector in the 1970s and the establishment of a black consciousness group at Sheffield university. Jasbir Singh from Malaysia, who was later a member of AYM (Sheffield), and Aneez Ismail from Uganda were two overseas students who were involved in the overseas student strike at Sheffield in 1977. This strike saw international students address British racism as a result of a fees hierarchy imposed without warning that tripled the fees of students already enrolled. As Jasbir recalls:

> There were a whole number of fees strikes, occupation of University administration buildings and so on... I had to pay something like £3,000 a year... I could hardly keep my head above water, I worked four nights a week, weekends in bars, so I could feel the direct pressure in terms of 'my god how am I going to pay the fees'... I kind of got pulled in because I was involved in the Malaysian society and knew some friends who were involved in it and through that my consciousness grew with regards to what Britain did to Malaysia and so on... (J. Singh 2006)

Aneez, who was at Sheffield University as a home student, was sympathetic to the overseas fees issue. Coming from a Ugandan Asian family who had lost their wealth when his father died and his relatives were forced out of Uganda in 1972, Aneez identified with the plight of the overseas students:

I just felt it was wrong. I wasn't affected myself, but.... because I was a British student, I knew the system. I was articulate and I discovered I had a knack for public speaking. I began to help and get involved....

The strike led to mass involvement by overseas students in political action

> We organised all the overseas student bodies. ... the fees strike was hugely successful ... We got the students union together to pass resolutions, we began occupations...

> What was significant was that we were such a well organised grass roots campaign. We were the only group that could organise a quorum in a general meeting,... we relied on mass, mass participation. (Ismail 2006)

It also encouraged the development of anti-imperialist alliances which was significant for the kind of AYM that was formed.

It was through this mass participation that the overseas students at Sheffield developed what they described as a 'black Caucus' in the NUS. Overseas students held controlling positions in the union for about three years, and this was the first expression of a black consciousness. It was a broad-based black consciousness with the involvement of diverse groups including many Chinese Malaysians. For Aneez and others the central issues were both anti-racist and anti-imperialist. Lots of different groups emerged that were highlighting the problems of Cambodia, Eritrea and later Iran, and debates were had on the different kinds of revolutionary movements that were being formed and what this could mean. As Aneez recalls:

> I remember it was the Iranian revolution at that time [1979] and Khomeni had just landed at Tehran airport and Joshi came and spoke and brought with him a group of IWA members... We had lots of Iranian students and we had a discussion at that conference on what the Islamic movement meant and so on.

However, as time went on, for some students the issue of racism which they faced everyday became more central than the international issues that the overseas students strike had inevitably raised. Anti-racist campaigners from London also influenced this development. In 1979 Pal Luthra (IRR) came to do a masters course in Sheffield and 'it was after that that we formed a Black Consciousness Group at the university around 1980... We produced newsletters and slowly started to have workshops on understanding racism and we became a big voice in the University' (J. Singh 2006). The establishment of the Black Consciousness Group (BCG) represented a move to focus more on racism than international issues which had been raised around the overseas student strike. This shift was partly a result of the passage of time through which the fees issue resolved itself. 'Everyone accepted the principle to pay the same fee, so that struggle disappeared. It had achieved its objectives' (Ismail 2006).

Through the BCG, students involved in the overseas student strike and anti-imperialist actions met local Sheffield students. For Aneez, the black consciousness group caused a division between the overseas and home Asian students. While there were overseas students involved in BCG, as time went on it became 'a predominantly British outfit' with mainly British students involved. As they began to establish links in Sheffield outside of the university, BCG made links with broad-based anti-racist organisations in Sheffield such as the Campaign Against Racial Discrimination, Campaign against Racist Laws and Sheffield Campaign Against the Immigration Laws. They made links with the established AYMs, organising meetings in support of the Anwar Ditta Defence Campaign. They also raised the issue of racist and fascist attacks mobilising for the New Cross Massacre demonstration in 1981 as well as trying to work with the Trades Council to raise issues about racist and fascist attacks. The BCG experienced the same racism that Matloub had become conscious of in the AUEW when they debated issues of principles and politics with the Union. 'I remember very clearly on one occasion', Aneez recounted, 'two henchmen of George Caborne [from the AUEW] were behind me and said, "If you don't shut up, we'll put you back on the boat". And that was the extent of the racism that existed, even in the trade union movement'.

The Sheffield Bradford 12 Support Group brought together local youths as well as young Asian students and members of the Black Consciousness Group at the university. Mukhtar Dar, who went to Sheffield Polytechnic to study fine art, remembers when he found out about the Bradford 12:

It was in late winter and I was walking through the corridors and I saw a poster about the Bradford 12 and it caught my eye. I stood there and looked at it. I was brought to tears. It said 'Until these twelve are free we will forever be imprisoned'. I took the poster off and rolled it up and decided that I was going to do whatever I could to support these Twelve... I went down and met a community leader and he didn't know about the Bradford 12 so he pointed me to a youth club ... and as I walked in, there were a number of Asian youth there and one of these young youths later to become a friend of mine stood up and spoke about the need to support these young guys in Bradford... I was very, very moved and I think I realised that what I'd experienced in terms of the racist abuse and racism, the insecurities I experienced, a sense of not belonging – that was shared by a whole group of individuals and it was not unique to me and I found a collective support and strength in that and from there things began to become much more politicised. (Dar 2006)

The success of the campaign and the principle of self-defence that it upheld encouraged the establishment of AYM (Sheffield) in 1982, which worked both in the city of Sheffield and amongst students, particularly in the Polytechnic. Matloub, one of the key members of AYM (Sheffield), also attend the Poly from 1983 and the Asian Youth Movement Society became an important group through which the youth mobilised support. Mukhtar recalls the powerful experience of being part of a group of young people who organised themselves to challenge oppression from a meeting at which Anwar Ditta spoke in support the Bradford 12:

The power with which she spoke really moved me,... I had tears running down my cheek. And then seeing my brothers, chairing the meeting, stewarding the meeting, suddenly we were taking control of our own lives, our destinies, and then the attack took place on a restaurant and I think that made us realise that we needed to have a permanent organisation.

The initial Asian Youth Council formed with the help of youth workers highlighted the role of state funding as a form of monitoring and the conflict between groups of young people that ensued as a consequence. As Mukhtar recalls:

what transpired was that these youth workers... were being paid and had their own interests. ... They began to use the threat that the youth were becoming more militant and organised and said to the City Council unless they gave some funding ... and gave them due recognition that things could escalate and get out of hand. And we walked into their offices and opened files and found out that they were writing minutes about meetings and we decided 'no', this was the wrong way. We're not here in anyway to be an appendage of the youth service and so we kicked them out and changed the name from the Asian Youth Council to the Asian Youth Movement. (Dar 2006)

The AYM in Sheffield maintained complete financial independence, apart from one grant to buy a Gestetner printer which was housed at Matloub's house, a hub of AYM activity and known to the youth as 'the bus stop'.

The desire to maintain independence from the state represented the spirit of the early AYM (Bradford) and the UBYL. The first campaign continued the theme of self-defence that these young people had organised around for the Bradford 12. The Ahmed Khan Defence Campaign was formed after a restaurant worker was charged with malicious wounding when 14 racist youth attacked the Shizan Restaurant in Darnall in 1982. The manager and four restaurant workers had tried to defend themselves when the police failed to arrive for 20 minutes, from a police station that was one mile away. As was often the case, one of the victims was arrested. The youth picketed outside the restaurant and at the magistrates court and organised a march against police harassment in Sheffield to raise the profile of the case and the injustice. The influence of the Bradford 12 victory can be seen in the posters and leaflets that were produced for the campaign. Leaflets for the Ahmed Khan case used the iconography of tied fists that was used so successfully in Bradford 12 posters and the slogan 'Self Defence is our Right' clearly resonated from the Bradford victory. The spirit of the Bradford 12 and the belief in independent black organisation can also be seen in the first edition of *Kala Mazdoor* (Black Worker), the magazine produced by AYM (Sheffield).

An article which asserts the importance of political independence in the first issue of *Kala Mazdoor* offers a critique of the CRE. The article criticises the lack of attention that the CRE gives to areas of crucial concern to black people including racist attacks, police harassment, poor housing and unemployment. AYM (Sheffield) were influenced by intellectuals such as Sivanandan who had spoken and written about the role of the Community Relations Commission (CRC) and the CRE, arguing that as arms of the state both organisations acted to contain dissent. AYM (Sheffield)'s attitude to the CRE encapsulates the attitudes of Sivanandan, who argued that the CRE could not challenge the racism of the state, but instead 'taught the white power structure to accept the blacks and ...taught the blacks to accept the white power structure' (Sivanandan 1982). The words of Sivanandan were recalled by AYM members: 'The politics of the CRE's equal opportunities was like first beating someone up so they can't walk and then giving them crutches' (Bassi 2006).

Kala Mazdoor carried this debate to its readers:

> by creating 'official channels' for dealing with the grievances of the black community, the CRE have diffused any possibility of the black community uniting and organising for their rights. It has contained the anger and frustration of black people... Why do you think they offer you free food and drink, why do you think they organise an expensive sports day for the youth – this is to distract our attention from the real problems that we face like poor housing, high unemployment, racial attacks and abuse, police harassment etc. (AYM Sheffield 1983)

This critical position on the CRE was reached by Sheffield both through the experience of council based organisations attempting to control AYM (Sheffield)'s development and organisation (as the experience of the Asian Youth Council exposed) but also through educationals which they held intermittently to inform members and encourage a critical understanding. The Black Consciousness Movement at the university had also played a part in young Asians seeing the value of educating themselves about black, working class and anti-imperialist struggle.

Like AYM (Bradford), AYM (Sheffield) tried to build links and solidarity through campaigns, often organising under umbrella organisations. The group organised for Ahmed Khan for example under the wider banner of the Campaign Against Racial and Police Harassment and repeatedly organised public meetings to build solidarity amongst all anti-racists. A meeting at the Mount Pleasant Community Centre on Sharrow Lane in April 1983 outlined this desire: 'The Asian Youth Movement is holding a public meeting aimed at uniting all anti-racists in the city and black people in particular, in the struggle against all forms of fascism and racism, institutional or otherwise' (tandana.org MH17). Like all AYMs, Sheffield set up broad-front organisations in developing their campaigns to enable mass participation and to liaise with other communities and other left organisations. They organised anti-police harassment campaigns such as The Ahmed Khan Defence Campaign; the Mohammad Iqbal

Defence Campaign, which raised the issue of the violence against taxi drivers; the Zafar Defence Campaign, which highlighted police harassment through stop and search policies; and the Pagehall Three campaign in 1986, which involved three Asian men who tried to defend themselves from street racists by simple actions such as standing with a broom in hand to stop racists entering a local shop (tandana.org MH232). They also supported the campaign for the Fargate Three, who were three African Caribbean men attacked by the police in the Fargate area in 1986. AYM (Sheffield) also organised in support of local families such as the Khan family in Highfields who were living with violence, fear and intimidation (tandana.org MH74). They linked with national campaigns such as the Newham 8 and Newham 7 as well as the campaign against the Police Bill. Later as former members of AYM (Sheffield) moved to other cities, other organisations such as the Sheffield Defence Campaign were established to mobilise black and white anti-racist activists who wished to work in independent anti-racist organisations in Sheffield. They continued to campaign against racism through broad-front organisations that mobilised communities, such as the Sharrow Action Committee against Racism.

While focusing on racism and police harassment, AYM (Sheffield) continued the struggle against institutional racism through support for anti-deportation campaigns such as the Ranjit Chakrovorty Defence Campaign, which they won. They also supported anti-imperialist struggles such as Palestine and the campaign against

7.1 Banner for Zafar Defence Campaign, against police criminalisation, Asian Youth Movement (Sheffield). Designed by Mukhtar Dar (courtesy Mukhtar Dar and Matloub Hussayn Ali Khan), MH2.

Union Carbide following the Bhopal disaster in 1984. The campaign in Sheffield against Union Carbide was particularly strong because of the company's ferrosilicon plant in the city which was used as an alloy by the steel industry. The Bhopal disaster was featured on the front page of one of the later newsletters that Sheffield (AYM) brought out in 1985 and 1986 called *Kala Sho-or: Black Consciousness* (1985b). Local and national trade union issues were also supported, including the strike at Aire Valley Yarns, Bradford, in 1983 (in conjunction with AYM Bradford) and the Miners Strike, which was particularly significant for Sheffield as a town near mining communities.

BIRMINGHAM YOUTH

The spirit of independent black organisation and a belief in self-reliance was also maintained by Birmingham youth at this time, who were also politicised by the events of 1981 and their involvement with the Bradford 12 campaign. They learnt through their own oppression to identify with the oppression of others. As Sheera Johal recalls:

> The pub in Southall burned down where fascists used to hang around and then I think we started to set up AYMs in Sheffield and Coventry and we set up our AYM here. ... We used to take a mini bus to Bradford during the trial. It was good... and then Bhupinder Bassi came from Canada, and he had been involved with the farm workers union and slowly we started discussing things, started to understand politics and international politics like apartheid and issues in Columbia ... and we started organising public meetings to make people aware... and we went to Ireland, because we came from the subcontinent where we were ruled by Britain and Ireland was still under British occupation so we had the links. (Johal 2006)

Birmingham Asian youth organisation was also heavily influenced by the IWA in Birmingham, the largest and most influential of all the IWAs in the country. Some members eventually left AYM and joined the IWA. Like many AYMs their relationship with IWA was contradictory. With the passing of their charismatic leader Jagmohan Joshi on a demonstration against the immigration laws in 1979, and the decline in membership of the IWAs in the late 1970s and early 1980s, the IWAs had begun to increasingly make alliances with the Labour Party in an attempt to maintain their influence in political life (Josephides 1990). While the youth reacted against this attitude, as Bhupinder recalls, 'we no longer had to pretend to like the Labour Partly because our parents expected us to vote Labour and the IWA propaganda about us all being workers no longer fit'; they were also influenced by the legacy of Joshi, the commitment to anti-imperialist politics, along with a commitment to class politics.

Asian Youth in Birmingham organised anti-deportation campaigns and strike support groups as well as events for international solidarity. They were particularly influential in the Baba Bakhtaura Defence Campaign, the Karamjit Singh Defence Campaign, the Kewal Brothers Strike Support Group and also took a leading role in the organisation of a black delegation to the North of Ireland (see Chapter 4). While the AYM in Birmingham was not formalised until the mid 1980s, activist youth in Birmingham worked closely with AYM (Sheffield) in the development of many of the above campaigns encouraged by family links between Sheffield students and Birmingham. The campaign in defence of Karamjit Singh (a young man threatened with deportation after having been charged with four other youths for petrol-bombing pubs that operated a colour bar following the riots in 1981) was organised collaboratively between youth in Sheffield and Birmingham. The campaign highlighted the double jeopardy for black people if they were found guilty of a crime. Not only did they serve their sentence, but they could then be deported as 'not conducive to the public good' (tandana.org MH118). Cases such as this enabled Sheffield and Birmingham to highlight the continuing racist nature of the immigration laws.

AYM (Birmingham) also articulated the continued commitment by many Asian Youth to unity across class and ethnic divides. While the 1980s saw a period when state funding led to ethnic divisions, with groups beginning to re-define themselves in the drive to claim resources, AYM (Birmingham) had Goan Christians, Punjabi Sikhs and Muslims as well as Bengali Muslims involved in the movement. The importance of unity across South Asians and other black communities was expressed in their magazine *Asian Youth News* published when the organisation eventually formalised in 1985 after the Handsworth Riots. It was at this time that the youth felt it was imperative for them to produce literature that would express their perspective. Like AYM (Manchester) who had worked to maintain unity between African Caribbean and Asian youth during the 1981 riots (Ramamurthy 2011b), AYM (Birmingham) worked to assert a similar perspective following the Handsworth riots after two Indian workers died in a fire at the post office. As their special report on Handsworth declared:

> The reports of Handsworth in the papers and on TV are almost the exact opposite of what actually happened... The Handsworth 'riot' was a rebellion against poverty, unemployment and police harassment – against the racism that confines us to the ghetto. Youth of all races took part in the attack on property and the police. It was not an attack by one section of the community against another and it is sad and tragic that two people died. On Wednesday 11 September Asian and African members of the community laid wreaths at the post office as a mark of respect.
>
> The police and the media are now trying to divide our community by making a pretence of sympathy towards the Asian shopkeepers who lost their businesses and their livelihoods. But the sympathy shown to Asians is pure hypocrisy – What have the police done to protect our communities in East London and elsewhere from racist attacks? What have they done to bring justice to the murderers of the Kassam family in Ilford? (AYM Birmingham 1985)

The paper evidenced police support for significant Asian business men who were hiring young Asian vigilantes to create fights with African youths. AYM argued that this was a deliberate attempt to try to create conflict in order to deflect people's attention from the poverty and harassment that they faced. To defend their position they noted how smaller business men on Lozell's Road had issued a statement saying that there was 'no enmity between African and Asian.' (AYM Birmingham 1985). The determination to maintain unity was keenly asserted and represented the continued attempt to assert a progressive, inclusive black identity, a position that was increasingly undermined as the 1980s drew on.

THE PATH TO STATE FUNDING

While Sheffield and Birmingham continued the militancy of the early AYMs, other areas embraced what appeared to be the possibility to consolidate official authority of their organisations by involving themselves in state structures. These developments led to different priorities which were to eventually erode the key objectives of the youth movements to struggle against police harassment, challenge the racism of the immigration laws, make links with anti-imperialist struggles world wide and keep the power and voice of the organisation with the community. The state created a trajectory which enabled the youth movements to be co-opted into the mainstream by offering spokespeople from the movements, roles in local council politics and the Labour Party. An emergent black middle class took these roles. As Harwant Bains noted in his analysis of Southall, a group of professional 'ethnics' emerged in the 1980s, the 'career militants', whose 'vociferous claim to represent the militant demands of their community ... secured them state patronage' (Bains 1988:240).

Gurnam Singh from AYM (Bradford) recalled the way the state wanted to talk to the AYM after the Scarman Enquiry:

> They wanted to talk to us,... incorporate us, give us grants and things like that. ... and I applied for this job – unqualified social worker, Section 11... They had 300 applications. I can remember going through five sets of interviews and people with PhDs applied for this job and I got the job! Cos in my interview with the manager I said that I was active in the Asian Youth Movements and that I was involved with anti-racist politics and all these things. And he said, 'You're the person we want'... for me it was a clear illustration of the incorporation of Black politics into the state. There were a number of us that got jobs, Marsha was working in the education department, ... Anwar got a job somewhere... and there were people like Jani Rashid .... We were all now being picked off the streets as it were and given jobs. And some of us then became suit wearing and totally abandoned the struggle all together, others took the struggle into the state and I think that's what I did. (G. Singh 2006)

While the acceleration of this process was apparent after 1981, it had begun much earlier, with the establishment of Community Relations Councils and the Commission for Racial Equality as Sivanandan had highlighted. The focus by the commission and later the CRE, on education and a philosophy of integration led to a focus on racism as an issue of ignorance and the need for 'mutual understanding' as opposed to acknowledging the needs of capital, the state and the exercise of power. In this way, as Sivanandan argued the creation of a 'black rhetoric' successfully took 'politics out of the black struggle and returned it to rhetoric and nationalism on the one hand and to the state on the other'. 'The Commission took up the black cause and killed it' (Sivanandan 1982:120).

AYM (Bradford)'s changing relationship to the state, and its grant giving bodies like the CRE was already apparent in the split which took place in 1981. The impact of this shift can be traced through a collection of minutes from 23 January 1983 to 17 March 1985. These minutes record the changing relationship between the Asian Youth Movement, the Labour Party and the local council, as well as the increasing use of energy by the movement on the establishment of a youth centre. It is clear that as state patronage required accountability, so minutes of meetings were taken and collected meticulously for the record and hence furnish evidence of the way in which the organisation was encouraged by certain members to shift its direction. The first meeting on 23 January began with a debate about 'Why Asian Youth should join the Labour Party' at which Marsha Singh (who was later to become MP for Bradford West, and was Chairperson of Asian Youth Movement (Bradford) in the late '70s and early '80s) introduced Keith Narey from Militant to the meeting. Narey argued that Asian youth should join the Labour Party on the basis that since this was a class struggle, 'together we would have a better opportunity of combating capitalism'. Unbeknown to his fellow comrades Marsha had remained a member of the Labour Party quietly undermining two of the fundamental principles around which the youth had organised until 1981 – (i) dual membership should not be permitted with the AYM because it enabled left parties to infiltrate the movement and (ii) that the Labour Party was as racist as the Tory Party as their slogan articulated: 'Labour Tory both the same, both play the racist game'. While both sides of an argument were aired, and Geoff Robinson (former member of IS) spoke on why Asian Youth should not join the Labour Party, highlighting the Labour Party's bad record of attacks on workers as well as immigration issues, the fact that such a debate took place in an Asian Youth Movement meeting is significant. Given that Marsha as Chair of AYM had enabled this discussion it is not surprising that at the following meeting the decision was made to allow members of the youth movement to join the Labour Party although it was recognised that 'the AYM as an organisation could in no way affiliate or work within the structure of the Labour Party, but as a pressure group we as the AYM would have the best effect' (AYM Bradford 6 February 1983). The AYM constitution that had originally incorporated socialist and anti-imperialist principles in its aims and objectives was also questioned and re-written in this period.

Marsha argued that the AYM fell between being a mass organisation and a cadre-based organisation, and the previous structure of AYM was too complicated with too detailed a constitution and that it needed simplifying. In essence, the changes that took place led to the dismantling of the cadre-based core to AYM (Bradford) that had made it the most powerful and influential of all the AYMs nationally (AYM Bradford 1983 Green Lane Youth Centre). The new aims focused on opposing discrimination, educating the youth about the relationship between discrimination and inequality and recognised the right of black people to organise independently, but there was no recognition in the new aims and objectives to the fact that 'the only real force capable of fighting racism was a workers movement, both black and white,' nor was there any commitment given to international solidarity. These aims and objectives fitted with the growth of a state based anti-racism which in the pursuit of funds divorced racism from class struggle.

In reflecting on the demise of AYM (Bradford), by the mid 1980s, as Anwar recalled, 'it was not a group with teeth anymore'. Anwar, a prolific and energetic organiser who had been involved in the organisation from its inception saw this trajectory as beginning in 1982:

> From 1982 onwards, AYM were on a slippery slope downwards... Marsha began to remove himself from the driving seat of the AYM in order to develop his own political ambitions while at the same time influencing a group of people that railroaded changes in the organisation that were in conflict with the constitution... what Marsha was doing was placing people within the organisation strategically... that he could control from behind the scenes. ... and I just felt 'this is going more and more Labour Party', the Labour Party started to have meetings in the Saathi Centre, everything started to revolve around the Labour Party... and it started to operate in a more dictatorial way. (Qadir 2006)

The shifting perspective can be seen in the leaflet for a picket against David Waddington organised by the AYMs and Bradford socialists, which was headed 'protest against the racist policies of the Tory Government'. The previous assertion of Labour and Tory as consolidating racist immigration laws was diffused through such an approach. As time wore on Anwar for example, who 'did not want to get used in the drive towards providing fodder for the Labour Party' resigned from the organisation in 1986.

The debates about the relationship between the Labour Party and the AYMs took place at the precise moment when black members of the Labour Party were debating the need for black sections within the party on the basis that autonomous organisation had been an 'organisational principle' amongst black groups over the previous decade. Shukra suggests that the organisers of LPBS '"forgot" that autonomous organisation emerged from debates about how to form a revolutionary consciousness' (Shukra 1988:71). Rather than forgetfulness, it could be argued that organisers within the Labour Party wished to develop a relationship between those organisations that had been associated with a revolutionary consciousness for their own political credibility. This can be seen in the way in which the Labour Party began to adopt the rhetoric of black struggle to attract members. A Labour Party Young Socialists leaflet for an Asian Youth Conference in Bradford in 1984 for example, contained a collaged collection of images of protesting Asian youth, some holding Bradford 12 placards, directly appropriating the history of independent black struggle (tandana.org MH193). This appropriation of their own history was not really challenged by the AYM. The only comment in the minutes about an invitation to participate was dissatisfaction with the way they were invited. While there is no evidence of any AYM member's involvement in the organising of the conference, the political ambitions of AYM leaders such as Marsha Singh were being carefully forged at this time. His political ambitions were apparent from the days when he and his school friends ran their own 'House of Lords'.

The shift in direction for the AYM from a militant/campaigning organisation to one providing social services can be seen from the list of roles ascribed to the executive committee at the Annual General Meeting held on 27 February 1983. Apart from the roles of chair, secretary and treasurer, these included sports secretary, social secretary and education officer. There was no designation for even one campaigns officer. The discussion on future activity listed 'Priority to be given on Centre' as the first activity, followed by the suggestion that a newsletter would go out every two months. The full time worker was given the role of keeping in regular contact with members and the sports and social secretary were to work towards the organising of social activities. The campaigning issues made up the last four points on the list of future activities and three of these were linked to council initiatives in terms of an equal opportunities programme, housing policies, education policies. Only the final point – the support of deportation cases up and down the country with a directive to support as many as possible – linked with previous AYM priorities.

It is clear from the minutes of meetings that follow over the next few months that campaigns continued to be run and supported over the next few years but as time went on the commitment to these initiatives dwindled. AYM (Bradford) supported the Ayre Valley Yarns dispute in which 22 Asian workers went on strike after their shop steward Liaquat Ali was sacked for attempting to organise a union in 1983 (tandana.org JR1 & JR3). They also played a central role in establishing the Dewsbury Defence Committee which campaigned to defend three Asian youth charged with actual bodily harm and damage to police property after the Asian community had been repeatedly attacked in Dewsbury with no police intervention or support (tandana.org SC49). The highly successful 'Defend the Bradford 18' campaign which saw 18 Bradford families facing deportation link together was also conducted in this period (tandana.org SC8 & SC9).

Yet inevitably with the development of a youth centre, the purchase of a building, the demands of the council began to take over. Even Marsha Singh, later MP for Bradford West, who was principally involved in steering the organisation onto its new path, recalls that after the Bradford 12 campaign: 'I think AYM had had its day by then.' The report of the full-time worker now employed for the AYM, Idris Bashir, in the Asian Youth Movement Newsletter from September 1983, makes the focus on the establishment of the new Saathi centre and its related activities clear:

> a large part of my work has been involved in looking for premises for our centre. Now that we have obtained the centre there is still much to be organised before it opens. ... Other work I have been involved in concerns the building of better communications between various voluntary groups, council officials and other youth workers in the city.

In Bradford the change from a militant organisation to what eventually simply became a youth centre took some years. The changing attitudes and perspectives of AYM (Bradford) were apparent to youth in Birmingham and Sheffield, as they tried to maintain their independence from the state. As Mukhtar from Sheffield commented:

we began to see Bradford in some ways disintegrate... Bradford Twelve had galvanised a generation, it politicised us, it brought out some of the politics around cooption. ... when we visited Bradford AYM we saw that they'd got this youth centre where they'd taken the posters of the martyrs off the walls because they had been given saunas and weight training rooms and some of these people began to dress in three piece suits. (Dar 2006)

One significant change of AYM (Bradford) after 1981 was the focus on local rather than international issues and a keen interest in education services. While local concerns and issues of education had always been at the centre of AYM activity, the youth had previously organised their own educationals, making substantial use of Bradford Central Library and using its café as a meeting place for debate. The early movement had also been active in making links between their own struggles and international ones, providing the organisation with a strong anti-imperialist perspective. As Sivanandan had declared in 1987, 'for us South Africa was not "out there", it was in our kitchens' (Sivanandan 1987, Workers Film Association 2011). Post-1981, some of the key campaigns in Bradford involved issues surrounding state education; this included a campaign against the racist head teacher Ray Honeyford who had attacked the post-Scarman development of a multicultural education policy in an article in the *Salisbury Review* and their support for a Bradford Council of Mosques campaign for halal meat for Muslim pupils in Bradford schools.

The campaign against Honeyford was both a strong grass roots campaign as well as one which enabled AYM to engage with the council on debates about education in a multicultural society. The AYM were instrumental in organising the Drummond Parents Action Group which picketed the school, demanding Honeyford's resignation after he condemned multiculturalism's policies of cultural enrichment as 'the approved term for the West Indian's right to create an ear splitting cacophony' and condemned bilingual education by distorting the facts to suggest that it prevented South Asian children from learning English and integrating into a crystallised construct of Englishness to which South Asian migrants would always stand outside (Singh 1984). The AYM produced policy documents such as *Reading, Righting, Rithmatic, Race* to challenge Honeyford's position, as well as the council's lack of attention to racist harassment at Eccleshill School. They argued that there were not just three 'R's, but four Rs, to include racism

(AYM Bradford 1984b). The interventions in educational policy were valuable but were the kinds of campaigns that were much easier to tackle when trying to integrate your organisation into state structures than campaigns that addressed issues such as police criminalisation. They could easily fit into what Sivanandan described as the creation of a 'black rhetoric' and an understanding of racism as ignorance as opposed to the operation of power relations. The production of policy statements for council use was indicative of the new direction for AYM (Bradford), where campaigning was eventually uprooted from the heart of their work. As Noorzaman commented, as time went on, 'you could see the AYM being seen to be more part of the wider network of local authority organisations'.

In engaging with council policy the AYMs did, however, play a role in counteracting the rising influence of conservative faith based organisations that were also receiving state sponsorship at the time. In 1981, the council had established the Bradford Council of Mosques and in 1984 the council approved support for both the Federation of Sikh Organisations and the Vishwa Hindu Parishad, both groups associated with the religious right in India. While the AYMs supported Bradford Council of Mosques' campaign for Halal meat in schools they opposed the call for separate religious schools arguing that such schools would lead to ghettoisation or segregation (AYM Bradford 1984a).

In Manchester the development was similar. Manchester, like Bradford, also got involved in debates over the kinds of education and schooling that should be developed, challenging the attempt by religious organisations to establish faith schools and single sex schools. In commenting on the effect of central and local government funding for community groups, Nilofer Shaikh recalls the new priorities that prompted her to leave the group after funding had been obtained for a youth centre with which influential members of the AYM had links:

... After it was set up they went for bigger funding to set up a youth centre for Asian youth which became the Tipu Sultan Centre. But one of the criteria for funding was that you couldn't be involved in political activities – at least not officially. I think that became a problem. A lot of people got involved and used their energies to run the centre. The group's time was taken up by organising activities to fulfil the criteria of the funding e.g. outings, youth centre sessions, playing pool, table tennis and the management of the project itself. We then had less time to do the campaigning work that we used to do before. It was around this time that I left the AYM. (Shaikh 2006)

The focus on funding absorbed so many individuals who believed that with the establishment of centres they could serve the community more effectively and in the minds of those involved the work towards establishing a centre became the narrative of achievement. For example at a National AYM meeting on Sunday 29 May 1983 one member reported how AYM (Bradford) had attempted to establish a centre since 1978, scraping money together to pay rent. For Junior Rashid, the centre appeared crucial to the development of the organisation, as the minutes list 'To build an organisation you need a base where you can meet on a daily basis'. An AYM (Manchester) member followed this contribution with a similar story about the efforts to get a base. Such a perspective did not go unchallenged, since for Anwar Qadir (from Bradford) the base could be seen in terms of people rather than premises. Anwar also articulated the importance of 'political finance' from members so that political, agitational leaflets could be made and the 'political side could be kept active'. Such debates indicate the conflicts and tensions in direction that emerged as the access to funds became widely available. As Noorzman reflected in relation to Bradford, by the mid 1980s 'you see the organisation was quite fixated on opening centres and trying to deliver solutions for local issues, ... in retrospect you have to decide what kind of an organisation you want to be. If you want to be an advocacy organisation it's less appropriate to look at funding. If you want to be a delivery organisation, then you apply for funding because that's what it's all about...'. By 1984, 'quite frankly [AYM Bradford] just became a community project... and that's why it actually collapsed, because it was no longer an advocacy organisation on quite challenging issues around... prejudice and discrimination etc. for the community.' The conflicts felt by the youth movements were also felt by women's organisations such as Southall Black Sisters. As Hendessi recalls, 'a section wanted SBS to be totally committed to the political struggle of black women. Others wanted more attention to be paid to the service provision side. The conflict erupted after a while.' (Hendessi 1989:11)

THE ATTEMPT TO ESTABLISH NATIONAL NETWORKS

The changing priorities of the various AYMs can also be identified as one of the key reasons for why a National Asian Youth Movement was never successfully established despite the fact that attempts to establish national networks of both the AYM and broader black caucuses were initiated by various groups from 1979 onwards. The desire to organise a black freedom march by AYM Bradford was the first attempt to establish a national network of organisations and was a fundamental reason for its organisation (see Chapter 5). As a leaflet for the march articulated,

> The most important net result of the march is expected to be the formation of a national black organisation in Britain. The basis for this will be laid down because of the unity in action that will be necessary from so many black organisations if this march is to succeed. (tandana.org SC1)

The failure of the initiative to take place is significant in terms of the failure to build a national organisation.

The success of the Bradford 12 campaign and the energy of those involved in the campaign in Bradford, London and Leeds again raised the possibility of a National Asian Youth Movement (NAYM) since it is hard to imagine that without networking on a national level the campaign could have achieved the success that it did. In 1982, following the acquittal of the 12, Manchester and Bradford AYM attempted to set up a national AYM once more. Meetings were held in Sheffield, Batley and Manchester to try to move this idea forward and involved groups of Asian youth of various sizes that existed in Sheffield, Dewsbury, Nelson, Bradford and Leicester. Jani Rashid from Bradford was appointed as the national convenor. He attempted to set up meetings in a variety of towns and cities to move the idea forward. Apart from the logistical difficulties of organising national meetings, minutes of meetings show the difficulties in establishing a network where groups had different priorities and some groups were more established and others were in their infancy. The constitution of the NAYM was also significantly different to the anti-imperialist and socialist principles of the Manchester and Bradford AYMs, which had both argued that 'the only real force in British society capable of fighting racialism and the growth of organised racism and fascism is the unity of the workers movement' and that they would support the struggle of the 'oppressed masses' in the Indian sub-continent. The constitution of the NAYM, while opposing colonialism and the struggle of oppressed nations, made no mention of the working class either in Britain or in 'oppressed nations' and focused more specifically on the issue of civil rights for all, demanding the end to unemployment and the need for equal pay. The programme was worthy but not revolutionary (NAYM 1983).

In London in 1983, Jasbir Singh, a former member of AYM (Sheffield) who started to work for the Newham Monitoring Project initiated another attempt at a network: the Independent Black Network. In organising on a national level, some of the problems with the unreconstructed term 'black' began to emerge – the acknowledgement of a class struggle so fundamental to the AYMs in the north such as Bradford, Manchester and Sheffield were not easily acknowledged amongst a wider network. The suggested aims and objectives were focused on supporting and campaigning against the racism and oppression of black people, building solidarity amongst black people and building a platform of activity controlled by black people. Some organisations and individuals clearly recognised the limitations of this agenda and asked: 'what about the mobilisation of progressive white movements,.. the question of class... of discipline...' and 'the question of and definition of black' (30 November 1984). Apart from what some participants described as the 'flimsy and inadequate' nature of the aims and objectives, the outcomes of the meeting also indicated the establishment of a national organisation to which any black individuals could affiliate. The initial proposal had been to establish a 'network of individuals *and* organisations' and hence the purpose of the network was overrun and inevitably led to the disintegration of the organisation.

The failure of these national networks is indicative of the conflicting agendas and political perspectives that existed amongst activists and organisations, between those that were prepared to work within the confines of state structures, whether this was the avenue through which they believed they could make the most effective change or because of the personal, financial and career benefits that were on offer to them and those that believed the only principled position was to campaign against all forms of racism from an independent position, where their beliefs could not be compromised.

8
New Organisations and New Identities

The shift in direction of some of the Asian Youth Movements from campaigning to service oriented organisations was part of a wider social and political process. In the 1980s the number of community organisations that began to emerge across county councils in the UK mushroomed, usually focusing on serving a particular ethnic minority's needs. There were ethnic minority units in the Greater London Council and other metropolitan councils, Section 11 youth projects, education projects and a vast array of cultural organisations. The drive to state funding had already begun in the late 1970s. In 1976, Southall Rights had been established in the wake of Gurdip Singh Chaggar's death. Funds for the Southall Monitoring Group had been granted following the death of Blair Peach and the conflict between the police and the community of Southall which ensued. Even the Indian Workers Association in Birmingham had opted to apply for state funds in 1978, setting up the Shaheed Udham Singh Centre to provide welfare and legal advice to the community. The establishment of the Tipu Sultan Centre by AYM (Manchester) and the Saathi Centre by AYM (Bradford) was just part of a much wider trajectory of state provision for ethnic minority organisations.

The demand for social service provision for minority communities was important and a right, but the process divided groups that once worked together. In Luton members of Luton Youth Movement established the Pakistani Youth Forum and the Bangladesh Youth League. By defining themselves in cultural rather than political terms, the course was set for funding and community differences were inevitably emphasised rather than minimised. While accessing state funds for services was just and this in itself had to be struggled for as the history of the Asian Resource Centre in Birmingham (which first sought funds from Cadbury's Barrow Trust rather than from the state) highlights (Asian Resource Centre 2003) it is the impact on political advocacy and campaigning that was significant. In absorbing themselves within welfare issues, the conflicts that young people faced on the street and the criminalisation and racism of young people by the police which had been a key reason for the development of the youth movements was often sidelined.

There were two organisations – Southall Monitoring Group and Newham Monitoring Project – that sought a different approach and attempted to use state funds to try to create some level of accountability by the state for their failure to deal with the racism confronted by communities. The belief was that communities could arm themselves with the evidence of neglect to demand change. AYM (Sheffield) explored the possibilities of establishing a monitoring project, although none was ever established. AYM (Bradford) also established the monitoring organisation Campaign Against Racist Attacks following the success of the Bradford 12 and the value of such information for the defence case. The monitoring projects attempted to maintain the broad black political identity of the AYMs and UBYL, but both organisations impacted on independent community activism. New organisations were formed but their success was diffused. As time went on, the influence of state funding and state agendas became more and more apparent as community identities changed. New geopolitical priorities were also responsible for these shifts as the 1980s wore on and the ideological support for socialist ideas that had been found in the Soviet Union began to collapse as the USSR itself began to disintegrate. This chapter will explore the ways in which South Asians responded to the shifting political climate to try to further the struggle against racism and police harassment in Britain. It will consider the ways in which both state priorities and changing geopolitics impacted on the ways in which they organised.

THE MONITORING PROJECTS

Both the Southall Monitoring Group and the Newham Monitoring Project were established following major conflicts with the police. Activists that had played a central role in campaigning during disturbances in the 1970s and 1980s were involved in their establishment. The development of the monitoring project in Southall arose out of the enormous chasm between the community and the police following the events of 1979 (see Chapter 3). Members of the Southall Defence Committee who had worked selflessly from the offices of Southall Rights (a legal advice centre that had been established after the death of Gurdip Singh Chaggar), worked to established the Southall Monitoring Group. The application for funds by activists in Southall in 1979 was similar to the decision by all youth movements to apply for funds during this period. After 1981, with the burning of the Hambro Tavern as a result of fascist provocation in the area, the funding of community groups increased even further. Such funding was to accelerate the disintegration of independent organisation.

In Newham, the death of Akthar Ali Beg in 1980 led to the formation of a number of campaigning organisations including the Newham Youth Movement, but the organisational force of this independent movement was minimised with the establishment of the Newham Monitoring Project (NMP). The political conflict between funded projects and independent campaigns had been recognised years earlier by youth in the East End. In 1978 the Bangladeshi Youth Movement for Equal Rights (BYMER) highlighted the impact of the race-relations industry in a pamphlet published after the death of Altab Ali and Ishaque Ali:

> As a tactic we had to find some 'respectable' corroboration of our 'plight' before it could be 'trusted'. Therefore, when the Trades Council expressed some concern in this respect the Youth Movement assisted in compilation of a 'dossier' of these attacks on which lots of people are attempting to launch their career within the race-relations industry. (BYMER 1978:4)

There is no doubt that many of the individuals that established and worked for organisations such as the Southall Monitoring Group and NMP were committed to the anti-racist struggle and its success. Many of them, having developed their organisational skills in anti-racist and campaigning groups, worked long hours to try to develop vibrant campaigns in the defence of the Newham 8 and Newham 7, for example. As Jasbir from Sheffield recalled:

> When I got the job at NMP, I remember I got paid six and a half thousand pounds ... I never felt it created conflict because we gave our hearts and souls to the work. We would be there first thing in the morning when everybody got up and were there well after midnight... because its what we believed in... although we were involved in police harassment cases in Sheffield... for me I really learned about it and felt about it when I was actually in Newham. The cases were phenomenal; some of them brought tears to your eyes. The big campaign at the time was the Newham 8, we publicised it and we got strongly involved with the families, not just the eight kids but also the parents, their mothers and

fathers and their brothers... to date I still know most of them... (J. Singh 2006)

The role of the funders, however, did impact on the way organisation took place across the country. Since Newham 8 and Newham 7 were effectively funded campaigns, they were able to pay for minibuses and coaches to be hired from Sheffield and Bradford to attend their demonstrations and pickets. While it was felt that this was the legitimate seizing of state resources, at the same time it impacted on the principles of self-reliance. In Bradford for example, while the AYM supported campaigns and pickets of the Newham 8 and Dewsbury Defence Committee, minutes of meetings indicate that they sent letters to the committees to ask for the costs of minibuses that were sent to the demonstrations (23 October 1983). While this was acceptable for the Newham 8 campaign that was run by Newham Monitoring Project, it was a different case for the Dewsbury Defence Committee. This change in direction is particularly noticeable since AYM (Bradford) had supported the development of the Dewsbury campaign. Prior to 1981 such requests for funding would not have been made, since groups raised the funds themselves in order to express the political solidarity of their members for others in struggle. AYM (Bradford) made tremendous efforts to organise the youth in Dewsbury with the hope that an AYM could be developed that would be 'active in issues affecting Dewsbury and not be like Dewsbury AYO'. Idris as full-time worker found it difficult to maintain the participation of the youth who left the work to him. One cannot help wondering if the position of Idris as paid worker did not influence their behaviour to leave the work to him. Yet the pressure on his time meant Idris found that he 'could not go on both doing the work for the defendants and the work for the AYM' (report by full-time worker, 1983). Campaigns and the AYM had become divided.

Jasbir from NMP has argued:

if the question is, would it have been a better world or would things have been significantly different and progressive if the funding was not there, I probably would have to disagree. The two organisations that come to mind are Newham and Southall and despite all the stories that have gone with regards to funding I think it did help... because people who were involved in some of these organisations were really solid people, they gave their hearts and minds to that work...

To members of the monitoring projects, it was organisations such as the CRE that had the most detrimental effect on anti-racist organisation. As Jasbir recalls,

> they were mostly white individuals who staffed the CREs... and they would always come down when there were racist attacks or any incidents and discuss things with the police, ... and in this way they took a lot of the anger and resistance out... We took a very hard line, we would talk to the police but we would not sit on any police liason groups or police consultative committees, ... because they were mainly there to diffuse tension, and they were the front line enemy, so how can you sit with your enemy and discuss your own issues? (J. Singh 2006)

It is clear that within the state structures different bodies represented conflicting positions, but all of these organisations formed part of an 'apparatus created by the state, to house a class of political middle-men' that would eventually 'sabotage the aspirations of the youth by activating the policy of "divide and rule"' by buying activists off the street (Mukherjee 1988:221).

The onset of funding even disrupted and effectively disintegrated organising methods amongst those who decided not to accept state funding directly. Members of AYM (Manchester) witnessed how:

> State funding came indirectly. Manchester City Council took a decision to provide coaches for immigration cases, so coaches were going free. You just informed them – we want to take a coach to Birmingham. And the number of people going on demonstrations began to fall. I remember there were coaches that would have eight or ten people going to Birmingham or London or Bradford for demonstrations. When you are trying to get the money yourself to take a coach you do much more work, now the only work was – publicise the coach, 'hey the coach will be going from Longsight at such and such a time' and no work was done. (Zulfiqar 2006)

The influence of funding meant that increasingly council funded initiatives rather than community initiatives could set the agenda about what issues activists should organise around.

In Newham, as time wore on, the priorities of state initiatives took increasing hold. By the 1990s dozens of different organisations began to form: London Against Racism and Anti-Racist Action

(ARA), for instance, which were London-wide groups. These groups were not community-based, but more and more of NMP's time and resources became absorbed in these initiatives, to the detriment of community action. So, as the community began to change from Pakistani to Bengali, then Tamil and Somali, NMP failed to address the changing landscape. As Jasbir noted,

> It was easy to get involved in the ARAs and the ARAFs and that kind of stuff. For me that changed some of its political direction ... I am not saying the Charles de Menezes Campaign is not important or the Stephen Lawrence campaign, they were critical campaigns... but you need to draw the links between what is happening there and Newham.

The tension over the direction and purpose of Newham Monitoring Project became apparent to many of its members. As members of NMP recognised, 'accepting GLC and local authority funding whilst preserving the community base was not without problems' (CARF 1991). The shift in name of Southall Monitoring Group to The Monitoring Group and then its shift in location from Southall to Holborn also expresses a moving away from its community focus to an independent advocacy and policy building organisation.

The changing directions of NMP and the Southall Monitoring Group express the way that local authorities, in taking up issues of 'anti-racism' often divorced them from black community struggles as a whole. Instead of welding groups previously excluded from the local state together to form a movement for socialism, local authority funding policies actually placed the groups in a competitive relationship with each other. In the black community, this accentuated the differences between Asians, Africans and Caribbeans and even divided the groups amongst themselves. The experience of Newham was similar to elsewhere. In negotiating a share of the limited resources available groups were continually identifying and arguing for their group or community's difference and distinctiveness. In this environment the broad-based concept of a political black identity that had been embraced by the youth movements struggled to maintain influence (Shukra 1998:221–2). As Kobena Mercer has argued 'one group's loss was another group's gain. In this zero sum game the only tangible consequence of diversity was dividedness' (Mercer 1998:47). Even academic theorising became embroiled in 'the politics of difference' as opposed to a search for strategies of unity between the oppressed which were interpreted by some as even hegemonic (Modood 1994a & 1994b). Whilst the first divisions were between Asians and Africans, as time went on, the splits and divisions increased along cultural, religious and ethnic divides. 'In making the local state the main vehicle for advancing anti-racist politics [these organisations]... confused and confounded the black community's capacity for autonomous self-organisation' (Gilroy 1990:60). In this process the core objectives to challenge state and street racism in all its manifestations got lost in a world where defining ones ethnicity ended up as the central pillar of concern.

Many of the people who were part of the AYMs got absorbed into the state's initiatives from the mid 1980s onwards. Some consciously set out to compromise their previous political visions or radically change their ideological perspective, the most notable being Marsha Singh who became Labour MP for Bradford West (1997–2012). For others the process was a gradual slide. Today, former members of the youth movements hold key leadership roles such as: Head of Diversity in Bradford, Chairman of Strategies for Change UK, Director of the Monitoring Group in London, Director of the Drum Arts Centre in Birmingham, Director of Equality Inclusion and Human Rights at NHS North West, Chief Executive of Coventry Refugee and Migrant Centre, and Director of the Asian Health Agency. While many attempted to keep their politics separate from their employment, as the Pakistani Workers Association was to suggest in the mid 1980s: 'sell your labour but not your soul', in the end as Naeem, a former member of PWA, reflects, 'none were able to keep the two separate. Those who joined the funded organisations ended up compromising their politics as their continued relation was always directly or indirectly, linked with their support for the state agenda' (Malik 2012a).

Preserving Independent Anti-Imperialist Organisation

If the state had begun to create a class of middle men then it was all the more important for activists to make the links between race and class and attempt to maintain autonomous anti-racist and anti-imperialist organisation. In the mid 1980s a sizeable group of activists continued to try to do this. For Sheera Johal in Birmingham, the AYMs in focusing primarily on racism were not able to develop a sophisticated class analysis. Joining the long-established IWA (GB) in Birmingham was, he felt, an expression of the development of his own politics. This was a direct challenge to the council-driven anti-racist politics spearheaded by Ken Livingstone's Labour-led

Greater London Council. Sheera reflected on the feelings of disillusionment that activists like himself felt about this shift: 'some
people started to join the Labour Party, like Marsha in Bradford...
and I think it just broke then.' Sheera's comment is significant
because it indicates the way in which despite the lack of a formal
national organisation, the influence and actions of individuals in one
AYM influenced other towns and cities. The mid 1980s saw former
members of the Asian Youth Movements join the Indian Workers
Associations, the Kashmiri Workers Association and Pakistani
members establish a Pakistani Workers Association.

The formation of the PWA in 1984 was the most significant
new development. Despite the size of the Pakistani communities in
the North there was no workers organisation to represent them.
Former members of AYMs from Bradford, Manchester, Sheffield
and Birmingham were all involved in the formation. Operating as
a workers' organisation made the class interests of the group clear.
Organising as Pakistanis, however, was a significant shift from the
broader framework of an Asian identity. The return to organising
amongst communities of national origin was not thought of by
these members as a retrogressive step but was seen as a way to
enable members to develop links with communist organisations in
Pakistan. This in turn would develop member's understanding of
the political situation in Pakistan. US support for military rule and
Islamicisation of Pakistani society under General Zia in exchange
for Zia's strategic role in coordinating the Afghan Mujahideen as
part of the US' war against the Soviet occupation of Afghanistan
had made the country geopolitically significant. The linking of
anti-imperialist and anti-racist issues had been a significant way in
which the AYMs had worked and was preserved in PWA along with
the belief in a black political identity. From 1984 to 1992, PWA
(GB) organised in Manchester, Birmingham and London. PWA's
grassroots activity remained focused on anti-racist campaigns.
The groups in Manchester and Birmingham organised campaigns
addressing racist attacks just as the AYMs had done previously and
were involved with some of the campaigns that Birmingham and
Sheffield AYMs in particular were supporting, such as the Baba
Bakhtaura Defence Campaign, Mohammad Idris Defence campaign,
the Khan Family Defence Campaign and the demonstration in
support of the Kassam Family who were suffering racist attacks in
Sheffield. They worked with former members of AYM (Manchester)
in the Ahmed Iqbal Ullah Memorial Committee. PWA also offered
solidarity with anti-imperialist struggles abroad such as those in

Palestine, Kashmir, South Africa, Eritrea and Ireland and educated their members and supporters on progressive struggles in South Asia, such as the Dalit Liberation Movement in India (PWA 1986 3:4) and the struggle against military rule in Pakistan (PWA 1985 2:4). Their aims and objectives were very similar to those developed by the early phase of AYM Bradford and Manchester, opposing all forms of racism including state racism, opposing all forms of discrimination, working for the unity of all black people and other national minorities, encouraging participation in the trade union movement, and organising cultural, political and social events to further the aims of the organisation. The key addition were aims that related specifically to Pakistan where they highlighted the importance of supporting the struggles of the Pakistani masses against 'all forms of imperialism, semi-feudal and semi-capitalist systems in Pakistan' as well the struggle for a democratic and secular Pakistan and women's struggles in Pakistan (PWA 1985 2:4:21). They produced the journal *Paikaar* to communicate their ideas both verbally and visually through photomontages which expressed the impact of neo-colonialism on Pakistan as well as agitational images that reflected the desire to smash racism and imperialism.

One of the most significant campaigns organised by PWA along with former members of AYM Manchester was the Ahmed Iqbal Ullah Memorial Campaign in Manchester. The stabbing to death of

8.1   Covers from Paikaar 1986–87, 1989 (courtesy Tariq Mehmood).

Ahmed Iqbal Ullah in the grounds of Burnage High School in 1986 after he tried to defend another Bengali school child who was being bullied sparked controversy over anti-racist educational initiatives and highlighted the imperative of linking questions of race and class. The Burnage Report headed by Ian Macdonald, which investigated the incident, highlighted the failings of anti-racist policies of the school, condemning the 'moral and symbolic anti-racism' that had alienated white pupils and working class males in particular by failing to address the interactions between class, race and gender. The report highlighted how the school had constructed all white pupils as racist and projected issues of anti-racism as a 'black problem' only addressing black pupils and their families in anti-racist initiatives – as though the solution to racism lay with them. It led to a press discourse that condemned anti-racist education policies, suggesting they 'had led to [the] killing' (*The Telegraph* 26 April 1988) and an airing of attitudes that suggested that 'so-called anti-racist policies only strengthened race prejudice', advocating that they should be abandoned.

Although the inquiry addressed the failure of state based anti-racism, for PWA the inquiry redirected the agenda from one which should have been about the right to self-defence, to one which argued about the type of anti-racist education policies by the education sector. This failed to address the key issue of turning to a state that had practised racism for hundreds of years as an institution that could find a solution to racism. The limits of such a perspective were even clear from the experiences of this campaign. To begin with, the Council had refused to acknowledge that the case was racist. They banned the Ahmed Iqbal Ullah Memorial Committee from organising a public meeting on any council premises because the committee had declared the incident racist. The council declared that this was sub-judice, although as Quamrul Kabir, from AYM (Manchester) and a member of the Memorial Committee pointed out, they had not declared that it was sub-judice for themselves and the police to declare that the case was not racist (Workers Film Association 2011). Rather than simply focusing on the individual racism of the school boy who killed Ahmed, or the failure of council initiated anti-racist initiatives, PWA emphasised the climate of racism created by the British state that fostered the conditions within which Ahmed was murdered, describing them as 'the main enemy'. They also highlighted the way in which the police as an organ of the state failed to respond quickly to racist attacks, which left Ahmed bleeding to death in the playground.

The increasing split between those within and outside of the race relations industry was highlighted by what PWA described as 'the farce of institutionalised "anti-racism"', which 'left the enquiry as the main focus of attention rather than the need of the youth to organise' (PWA 1986/7 3:4). PWA emphasised the right of the youth to self-defence and the importance of organising. They adopted some of the key slogans of the early AYMs and the UBYL 'Self Defence is No Offence' and like the early AYMs borrowed the position of the youth in Soweto: 'Don't mourn, organise'. For members of PWA, the strength of the campaign was muted by the redirection of energies into the inquiry.

During the late 1980s PWA also organised meetings to inform members on political questions in relation to Pakistan, but their core campaigning work remained focused on Britain. They organised a campaign for justice for Mohammad Siddique, killed by racists; a campaign for Tahir Akram, also killed by racists in Oldham during the Rushdie affair; and in Birmingham they campaigned for justice for Tasleem Akhtar, a young girl murdered on the street. In focusing on racist murders and violence they continued to focus on the issues that were core to independent AYMs and continued to identify themselves as black. Along with these campaigns against racism PWA continued to offer solidarity to international struggles such as Ireland, South Africa and Palestine.

The lack of anti-imperialist perspectives amongst the burgeoning number of council funded anti-racist initiatives also encouraged the founding of South Asia Solidarity Group (SASG) in 1989. One of their first pamphlets, *Asian Culture: Black Resistance*, offered a critique of British multiculturalism, analysing it as a form of social control and a way to manage black struggle particularly in relation to black identities and culture:

This culture is now being defined by the state in a form which is entirely static and unconnected with black people's everyday struggles in Britain. Through multicultural teachers in schools and multicultural projects in the community we are fed 'Asian' culture ... which consists of traditional food, religious festivals and traditional clothes, saris and samosas in other words. ... At the same time a whole new stratum of black community leaders whose salaries are paid by the central or local state ... while appearing to provide leadership to the community effectively serve to diffuse the struggle of the black working class and black unemployed. (SASG 1989a)

8.2   Photograph of a demonstration to protest against the murder of Tasleem Akhtar, organised by Pakistani Workers Association. (courtesy Matloub Hussayn Ali Khan).

SASG emphasised the way in which ethnic identities provided the criteria of funding, leading to acrimony and the development of strong, narrow ethnic nationalist approaches. So while 'black nationalism ... was once regarded as a threat to the state', a narrow form of nationalism began to be encouraged by the state as a means of controlling and dividing black people (SASG 1989a). SASG explored the meaning of anti-imperialist and progressive culture, as a culture that was not easily packageable and commodified. Throughout the 1990s the group produced a journal, *Inquilab*, that raised awareness about struggles in South Asia as a whole. As one of the founding members of this group had been a key organiser in Awaz and other black women's organisations, the organisation encouraged and enabled the participation of women particularly and were strategically involved in strikes involving Asian women workers such as the Burnsall strike in 1992. This strike in a Birmingham sweatshop began when 19 black workers, most of them Asian women, walked out demanding union recognition, equal pay, and basic health and safety. As with Grunwick's in 1976 and Imperial Typewriters in 1974, the workers had to turn to the Asian communities to offer solidarity to their struggle. The local and national leadership of GMB (Britain's General Union) eventually betrayed the workers when they called off the strike on the eve of a national demonstration in support of the workers (Johal 1993/4). Linking the production of culture to struggle, SASG helped to write a song for the strikers, '*Hartalian na Kaina usi hoon nahin behna*' ('The strikers say they will not now sit down'), based on an old Noor Jahan song '*Kehnde Ne Naina*' ('Your eyes say').

In 2005 South Asia Solidarity Group once again supported a strike by Asian women workers at Gate Gourmet who protested at the introduction of agency workers on the production line and were then locked out of the factory. The strike was supported by baggage handlers, bus drivers and ground staff at British airways who held a solidarity strike for 48 hours until their union declared that such secondary action was illegal. While the union, TGWU, made an agreement with the company within 16 days which would permit some of the workers their jobs back on new contracts and voluntary and compulsory redundancy for the rest, it was left to anti-racist activists including SASG to offer support to the workers in the following weeks. In taking an anti-imperialist and anti-racist approach to the strike, SASG offered an analysis of the events which exposed how Gate Gourmet was not really making the losses that they declared, since as a multinational they had profits of £1.05 billion and assets of £15 billion internationally. The action by Gate Gourmet had as much to do with the Texas Pacific Group who had taken over of the company in 2002, an organisation that owned Burger King and had a history of smashing unions in Texas. For SASG, the strike also showed the possibilities of international solidarity with US Gate Gourmet workers raising large funds for the workers at Heathrow (SASG 2005)

While small independent organisations such as SASG have continued to exist, independent political organisations with a mass community base disintegrated in the early 1990s. Even organisations such as Indian Workers Association in Birmingham that had a mass base in the 1970s and 1980s ceased to have such influence. The problems of social depravation, poor housing, unemployment and poor education however persisted. Police antagonism also persisted. Changing geopolitical priorities changed the way in which South Asians have perceived themselves and organised their communities. This climate has challenged the broad-based political blackness that the youth stood for, although it could be argued that the need for such identities are just as strong today.

SHIFTING IDENTITIES AMONGST SOUTH ASIANS IN BRITAIN

As multiculturalism encouraged an inward looking approach to identity that did not seek to build links between communities struggling against discrimination but rather provided services based on what community leaders defined as a community's cultural requirements, many young people who had first identified with the broad-based black identity of the 1970s and early 1980s began to redefine the way they thought about themselves. As Mukhtar Dar reflected, 'what is significant is the process by which the AYM's symbolic black secular clenched fist split open into a submissive ethnic hand with its divided religious fingers holding up the begging bowl for the race relations crumbs.' The change in identity took place at a time of changing global political realities that also impacted on these shifts. The collapse of the Berlin war in 1989 and the demise of the Soviet Union were significant developments that led to a questioning of Marxist ideology. The increasingly widely held belief that Western liberal democracy would provide the final form in ideological development and human government (Fukuyama 1989) led many to believe that multiculturalism and the increasing shift into identity politics, was proof of the openness of Western liberalism (Taylor 1992). Any challenge to Western liberal culture began to be seen as a challenge to human freedom.

There were a number of key moments of particular significance for South Asians in the 1980s and 1990s that shifted the identity of many from 'black' to religion and culture: (a) the rise of the Bharatiya Janata Party in the 1980s that campaigned for 'Hindutva' and the demolition of the Babri Masjid that was eventually destroyed in 1992; (b) the increasing popularity of the Khalistan movement amongst Sikhs in the diaspora in the late 1980s after the storming of the Golden Temple in 1984; (c) the demonisation of Muslims in the late 1980s, crystallised by the Rushdie affair in 1989.

This is not to suggest that religious groups had not organised previously but the changes in state policy gave them greater authority. In Bradford by the late 1980s even business organisations were divided on religious lines with the establishment of the Institute for Asian businesses in 1987 which was largely Hindu and Sikh, the Hindu Economic Development Forum in 1989 and the Asian Business and Professional Club in 1991 (Modood & Werbner 1997:130). In the late 1970s in Bradford, one AYM member recalls the fact that the Hindu cultural society were already organising and giving paramilitary training to Hindu youth as part of the RSS (Rashtriya Swayamsevak Sangh). Muslim youth were also being encouraged to fight in Afghanistan, as Mumtaz personifies in *Hand on the Sun* (Mehmood 1983).

Identification with religious political organisations were partly a response against the policies of integration by young people who wanted to value their roots and resist assimilation into British society which had denigrated South Asian culture during colonialism and beyond. Amongst Sikhs, organisations such as the Indian Sikh Youth Federation – the UK wing of the All-India Sikh Students Federation – began to gain support amongst young people in the UK after the attack on the Golden Temple. The conflicts in India were to spill on to the streets of Britain, with IWA and pro-Khalistani youth fighting on the streets of Handsworth in the mid 1980s, as the polarisation of political opinions intensified. One member of the AYM in Bradford joined the All India Sikh Students Federation becoming its vice president for a short period in time. Gurnam articulates his involvement with Sikh political youth as a response to racism. He remembers how his father brought him up in a secular environment and was from a family of shaven Sikhs. As he became involved with Sikh groups, Gurnam began to learn more about Sikh and Punjabi culture in his attempt to value his roots and began wearing a turban and learnt how to play the *tabla* and harmonium. Involvement with the Indian Sikh Youth Federation was also an internationalisation of politics for Gurnam. Gurnam's understanding of Marxism and left politics from the educational discussions in the AYM however, eventually led him to leave the Indian Sikh Youth Federation.

Although the cultural and religious turn in identity affected all South Asian youth, it was Muslim youth that were affected the most by the changing climate. This shift should not be seen as an example of a community turning inward (Alam & Husband 2006:14–16), but the result of shifting global attitudes in a period in which the

US was declared as the only remaining superpower and Islam began to be constructed as the political and cultural 'other' of the West – monolithic, static and unresponsive to change (Huntington 1993; Conway et al. 1997). Such an image maintained the Orientalist construct of the East as the opposite of Western rationalism that was associated with scientific progress. While the Orientalist image can be traced throughout the colonial and post colonial periods, the Rushdie affair in 1989 provided reinforcement of this negative stereotype and led to many British Muslims reorganising to defend themselves along religious lines.

Salman Rushdie's publication of the novel *The Satanic Verses* was seen by many Muslims, especially in South Asia, as an attack on their faith and as blasphemous, although as Parekh points out this concept does not exist within Islam. It was also a book that many British Muslims argued added to the myths that the West had created about Islam for centuries (Parekh 1990:699). Before the publication of Salman Rushdie's book, Penguin India had warned of its inflammatory nature and banned the book. When British Muslims across the UK first protested against the publication of the book there was little interest in their peaceful demonstrations, such as a march in Bolton that attracted 8,000 people on 2 December. It was only when members of Bradford's Muslim community decided to burn a copy of the book as a symbolic protest that the media – suddenly confronted with a sensational image that could construct Muslims as backward, barbaric and the antithesis of the West – took interest. Bradford Muslims were even compared to Nazis by a press that set out to vilify them. Attacked along religious lines, Muslims began to increasingly organise along such lines. The formation of the UK Action Committee for Islamic affairs took place in 1989. For young people both in and outside the youth movements who had forged an anti-racist black identity that had always been secular, the Rushdie affair raised contradictions and conflicts that led to exacerbated divisions that were already manifest of class, gender and anti-imperialist politics. Ayatollah Khomeini's fatwa against Rushdie polarised opinions further. A number of organisations, focusing entirely on the question of the defence of free speech set up the International Committee for the Defense of Salman Rushdie and His Publishers to argue for the abolition of the blasphemy law that only protected Christianity. Muslim groups argued for an extension to the law. The polarised nature of these conflicts led to debates about the nature of 'multiculturalism' (Weller 2009) from both the right and the left, and created a media space that permitted outpourings of racist attitudes and actions such as that of Robert Kilroy Silk who complained about 'uncivilised foreigners' corrupting British traditions. In January 1989 the Monday club took the opportunity to distribute 3,000 leaflets calling for the end of immigration and repatriation. The National Front argued for the repatriation of Rushdie himself (PWA 1989a:7). Racist violence also escalated. In the summer of 1989, three racist murders took place in the East end of London, and in Oldham Tahir Akram, a 14-year-old school boy, was shot dead by racists with an air rifle as he walked home in the predominantly Pakistani area of Glodwick.

The independent community organisations that had tried to preserve an anti-imperialist and class based perspective, such as PWA and SASG, argued that it was not possible to simply rally around the question of free speech and that the whole conflict raised a series of issues that needed to be explored together – the rights of minorities, racism and racist violence, questions of free speech as well the international response. For both PWA and SASG, the polarisation of attitudes to 'Are you for Rushdie or the Ayatollah?' was not acceptable and the failure of the media to permit a more diverse set of responses to the issue proved media racism. As SASG argued in their leaflet 'Unspoken Verses':

> The excessive self-generated media coverage given to the Rushdie affair has juxtaposed images of the Bradford book burnings with fist-shaking frenzied mobs in Iran. Through this selective choice of images, Muslims in Britain are being represented as a homogenous group with an alien 'anti-British' culture. (SASG 1989b:1)

Both SASG and PWA also drew attention to the way in which the word Muslim had started to become a term of abuse and synonymous with the term 'Paki'. They highlighted the racist violence that had taken place and the failure of the media to draw attention to these murders (PWA 1989b:5). In essence, both organisations argued that the racism that had been unleashed was more significant than the debates about free speech which only appeared to operate to fuel racism. As SASG highlighted, the Thatcher government had been happy, for example, to ban Peter Wright's *Spycatcher* in 1987, which detailed activities of M16 including a plot to assassinate President Nasser during the Suez crisis. During the 1980s, Thatcher had also curtailed the ability of elected Irish politicians, such as Gerry Adams, from speaking in their own voices and banned the promotion of homosexuality in 1988 with Section 28 of the Local Government Act. The defence of free speech was hypocritical.

Both PWA and SASG also drew attention to the internal dissent that existed within Islam in Sufi poetry for example, but highlighted the way in which this dissent critiqued the institutions of the faith not Muhammad himself and came from within communities where they had a strong artistic and cultural base. While more recently Sufism has been used to construct the concept of 'good' Islam as opposed to 'bad' Islam, PWA and SASG saw it as an expression of dissent within Islam that represented it as a culture with dynamism and change. Rushdie as the classic 'post-colonial', border intellectual did not have such links and wrote as an outsider from both the West and the Third World. 'The ascendancy of postcolonial theory... has had an ambiguous effect', as Anouar Majid has highlighted,

> for though it has brought the concerns of the hitherto marginalized people to the front of intellectual debates, it has also, by the same token, managed to obfuscate some of the enduring legacies of colonialism, including the pauperization of the Third World in the age of late capitalism. (Majid 1995–96:5)

Majid's comments highlight the distance that the 'post-colonial' intellectual and rising middle class in England had with the black working class in Britain. Multiculturalism had enabled the distancing of the relationship between race and class in both government and academic discussion, but the actual poverty and alienation felt by Pakistanis and Bangladeshis were tangible realities for black workers, many of whom were Muslim. Throughout the 1980s, of the nine non-white groups identified in the Labour Force Survey, Pakistanis and Bangladeshis had the highest rates of unemployment, the lowest number of educational qualifications and the highest profile in manual work. This was the case for men and women in both first and second generations. Pakistanis and Bangladeshis also experienced some of the worst effects of the immigration legislation, lived in some of the worst housing and experienced high levels of racist violence. The largest percentage lived in the North and Midlands where the decline of mills and factories affected the communities the most (Modood 1990:145).

The outcry against the Satanic Verses was a response from communities that were marginalised economically and culturally. As SASG argued, Rushdie, as a middle class intellectual was supported by a publishing industry that only wished to evoke a limited range of images of the 'Third World'. 'This market does not welcome working class Asian writers, but excludes them, and by doing so limits and controls images through which the Indian subcontinent and Asians in Britain are portrayed'. These positions shifted the debate from one that many argued were between liberalism and fundamentalism to one that suggested the need to consider questions of class and imperialism.

At the same time, the Rushdie affair challenged the 'multi-cultural consensus'. While the 'new class of "ethnic representatives" who entered the town halls from the mid-1980s onwards', as Arun Kundnani argues, 'entered into a pact with the authorities'; in return for 'managing and containing anger from within the ranks of black communities' the authorities gave them 'free rein in preserving their own patriarchy' (Kundnani 2001). Such patriarchy did not go unchallenged. Southall Black Sisters and the Iranian Women's Organisation in Britain challenged religious 'orthodoxies' in the interests of women's rights, setting up Women Against Fundamentalism (WAF) in the wake of the Rushdie affair. They argued that current multicultural policies 'would deliver women's futures into the hands of fundamentalist "community leaders" by seeing them as representatives of the community as a whole' (WAF 1990). While the right to resist fundamentalism was particularly important in a climate where US funded Islamicisation held sway in Afghanistan and Pakistan, WAF's protest against the London demonstration that called for the banning of *The Satanic Verses* left them standing next to fascists on that day. While WAF had legitimate concerns about women's rights and SBS had played a crucially important role in raising questions of domestic violence and the rights of women within black communities throughout the 1980s, their presentation of all those that opposed Rushdie's book as fundamentalists fed a view of Muslims as a homogenous group opposed to Western liberalism and served the interests of Western imperialism. It ignored the class dynamics and feelings of alienation that created the outcry. Western popular discourses surrounding its own secularism were constructed as liberal and inclusive rather than acknowledging how deeply they had been shaped by US security and foreign policy concerns in the Muslim world (Mahmood 2006).

This polarised view of Muslims fostered by the media was to have a fundamental impact on the way in which British Muslims were to see themselves and the way others saw them. As a result of the attacks on Islam, Muslims across the UK began to organise to defend their culture and identity. The one day conference on 'The

Future of Muslims in Britain' in 1990 that was to establish the Muslim Parliament in 1992 was subtitled 'a strategy for survival'. As the 1990s wore on, a whole host of Muslim organisations were formed: UK Action Committee on Islamic affairs funded by Saudi Arabia, Islamic Human Rights Commission in 1997 as well as the Muslim Association of Britain and the Muslims Council of Britain in the same year. As Aki Nawaaz, a musician from Fun-Da-Mental who identified with Asian Youth Movement politics as a school child and tried to join the AYM with his brother when he was at school, but was told to come back when he left school, remembers:

> Rushdie was the first time we felt that rather than just black and Asian we were Muslims. Before it didn't really exist. But with Rushdie there was the wholesale demonization of Muslims. It wasn't any different to what they did to black people but in terms of Islam there was a whole generation who brought their kids up with liberal values around Islam. Some were influenced by communism. Even they started to be dragged back into a Muslim identity. They could not handle the attack on their Muslim identity. We were young and hung around with anarchists, punks and Hells angels and they would ask us questions about why we felt so strongly about Rushdie and we didn't have all the answers. ... but we had always been told you can't insult the prophet, and it was in fact a Sikh employee of Penguin India that argued that Rushdie's book should not be released, and we never heard Hindus make jokes about their religion. We always kept it sacred... that was the bomb of Rushdie... . (Nawaaz 2012)

The politics of Fun-Da-Mental represent the continuities and the shifts in South Asian identity, because while 'we were totally identifying with our Muslim identity we were still influenced by black politics. As *Seize the Time* articulated "all they are doing is telling us black kids and all us minorities that our lives isn't worth anything"' (1994). While the band Fun-Da-Mental is often identified with Islamic politics, there were Sikhs in the band and, as Aki Nawaaz explains, although they felt the response to the Rushdie affair was 'a bit mad' they believed that they would feel similarly if someone insulted Guru Nanak. Fun-Da-Mental represented a hybrid musical style drawing its roots from everything including punk, hip hop, Qawwali and dance music to create a radical anti-imperialist expression, influenced by Black Power politics that was not exclusively Muslim. It was simply that in the contemporary climate being Muslim became a factor.

> So seek and you shall find the time
> Subhanallah, al hamdhu lilah to my leader
> Abuse, refuse to acknowledge the truth
> You say Islam and it's sexism
> But you're blind, when it comes to global masochism
> There's hesitance when you gotta see the essence
> Of where I'm coming from, I know, I see
> I learn and tried to learn from you
> But my spirituality determines reality

('Dog Tribe' MC Mushtaq, *Seize the Time*,
Fun-Da-Mental 1994)

The lyrics argue the right to express a religious identity, assert the impact of global politics on Muslim identities and recognise, although rather defensively, the gender debates that existed at the time.

The Rushdie affair was the first in a series of moments that created divisions that were to shatter the strength of the Black political identity that South Asians within the AYMs had affirmed so effectively in the late 70s and early 80s. The continued attack on socialist and communist principles which led to the collapse of the Communist Party of Britain in 1991 led to disillusionment amongst many activists – black and white – and affected the ability of such organisations to sustain membership. At the same time, the attack on Muslims continued with press coverage of the Gulf War that borrowed all the racist stereotypes of the previous decades and combined anti-Muslim sentiments with anti-immigration sentiments that were well summed up in *The Sun*'s 'A is for Ayatollah' alphabet published in November 1991 (Conway et al. 1997:16). In cartoons, Muslims were seen 'infiltrating' Britain, seeking to take it over (Abbas 2000:66–7). The following year the Bosnian War saw an attack on a Muslim majority community in Europe. As Fahim Qureshi, a member of Luton Youth Movement and later PWA, recalls, 'the whole Bosnian experience... seeing Muslims in concentration camps, that had a profound effect on me' (Qureshi 2012). Increasingly, young people who had supported anti-racist campaigns that the AYMs and PWA had organised had the same urge to support justice for Bosnia. Living in areas of high depravation such as East Manchester with little opportunity for paid work, a proportion chose to support Muslim Solidarity Campaign's aid convoys to Bosnia. In working with the convoys, these young people were not simply jettisoning the anti-imperialist and left politics that they had been introduced to in previous organisations, since the Muslim Solidarity Campaign formed part of the Workers' Aid for Bosnia campaign. This campaign provided both humanitarian aid as well as advocated the raising of the UN-imposed arms embargo, which effectively left Bosnians defenceless against better armed Serb nationalists. The genocide of Muslims at Srebrenica in 1995 further cemented the belief by Muslims, many of them South Asian, that the focus of the struggle for social and human rights should be centred around a defence of Islam. Huntington's 'clash of civilisation' debate forced the notion of global conflict as a conflict of cultures, namely those of the West and Islam, rather than one between the haves and the have nots. It became increasingly difficult not to speak about the struggle against oppression as a non-religious one. As Sivanandan put it at a protest meeting against the Gulf War in 1993, 'We are all Muslims now'.

9
The Asian Youth Movements and Politics Today

Shifting political identities from 'black' to faith-based did not come overnight. The term 'black' continued to be used by Pakistani Workers Association, South Asia Solidarity Group and Southall Black Sisters, for example, in the early 1990s as well as in trade union forums. The issues that the AYMs were concerned about – street racism, institutional racism, the criminalisation of minorities and police racism – have continued. While the new language of racism in the late 1990s and 2000s presented the root of the 'problem' for young Asians as ethnicity and culture and promoted a 'national story of Britishness ... around a set of core values to which minorities must assimilate', the old forms of racism in which colour played a crucial role have never been far away (Conway et al. 1997:5). The concept of assimilation pushed in the 1990s was not new but was the reassertion of a policy that had been promoted amongst conservatives in the 1970s and 1980s. It drew on a wider anti-Muslim political culture associated with the 'war on terror', which suggested 'self-segregation' and alien values as the key problem rather than imperialist aggression and institutional racism (Kundnani 2007: 24). This discourse, along with the intensification of struggles from civil rights to human rights, have left Muslims, suffering criminalisation and harassment, isolated. Anti-racists have not built the broad-based links that were developed during the 1970s and 1980s. Attacked as Muslims, many have organised around this identity.

RIOTS AND RACISM IN NORTHERN TOWNS

Social and economic research reports for Bradford and Oldham in the late 1990s and 2000s present a picture of institutional discrimination, poverty and street racism as conditioning the lives of South Asians in the north. A report on housing in Oldham by the CRE in the early 1990s highlighted the council's unlawful practices. Asians had to wait longer than others to be re-housed, were more likely to be housed on one or two estates in Oldham and were likely to be offered older, unimproved properties (CRE 1993:5–7). In 2001, Oldham Council still only had 2 per cent of Asian employees although they constituted 11 per cent of Oldham's population (Chrisafis 2001). They were the town's biggest employer. In Bradford in 1995, youth unemployment was 37 per cent in Manningham compared with 22 per cent for the city as a whole. In 2000, 80 per cent of Muslims (mainly Pakistanis, Kashmiris and Bangladeshis) and 45–50 per cent of Hindus and Sikhs were living in areas classified as 'struggling'. These were typically inner city areas of Bradford (Phillips 2001:3).

Harassment and aggression from the police also continued with Islamophobia and old style racism going hand in hand. During the weekend of the 1995 Manningham riot police refused to negotiate with community leaders over styles of policing and police were heard shouting comments such as 'Pakis go home' (Ali 1996:28). 'Colour, historical national identity, minority ethnic identity, cultural identity and Islam are ... fused in contemporary British Islamophobia' (Alam & Husband 2006:2). Official reports of the Manningham riots argued that they were the result of anti-social elements, (*Yorkshire Post* 12 June 1995, Channel 4's *Black Bag* 31 August 1995) dissenters argued that they were sparked by antagonistic and aggressive policing (Bagguley & Hussain 2003). The new police station in Manningham, which looked like a fortress, was symbolic of such police antagonism. Reports noted that 72.5 per cent of young people identified the police as a group from which they experienced racial prejudice and that police aggression was directed against Muslims in particular. Young people were also being harassed by the police while they were on the streets playing football, and were asked if they belonged to proscribed organisations such as Hamas (Foundation 2000).

The media attitudes to the 2001 riots in Burnley, Oldham and Bradford collapsed discourses of class and underclass with arguments about social exclusion and poverty being elided with debates surrounding cultural divides that included generation gaps, gang cultures, vigilantism and criminality (Alexander 2004:530–1). This focus has played down the fascist antagonism as well as police aggression that provoked the violence. In Oldham, fascists and racists attacked Asian businesses and chanted racist abuse in the Pakistani and Kashmiri area of Glodwick in May 2001. This was the area in which Tahir Akram had been killed following racist violence unleashed during the Rushdie affair. Official debates constructed discourses about Asian violence against whites, with little interrogation of statistics that suggested whites were suffering a higher percentage of attacks from Asians. Headlines such as 'A Rash of Attacks by Asian Gangs' in the *Guardian* and 'new efforts to curb racist attacks on white people' in *The Times* on 20 April 2001 framed the problems in Oldham as Asian vigilantism. Yet as the Campaign for Racism and Fascism reported, 'The Q Division of Greater Manchester Police, which operates in Oldham has a history of indifference to racial attacks by whites in the area and Asian youths are themselves regularly harassed by the police (recently a young Asian boy was seriously wounded when, having already surrendered to the police, he was mauled by police dogs)' (CARF 1999).

The Bradford riots of 2001 were represented in the media as 'simple thuggery' and 'mindless violence' (BBC 9 July 2001). Even Marsha Singh, MP for Bradford West, whose political career had been made on the back of the Asian Youth Movement, towed the Labour Party line and condemned the youth saying 'strong action' was needed, advocating the use of water cannons to prevent disorder. Such reactions emphasised anti-social behaviour rather than the root causes of discontent. The fact that the 'targets' of the rioters were overwhelmingly the police and white-owned property highlights the riots as representative of the frustration that many Asians felt about the discrimination that their communities face on a day to day level.

Caught up in the aftermath of 9/11 and new policy agendas, young Muslims with no previous criminal record were subject to draconian sentencing. Media representations of Pakistani Muslim males as problems (Choudhury 2005) with discourses reminiscent of the myth of black criminality popular in the 1970s and 1980s were reproduced constructing the 'new Asian folk devil' and enabling excessive sentencing to take place (Alexander 2000, Gilroy 1987a). This image was strengthened by the police publication of photos of 'Wanted' rioters as well as the action of 'community leaders' in naming the young men concerned and turning them over to the police (Allen 2003). Wider popular discourses have also constructed Islam and 'cultural tradition' as problems that position Asian women and mainstream society as in need of being defended from the Asian man, his 'culture' and his violence (Bagguley & Hussain 2008). In this context the history of resistance to police racism and victimisation has been constructed as the problem of Asian male culture. Culture continues to be represented here as static in contrast to the AYM attempts at revolutionary and dynamic cultural expressions. These discourses have constructed representations of young Asian men as 'both produced by, and as standing outside, their cultural community – a depiction that denies the continuities across genders and generations and reduces the validity of disturbances as legitimate political concerns.' (Alexander 2004:537). Macey has even sought to represent the Bradford 12, for example, as having 'created a legacy of distrust of the police', rather than this distrust being recognised as the result of police actions. She also constructs the campaign for halal meat in schools as a signifier of increasing Muslim 'demands' on the white establishment, rather than a campaign to service the legitimate needs of particular communities (Macey 1999).

Unlike the Bradford 12 defendants, the young men involved in the 2001 disturbances did not belong to independent political organisations that could represent them, defend them, or advise them about effective political action. Families were left isolated and there was no campaign against the criminalisation of the youth. The only time the community seemed to come together was when they felt shocked by the sentences handed out. As Ruth Bundey notes, these sentences were,

> a matter of policy. This is where policy and law come together.... when the community found that youngsters with no previous convictions with great school records, very well thought of by everybody, never done anything wrong in their lives, living at home, for an offence of picking up a stone, maybe throwing it, maybe not even hitting anything, but on the spur of the moment with the adrenalin of the crowd ringing their ears were being sent to prison for four years for riot. That did stir people up and there was a huge feeling of resentment at the length of the sentences, which were policy driven. (Bundey 2006)

In response to such a policy of criminalisation, the Fair Justice for All Campaign was set up to highlight the young people as 'victims twice over: of violent racist attacks against their communities by fascist gangs; and of the institutional racism that they subsequently met'. The campaign argued that white youths in similar circumstances have routinely faced less serious charges, resulting in significantly more lenient sentences: 'Such double standards are unacceptable, unfair and unjust.' Supported by Aki Nawaaz from Fun-Da-Mental, the journalist Yvonne Ridley, the solicitor Imran Khan and Suresh Grover from The Monitoring Group, the Fair Justice for All

Campaign mobilised community support and just as the Bradford 12 trial brought 800 people to a meeting in their defence shortly after the arrests, so this campaign mobilised large numbers when they first came together. Like the AYM campaigners, Fair Justice for All put the families, namely the mothers, at the front of the campaign, but the relationship between the lawyers and the campaign was not as strong or as unified as in the Bradford 12 case. While solicitors such as Imran Khan worked with the campaign, there were other solicitors who argued against the value of a campaign, treating the cases as those of individual petty criminals and not recognising the social and political contexts of the actions of the young people. 'People were scared and frightened. Do they become involved and then the judge may give their son's a bigger sentence. There were legal reps that were saying keep your heads down' (Nawaaz 2012). This division amongst legal representatives weakened the power of the campaign considerably. As Ruth Bundey reflected, while it was 'the sons of the community that were on trial' in 1981, the same feeling did not exist in 2001. The professionalization of campaigners also influenced the process. Although there were individuals such as Suresh Grover who had been instrumental in the development of the Bradford 12 campaign supporting Fair Justice for All, their role was primarily as case workers rather than campaigners.

The breadth of support that existed for the Bradford 12 in terms of national and international solidarity did not exist for the young people in 2001. The women organised themselves but as Aki Nawaaz recalls, 'when we were campaigning Muslims came but no left – even the big meeting, it was just Pakistanis and Yvonne Ridley'. Aki notes how they did try to discuss and liaise with the left but along with 'a cautiousness about getting involved with the left', there was a general lack of left support anyway: 'There was one woman from Anti Fascist Action that came but she was quite helpless and her style was very different to the other women in the campaign'. The climate of Islamaphobia and the decline of the left were both significant factors in the difficulty in building broad-based alliances. The 'war on terror' and the policy agendas of 'community cohesion' that were to develop following 2001 shifted the blame for racism to the communities themselves and ensured the disintegration of support for the minority that was the most victimised in the UK. The official reports and enquiries after the riots in Oldham, Burnley and Bradford in 2001 coming after 9/11, emphasised the fragmentation of communities along social, cultural, ethnic and religious lines, and went so far as to suggest that communities were deliberately self-segregating, rather than acknowledging the oppressive role of the police (Cantle 2001). As the Bradford blogger Atif Imtiaz put it 'the race agenda was turned on its head, the problem was not institutional racism but certain obstinate communities' (Imtiaz 2005).

What was meted out on minority communities in 2001 was passed over to majority communities in 2011 when draconian sentences were given to many working class white youths involved in the summer riots. Those involved in the 2011 riots, black and white, were described as 'thugs' and 'criminals' just like the youth of Bradford. The crucial role that police violence had played in the riots in Tottenham with the death of Mark Duggan, and the riots in Birmingham because of existing tensions following the death of Kingsley Burrell in spring of 2011, which also highlighted the role of racism as a factor with the 2011 riots, was played down with the media representing working class youth as 'feral' and without proper parental guidance, instigating similar moral panics to those that had been developed in 1981 (Alleyne & Ford Rojas 2011).

THE INSTITUTIONALISATION OF ANTI-ISLAMICISM

Since 2001, 'community cohesion' has been at the forefront of council and educational agendas. Muslims have been represented as refusing to integrate into Western liberalism and as antagonistic to its 'freedoms'. Yet for anti-imperialists in Britain, Muslim and non-Muslim, it is the occupation of countries with majority Muslim populations in Iraq, Afghanistan and Palestine and the refusal to allow a Muslim majority country in Europe in the shape of Bosnia or Turkey that is central to the conflict. The demonisation of Muslims in British society increased further after the London bombings of 2005. The 'Prevent' agenda launched in 2007 legitimised the targeting of Muslims by the police and the state to the point where stop and detain counter terrorism measures have meant that people of Asian origin are 42 times more likely to be stopped than other people (Fisk 2012). Yet Marsha Singh, former chair of AYM and well-established MP for Bradford West by 2005, voted for the extension of the detention period for terrorist suspects to 90 days. As the blogger Atif Imtiaz noted,

> A political concern remains unrepresented because our MP doesn't have the gravitas to say 'Mais non' to the whip. It is the politics of the 'Yes men'. If the political system does not

represent the political consciousness of its constituencies, then that consiousness will simply go elsewhere. (Imtiaz 2005)

It is significant that when Marsha Singh resigned in 2012 on the grounds of ill health, Bradford West voted in the only MP who has stood firmly against imperialist *awars*. The centrality of politics rather than faith can be seen in the election first of Marsha as a Sikh and then Galloway in a primarily Muslim ward.

While blaming communities for their refusal to integrate was a dominant narrative in the 1970s and 1980s, as Margaret Thatcher's 'swamped' speech exemplified, the policy of multiculturalism in the 1980s had encouraged Roy Jenkins' philosophy of 'cultural diversity in an atmosphere of mutual tolerance' amongst liberals in Britain (Jenkins 1966). After 2005, it was not just conservative voices who argued that lack of assimilation was the key conflict, but liberals too. 'Integrationism normalised an anti-Muslim political culture' (Kundnani 2007:24). While the AYMs and anti-racists had challenged the policies of state multiculturalism as failing to address the power base of racism, which they saw as embedded within the British State, in the 2000s multiculturalism had to be defended (Lerman 2010, Hasan 2012). Once again, 'British values' have been increasingly defined as homogenous and the anti-terrorist legislation of the 'war on terror' has institutionalised anti-Muslim racism in the structures of the state (Fekete 2004).

The events of 9/11 were a turning point. Fun-Da-Mental attempted to give expression to the demonisation that was felt by Muslims at that time: 'I remember all the gigs we used to do, there was a complete mixture of backgrounds. 9/11 changed the landscape. After 9/11 not many promoters would put us on' (Nawaaz 2012). The album *All is War (The Benefits of G-Had)* highlighted the abuse of Iraqi prisoners, with a hooded statue of liberty on its cover using similar iconography to the Stop the War photomontagist Leon Kuhn. The album called on the listener to consider the gravity of the crimes of the suicide bomber, a renegade academic offering information to the highest bidder and a government scientist paid to come up with new ways to kill. Through their music, Fun-Da-Mental sought to show how, constructed as the outsider, Muslims were criminalised (Campion 2006).

By suggesting that communities were refusing to integrate and that Britain was 'sleepwalking to segregation' (Phillips 2005) the experience of discrimination has been ignored and the legitimate interest that young people expressed in global injustice has been represented as anti-British. Yet young people that were interviewed after the riots in Bradford in 2001 did not express a desire to extricate themselves from British society. They saw themselves as British and here to stay. As youth in their twenties articulated:

> they [the elders] always saw themselves as outsiders whereas the youth of today believe that they have a right to stay here, we were born here. We contribute to society, to the communities, this is our home. We might be a Pakistani minority but we are British citizens and we are British so we deserve equality and everything.

> Our parents' intentions were to come to the UK, earn a living and go back home and settle back down at home. And then as we have been born and grown up we have more or less decided that this is our home and that it is not back in Pakistan. So we see it as in thirty years time, forty years time still being here and our parents didn't think of that. So we would like to more or less make it known that we are here to stay. (Cited in Bagguley & Hussain 2003).

What is notable about the comments that these young people make is that their parent's generation – those that established the AYMs – were saying the same thing. The ideas and slogans from the AYMs resonate with these young people's comments: 'Come what may, we're here to stay!', 'Black People have the right, Here to stay, Here to fight!' These young people from a third generation articulate similar desires to their parents, for a space within Britishness, a desire to belong and be treated equally. The question has to be asked, why are these young people still struggling for the same thing? Rather than the issue of self-segregation, Sukhtant Chandan argues, 'for young people and not so young people who have come from other parts of the world and live here, who have travelled and made this their home... It remains a question whether non-white people can be accepted *as who they are* in the West' (Chandan 2011). The current assimilationist agenda of 'community cohesion' structures authentic Britishness as not only monocultural rather than multicultural but also as containing political 'values' that demand allegiance.

SECULARISM AND ITS DISCONTENTS

Authenticity in what it is to be British mirrors the conservative debates about authenticity of South Asian identities, which have been repeatedly constructed as religious and culturally conservative. The polarisation of identities within the Asian community into religious ones was problematic for many individuals who had been part of the Asian Youth Movements and other anti-racist organisations. Suddenly the term 'faith communities' began to be used increasingly to describe ethnic minorities in the 1990s. The assertion of faith as a defining feature of the identity of non-white migrants in Britain by both the state and sections of minority communities, led to some non-religious South Asians from a Muslim background to use the term 'secular Muslim' in order to try to define themselves as not defined by faith (Sullivan 2011).

Yet such a construct maintains the shift in an interpretation of conflict from politics to culture as set out by Huntington (1993) and has not challenged the state's demonisation of Islam and Muslims. It has maintained the dichotomy of 'good Muslims' and 'bad Muslims', which President Bush, Tony Blair and others sought to construct in an endeavour to avoid the criticisms of racism and Islamaphobia that were asserted when they suggested the 'war on terror' as analogous to the crusades. Bad Muslims were those associated with terrorism and good Muslims were keen to clear themselves of any identification with it, and would support 'us' against 'them'. As Mamdani has highlighted, the central message of such a discourse suggested,

> unless proved to be 'good', every Muslim was presumed to be 'bad'. All Muslims were now under obligation to prove their credentials by joining in a war against 'bad' Muslims. Judgements of 'good' and 'bad' refer to Muslim political identities, not cultural or religious ones. (Mamdani 2005)

The term secular Muslim in this context has operated to enable individuals to distance themselves from what has been constructed as the archetypal Muslim – the 'bad Muslim'.

Individuals, however, are not secular – it is the state that is either secular or not and can discriminate against its citizens. No other group in Britain has felt the need to use such a term and describe themselves as 'secular Christian', 'secular Hindu' or 'secular Jew'. Increasingly, 'secular Muslims' have aligned themselves with the British state's anti-Islamicism agendas in which Muslims have been criminalised for being Muslim and faith and ethnicity have frequently been elided by politicians and journalists who have referred to relations between Muslims and whites (Kundnani 2007:30). These organisations include Muslims for Secular Democracy and the Council of ex-Muslims in Britain who argue that they represent 'a branch of a growing network of secular "ex-Muslims" who oppose the interference of religion in public life' (Council of ex-Muslims in Britain 2012). This suggests that secular democracy is a character of British society. Yet the British state is not free of religious ideology. Its institutions are intrinsically linked to the church. The queen is the head of the church and the state, and the relationship is further entrenched with 26 bishops holding unelected seats in the House of Lords.

The policy objective in criminalising and isolating Muslims as the 'problem faith' can be seen, for example, in the appointment of Ramesh Kallidai, secretary general of the Hindu Forum and a man known to have links with right-wing Hindu organisations such as Vishwa Hindu Parishad, to New Labour's Committee on Integration and Cohesion, following the 7/7 bombings. This appointment was not simply another example of the alignment of the state with conservative religious groups but can be seen, Wilson argues, as the symbolic adoption of a series of interlinked tropes between a right-wing Hindutva ideology and Western imperialism's Islamaphobia in which the threat to the nation was embodied in stereotypes of Muslims as terrorists, fanatics, aligned with forces external to the nation, illegal immigrants, rapid population growth and women's subordination (Wilson 2012:234). If this was to define 'what we have in common, rather than obsessing with those things that make us different' as the brief for the Committee on Integration and Freedom suggests, Muslims did not stand a chance. To style oneself as a 'secular Muslim' was to suggest that you could be integrated and be 'properly' British in comparison with practicing Muslims who could not.

The shift of the secular voice to the imperialist camp is encapsulated in Kenan Malik's attack on shifting political identities amongst Muslims in his book *From Fatwa to Jihad* (Malik 2010). Malik condemns some former members of the anti-racist movement for turning to religiously defined political identities without recognising the geo-political shifts that have created these changes, nor the continuing impact of racism in the lives of South Asian communities. As Naeem Malik has argued,

if one looks at the countries leading occupations Western countries are in the lead. From Palestine to Afghanistan the countries occupied are all Muslim countries... we need to ask what kind of civilisation accepts Drone attacks killing civilians and calling it collateral damage. Anger over sustained injustices from Guantanamo, Belmarsh, Palestine, Libya, Syria, Iraq, Iran, Pakistan and Afghanistan over many decades takes all forms and what ignites that anger may not be understandable. Unless the West ends its occupations of Muslim lands I would say that Muslims would find it difficult to see that the West is not at war with Islam. (Malik 2012a)

What is secularism anyway, what does it mean to be secular? What position should it have in anti-imperialist struggles? Secularism is not free of ideology. Secularism only means the avoidance of religious ideology from the state. In European societies, as Arun Kundani has pointed out, 'that are marked by structural anti-Muslim racism, it is natural and necessary that Muslims organise *as Muslims* in fighting the specific racism they face. In this, they are not breaking with the tradition of black anti-racist politics, as has often been assumed but rediscovering on a new level its original lesson' (Kundnani 2008:40). That original lesson was to struggle against racism and give solidarity to those both nationally and internationally that suffered discrimination and victimisation. It was a struggle against colonialism and imperialist domination. These were the 'values' that the AYM wished to integrate with, as Tariq remembers: 'The British culture that we loved and adored was the culture of those who were fighting against British capitalism, British colonialism and there were many of those, its not like today where we seem atomised into many different groups' (Mehmood 2007).

In keeping these principles as their core motivators for political action, those former members of the Asian Youth Movements that have sought to maintain an anti-imperialist stance have ended up in antagonism with former comrades who have become immersed in an interpretation of South Asian arts and culture easily absorbed within the 'Prevent' agenda, whose entire premise is based on the idea that all Muslims are potential terrorists and ignores the primary motivations of individuals to resist an unjust and oppressive foreign policy. In one instance, the left-wing revolutionary Pakistani poet, Faiz Ahmed Faiz was interpreted as representing 'peace and social justice' and 'against extremism' during the centenary celebrations for Faiz in England. Yet historically, Faiz's poetry offered a spirit of resistance and he has acted as a motivator and supporter of anti-imperialist struggle including the Palestinian struggle for self-determination. His poetry recognises the legitimacy of armed struggle against oppressors in order to achieve world peace and the prosperity of its people as the poem *Let us Walk in the Bazaar in Shackles* highlights:

> *Khak bar sar chalo, khoon badaman chalo*
> *Rah takta hai sub shehr-e-janaan chalo*
> *Hakim-e-shehr bhi, majma-e-aam bhi*
> *Teer-e-ilzam bhi, sang-e-dushnam bhi*
> *Subh-e-nashaad bhi, roz-e-naakaam bhi*
> *Unka dum-saaz apnay siwa kaun hai*
> *Shehr-e-janaan main ab baa-sifa kaun hai*
> *Dast-e-qatil kay shayan raha kaun hai*
> *Rakht-e-dil bandh lo, dil figaro chalo*
> *Phir hameen qatl ho aain yaro chalo*

> Go with dust on head and blood on garb
> Go as the city of my beloved is waiting
> City's ruler and crowd of commoners
> Arrow of false charge, stone of accusation
> Morning of sorrow, day of failure
> Who is their friend except me
> Who is untainted in the city of beloved
> Who deserve the killers or executioners hand
> Get ready for the journey of heart, go wounded heart
> Let me go to be executed

(Faiz Ahmed Faiz, Lahore Jail, 1951–3)

The anti-Islamic framework in which we live has also been brought home by Robert Fisk in an article prompted by the violence in the Arab and Muslim world following the release of the Islamophobic film *Innocence of Muslims*:

> A New Zealand editor once proudly told me how his own newspaper had re-published the cartoon of the Prophet with a bomb-filled turban. But when I asked him if he planned to publish a cartoon of a Rabbi with a bomb on his head next time Israel invaded Lebanon, he hastily agreed with me that this would be anti-Semitic. There's the rub, of course. Some things are off limits, and rightly so. Others have no limits at all. Several radio presenters asked me yesterday if the unrest in Cairo and Benghazi may have been timed to 'coincide with 9/11'. It simply

never occurred to them to ask if the video-clip provocateurs had chosen their date-for-release to coincide with 9/11. (Fisk 2012).

Such attitudes indicate the ideological nature of Western liberalism and the secularism it professes. Whatever one can say about the film, it was done to provoke and it did. However as Naeem has argued, 'if there were no occupations the provocation would not have worked' (Malik 2012a).

A RETURN TO INTEGRATIONISM

The ideological nature of Western liberalism is explicit in Cameron's criticism of state multiculturalism as a failure in 2011 at a security conference in Munich, in which cultural assimilation is seen as a mark of political harmony. In December 2012, despite Labour leader Ed Miliband arguing that Britain should embrace being a 'multi-ethnic diverse' Britain, the discourse of immigrants as problems was reasserted as an 'anxiety' which is economic in order to defend the Labour position from racism. In his speech Miliband has pushed an integrationist agenda which places the responsibility for integration with migrants, by questioning the right of migrants to live in separate communities and emphasising the learning of English and the need for citizenship education as key markers of fitness for citizenship. He also emphasises culture and politics as markers of loyalty. Both 'race' and chauvinism are unspoken undercurrents in his speech in which he highlights statistics that indicate a growing number of children for whom English is not their first language (Miliband 2012).

Miliband has found support in strange places. Sivanandan, the founder of the Institute of Race Relations who offered inspiration through his writings to the AYMs has responded positively to the Labour leader. Sivanandan has argued that Miliband's need to limit immigration is not about race, 'because immigration at a time of unemployment brings down wages and helps the employer and not the worker – which is why the concept of a living wage is such an important one' (IRR News Team 2012). Yet black workers and anti-racist activists in the 1970s took up struggles to challenge such notions. Black workers and migrant workers, they argued, did not bring down wages. It is capitalism which encourages wage differentials and the economic divisions created by imperialism lead to the need for workers to move to the sources of capital. The most effective way for trade unions to win struggles for better wages and conditions was for white workers to join with black workers to ensure a united struggle. Black workers organised themselves despite the lack of unity. The strikes at Imperial Typewriters and Grunwick's were about black workers demanding the same conditions as white workers including the right to join a union.

Sivanandan rationalises Miliband's assertion about 'fitness' for citizenship by suggesting that this is just about the British need for 'pomp and circumstance'. Yet the structure of Miliband's speech juxtaposes concern over the disturbances in Bradford and Oldham with concern over separation and isolation which is then followed by remarks on English language and citizenship. Although the statistics about language to which Miliband refers relate to migrants from Europe, the questions of citizenship are not about European migrants. The eliding of the two issues acts to create anxiety over non-white participation in British society. Sivanandan suggests that Miliband just needs to add 'a coherent policy on outlawing racism' to make his ideas on integration work. This ignores such integrationist policies as part of the state's racist structures.

A SPIRIT OF RESISTANCE

The Asian Youth Movements and the United Black Youth League represented a spirit of resistance that was widespread in 1981. As Anwar Qadir reflected on the AYMs, 'We were a small organisation with a great big part to play nationally' (Bradford 12 Thirtieth Anniversary Commemoration, 16 July 2011). In July 2011, on the thirtieth anniversary of the Bradford 12, two commemorations took place in Bradford and London. In planning for these events, debates took place that ranged from the importance of looking at the rise of political Islam to those that rejected this and argued that the relevance of the core objectives of the AYMs and UBYL for today should be discussed, namely challenging racism, state oppression and imperialism. The commemorations focused on the latter because of the belief that the key issue affecting South Asian communities was racism, Islamaphobia and state criminalisation. The links between past and present experiences of criminalisation were directly drawn through the experience of Saber Hussain (a former Bradford 12 defendant) whose son was jailed for twelve years under the new terrorism legislation. The final platform of speakers highlighted the commitment to independent political organisation which offered unconditional solidarity to those in struggle, both nationally and internationally. It considered the importance of strategy in organisation as well as an analysis of the current global politics. The shift from concerns over civil rights to ones of human rights was also raised, as was the politics of funding. The themes of the meeting provide a framework with which to explore both the inspiration and the legacies of these organisations.

As Amrit Wilson highlighted, for many, it was 'a period of intense struggle... there was a lot of repression but people did actually fight back... The campaigns were ours, they were not run by professionals, we owned them and were propelled by a sense of justice which gave rise to a very powerful solidarity' (Wilson 2011). This was a solidarity not limited by official criteria's belonging to state funded cultural, social or policy organisations. This was a solidarity that was not bound by the limitations of the legal system. If Anwar Ditta, for example, had no legal avenue left to appeal through then as far as the AYMs were concerned the law was wrong and they would struggle for justice anyway. If the state attempted to try those that fought in self-defence as terrorists, as in the Bradford 12 case, campaigners and defendants stood strong and argued, they were not terrorists, but 'victims of terror' (Bradford 12 Internal Bulletin, No. 12, 3 June, p. 4). They worked with lawyers that recognised that law and politics were intertwined and that campaigns alongside supportive legal teams would have the best results. The legacy of the youth movements' strategies and approaches has influenced a wide variety of campaigns. Dan Glass, an environmental campaigner and member of Plain Stupid, spoke about the way in which the Bradford 12 campaign represented the right to protest. When facing conspiracy charges over environmental protest, the Bradford 12 campaign and trial provided inspiration to him in terms of campaigning tactics in which the struggle from the courts of the people to the courts of law were linked. It influenced the slogan, 'climate self-defence is no offence', which environmental activists coined to highlight the inadequacies of the law in protecting the earth. The Bradford 12 has also influenced other campaigns. Suresh Grover of The Monitoring Group has commented on how the Bradford 12 case influenced the Stephen Lawrence campaign in terms of the strong relationship between the legal team and the campaign in terms of the way in which strategies of cross examination were used in the Bradford 12 case, as well as the pressure placed by the campaign through the public gallery, with a public gallery spokesperson who issued statements to the press on a daily basis to emphasise a wider public's position and concerns. These were strategies that were learned from the Bradford 12 case.

The legacy of self-defence as a right and protest as a right is also important in a political climate where the struggle has shifted from one about social to human rights. The incarceration of Babar Ahmed and Talha Ahsan without trial and their subsequent extradition, the arrests of ten Pakistani students in 2010 in North West England on terrorist charges and their deportation to Pakistan and, in the case of Abid Naseer, to the US, despite all cases against them being dropped, highlights the human rights abuses against Muslims in Britain that are both British and overseas citizens. By integrating Talha Ahsan's prison poetry into the thirtieth anniversary commemoration, activists asserted the way that the spirit of the UBYL and the early AYMs did not shy away from challenging the state on key issues such as who is the terrorist. They also continued to mobilise and organise for campaigns where legal rights were denied. Talha's poem, *Mind the Gap* gives evidence of the denial of human rights in Britain today through a very British experience of hearing the recorded voice say 'Mind the gap' on the London Underground.

> ( ) until proven ( ),
> ( ) and ( ),
> anti-( )
> some allegations
> the firmer denied
> the greater proven,
> the chasm between
> ( ) and ( ) widens,
> jump it,
> don't fill it

(Ahsan 2011)

The difficulties of mobilising support for campaigns such as those of Babar Ahmed and Talha Ahsan are indicative of the changing circumstances in which we live where the right to know the evidence against you, the right to an open trial with a jury of one's peers is no longer a right given to all citizens. Anti-Islamic discourses are so widespread that it has left the campaign for Talha Ahsan and Babar Ahmed with a muted anti-racist analysis and many Muslims fear being targeted if they offer solidarity. These conditions highlight the importance of independent anti-racist activism which is broad based and challenges state oppression.

The need for organisations independent of the state is the key lesson of the Bradford 12 and the independent AYMs. Such organisations have been able to make much more consistent demands for accountability. The principle of building solidarity that was national, international and anti-imperialist could not be maintained by state funded organisations.

A recent example of this can be seen in the work of the United Family and Friends Campaign (UFFC) that works to campaign for justice for individual families that have suffered as a result of the racism and systemic violence within the police force. During the Charles de Menezes Campaign, the state funded Newham Monitoring Project restricted contact between Menezes family and UFFC. UFFC tried to establish a 'no shoot to kill' campaign at the time, but the opportunity to link the death of Menezes to that of police violence more broadly was lost (Ken Fero 2012). NMP also did not raise the issue of the inevitability of state violence in this period of Islamaphobia and Anglo–American led aggression. In this sense the principle of building solidarity from *all* areas that had been so fundamental to the success of AYM campaigns against racist violence, in support of divided families and in support of the Bradford 12 was not developed.

The question of political independence and the influence of state sponsorship was a key debate at a thirtieth anniversary commemoration of the Bradford 12 in London in July 2011. The discussions and debates were not just situated around Britain but also made links between the British experience and the global role of NGOs often sponsored by American and British Aid. As Naeem Malik has pointed out, 'NGO's today are the key instrument, but not the only instrument, for administering the empire in the neo-liberal era.' British Aid for example has funded 'unique' research in the Federally Administered Tribal Areas of Pakistan to justify the idea that people in the region support drone attacks and believe they play a positive role in the fight against terrorism (Malik 2012b). Finally as the AYMs and UBYL did, the Commemoration expressed a commitment to national liberation struggles by inviting the Palestinian freedom fighter Leila Khaled to speak through Skype who called for anti-imperialist unity.

There are valuable lessons to be learned from the experiences of the independent AYMs, their methods of organising, the conflicts and difficulties that arise as a result of alignment with political parties and the impact of the shifting political positions of individuals as political climates and allegiances change. As Tariq and Amrit asserted, 'we believed a better world was possible,' 'there was a feeling... that we could fight and win...'.

Bibliography and Interviews

BIBLIOGAPHY

Abbas, Tahir 2000 'Images of Islam', *Index on Censorship*, No. 5, pp. 64–8.

Ahmad, Noshin (1998) 'Hijabs in Our Midst', in Jonathan Rutherford (ed.), *Young Britain: Politics, Pleasures and Predicaments*. London: Lawrence and Wishart, pp. 74–81.

Ahmat, Y., Hussain, A., Gata Aura, T. and Clarke A. (1983) 'The textile industry and Asian workers in Bradford', *Race Today*, Vol. 14 (March–April 1983), pp. 215–18.

Ahsan, Talha (2011) *This be the Answer: Poems from Prison*. Edinburgh: Radio Ramadan.

Alam, M. Y. and Husband, Charles (2006) 'British–Pakistani men from Bradford: linking narratives to policy' report, York: Joseph Rowntree Foundation. Available from: http://www.jrf.org.uk/sites/files/jrf/1585-pakistani-men-bradford.pdf

Alexander, C. (2000) '(Dis)Entangling the Asian Gang', in B. Hesse, *Unsettled Multiculturalisms: Diasporas, Entanglements, Transruptions*. London: Zed Books, p. 135.

Alexander, C. (2004) 'Imagining the Asian gang: ethnicity, masculinity and youth after "the riots"', *Critical Social Policy*, Vol. 24, No. 4, pp. 526–49. DOI: 10.1177/0261018304046675.

Ali, Shanaaz (1996) *An investigation into the causes of the Bradford riot on the weekend of 9th–11th June 1995*. MA Thesis, Leeds University, Leeds.

Allen, Chris (2003) *Fair Justice: the Bradford Disturbances, the Sentencing and the Impact*. London: Forum Against Islamophobia and Racism.

Alleyne, Brian (2002) *Radicals Against Race: Black Activism and Cultural Politics*. London: Berg.

Alleyne, R. and Ford Rojas, J-P. (2011) 'London riots: mother condemns "feral rats" who attacked Ealing store', *The Telegraph*, 10 August. http://www.telegraph. co.uk/news/uknews/crime/8692439/London-riots-Mother-condemns-feral-rats-who-attacked-Ealing-store.html

Anwar Ditta Defence Committee (1980) 'Bring Anwar's Children Home' pamphlet, AD241. www.tandana.org

Anwar Ditta Defence Committee (1981) 'Victory Celebration' leaflet, AD56. www.tandana.org

ARAF (1981) 'Asian Youth Movement', *Araf: South Manchester Anti-racist and Anti-fascist paper*, No. 1, October.

Asian Resource Centre (2003) *Across All Boundaries: Silver Jubilee Review – 25 years of Asian Resource Centre in Birmingham*. Birmingham: Asian Resource Centre. http://www.asianresource.org.uk/anniv-book.pdf

Athwal, Harmit (2007) 'The Hounding of David Oluwale', Institute of Race Relations, London. http://www.irr.org.uk/2007/may/ha000008.html

AYM (Birmingham) (1985) 'Handsworth 1985', *Asian Youth News: Birmingham Asian Youth Movement*, September.

AYM (Bradford) (1979) *Kala Tara*, magazine of the Asian Youth Movement (Bradford).

AYM (Bradford) (1983) Minutes of meeting, Green Lane Youth Centre, Saathi Centre Collection.

AYM (Bradford) (1983) Minutes of meeting held at CRC, Saathi Centre Collection, 23 January.

AYM (Bradford) (1983) Minutes of Annual General Meeting Asian Youth Movement, 27 February.

AYM (Bradford) (1983) Minutes of meeting, Saathi Centre Collection, 6 February.

AYM (Bradford) (1983) 'Report from full time worker', Newsletter, September.

AYM (Bradford) (1983) Minutes of AYM Meeting, Saathi Centre Collection, 23 October.

AYM (Bradford) (1984a) *Policy Statement on Separate Religious Schools*, Asian Youth Movement, Bradford.

AYM (Bradford) (1984b) *Reading, Righting, Rithmetic, Race: Racism and Schools*, Asian Youth Movement, Bradford.

AYM (Manchester) (1981a) 'Black workers and trade unions: Imperial Typewriters strike', *Liberation*, Vol. 2, No. 1, April.

AYM (Manchester) (1981b) 'Black Jews in the racist state of Israel', *Liberation: Organ of the Asian Youth Movement (Manchester)*, April.

AYM (Manchester) (1981c) *Liberation: Organ of the Asian Youth Movement (Manchester)*, July.

AYM (Sheffield) (1983) *Kala Mazdoor*, Issue No. 1.

AYM (Sheffield) (1985a) *Kala Mazdoor*, Issue No. 2.

AYM (Sheffield) (1985b) *Kala Sho-or: Black Consciousness*, December 1985.

Bagguley, P. and Hussain, Y. (2003) 'The Bradford riot of 2001: a preliminary analysis', paper presented to the 9th Alternative Futures and Popular Protest Conference, Manchester Metropolitan University, 22–4 April.

Bagguley, P. and Hussain, Y. (2008) *Riotous Citizens: Ethnic Conflict in Multicultural Britain*. Aldershot: Ashgate.

Bains, Harwant (1988) 'Southall youth: an old fashioned story', in Philip Cohen and Harwant S. Bains (eds), *Multi-Racist Britain*. Basingstoke, Macmillan Education, p. 221.

Bashir, Idris (1983) *Asian Youth Movement Newsletter*, September.

BBC News (2001) 'Labour at odds on Bradford riots', 9 July. http://news.bbc.co.uk/1/hi/uk_politics/1430437.stm

Benson, S. (1996) 'Asians have culture, West Indians have problems: discourses in race inside and outside anthropology', in T. Ranger, Y. Samad and O. Stuart (eds), *Culture, Identity and Politics*. Aldershot: Avebury, pp. 47–56.

Benyon, John (ed.) (1984) *Scarman and After: Essays Reflecting on Lord Scarman's Report, the Riots and their Aftermath*. Oxford: Pergamon Press.

Black Panther Movement (1971) 'Black People Have the Right to be in Britain' leaflet for the National Conference on the Rights of Black People in Britain, 22–3 May.

Bradford 12, Internal Bulletin, No. 1, Saturday 1 May 1982.

Bradford 12, Internal Bulletin, No. 2, Tuesday 4 May 1982.

Bradford 12, Internal Bulletin, No. 3, Saturday 8 May 1982.

Bradford 12, Internal Bulletin, No. 4, Monday 10 May 1982.

Bradford 12, Internal Bulletin, No. 5, Wednesday 12 May 1982.

Bradford 12, Internal Bulletin, No. 6, Tuesday 18 May 1982.

Bradford 12, Internal Bulletin, No. 7, Thursday 20 May 1982.

Bradford 12, Internal Bulletin, No. 9, Thursday 27 May 1982.

Bradford 12, Internal Bulletin, No. 10, Tuesday 1 June 1982.

Bradford 12, Internal Bulletin, No. 11, Wednesday 2 June 1982.

Bradford 12, Internal Bulletin, No. 12, Thursday 3 June 1982, p. 4.

Bradford 12, Internal Bulletin, No. 12, Friday 4 June 1982.

Brah, Avtar (1989) 'The early days', in Southall Black Sisters (eds), *Against the Grain: Southall Black Sisters 1979–1989*. Southall: Southall Black Sisters.

Brown, Ruth (1995) 'Racism and Immigration in Britain', *International Socialism Journal*, Issue 68, pp. 3–35.

Bunsee, B (1973) 'Mansfield workers' new step against racialism', *Tribune* magazine. http://archive.tribunemagazine.co.uk/article/4th-may-1973/10/mansfield-workers-new-step-against-racialism.

BYMER (1978) 'Bangladeshi Youth Movement for Equal Rights: New Office Opening Celebration' pamphlet. 9 December.

CAIL (1980) 'CAIL News: Newsletter of the campaign against the immigration laws', Spring.

Callaghan, John (1990): Rajani Palme Dutt, 'British communism, and the Communist Party of India', *Journal of Communist Studies*, Vol. 6, No. 1, pp. 49–70.

Campion, Chris (2006) 'Fundamental: all is war', *The Observer*, 16 July. http://www.guardian.co.uk/music/2006/jul/16/11.

Cantle, Ted (Chair) (2001) 'Community cohesion: a report of the Independent Review Team' (The Cantle Report). London: Home Office. http://resources.cohesioninstitute.org.uk/Publications/Documents/Document/Default.aspx?recordId=96

CARF (1981) *Southall: The Birth of a Black Community*. London: Insitute of Race Relations/Southall Rights.

CARF (1991) *Newham: The Forging of a Black Community*. Newham Monitoring Project/ Campaign Against Racism and Fascism.

CARF (1999) *The Politics of Numbers: Police Racism and Crime Figures*, Campaign Against Racism and Fascism, CARF report No. 50, June/July.

CARL (1981) 'Here to Stay' Newsletter, Campaign Against Racist Laws, Spring, p. 2–3.

Carruthers, Susan (1995) *Winning Hearts and Minds: British Governments, the Media and Colonial Counter-Insurgency 1944–60*. Leicester: Leicester University Press.

Carter, B., Harris, C. and Joshi, S. (1987) *The 1951–55 Conservative Government and the Racialisation of Black Immigration*. Warwick: Centre for Research in Ethnic Relations, University of Warwick.

Carter, Trevor (1986) *Shattering Illusions: West Indians in British Politics*. London: Lawrence and Wishart, p. 140.

Castells, Manuel (1983) *The City and the Grassroots: A Cross-cultural Theory Of Urban Social Movements*. Berkeley: University of California Press.

Chandan, Sukhant (2011) 'Taking Over the West', *MRZine, Monthly Review*, 9 April.

Choudhury, Barnie (2005) 'Asian Vigilantes', online report. BBC Radio 4, 16 August. http://www.bbc.co.uk/radio4/today/reports/archive/politics/oldham1.shtml

Chrisafis, Angelique (2001) 'Mean streets in a divided town', *Guardian*, 12 December. http://www.guardian.co.uk/uk/2001/dec/12/race.politics.

Clayton, Gina (2010) *Textbook on Immigration and Asylum Law*. Oxford: OUP. Especially 'History and sources of immigration law', pp. 5–36.

Cohen, Abner (2004) *Urban Ethnicity*. London: Routledge (first published 1974).

Cohen, Steve (2003) *No One is Illegal: Asylum and Immigration Control Past and Present*. London: Trentham Books.

Conway, G. (Chair), et al. (1997) *Islamophobia: A Challenge for Us All*. Report of the Runnymede Trust Commission on British Muslims and Islamophobia. London: Runnymede Trust, p. 5.

Copsey, Nigel (2000) *Anti Fascism in Britain*. London: Macmillan.

Council of Ex-Muslims in Britain (2012) 'Challenging Forced Religious Identities – The Case of Secular Muslims in France and ex-Muslims in Germany and the UK', Press Release, 5 December.

Cox, Derek (1970) *A Community Approach to Youth Work in East London*. London: Young Women's Christian Association.

CRE (1993) *Housing Allocations in Oldham: Report of a Formal Investigation*. London: Commission for Racial Equality.

Dahya, B. (1974) 'The nature of Pakistani ethnicity in industrial cities in Britain'. In A. Cohen, *Urban Ethnicity*. London: Tavistock.

Denham, John, Eagle, Angela, Ainsworth, Bob, et al. (2001) 'Building cohesive communities: a report of the Ministerial Group on Public Order and Community Cohesion' (The Denham Report). London: Home Office. http://resources.cohesioninstitute.org.uk/Publications/Documents/Document/Default.aspx?recordId=94

Denham, Jim (2004) 'Learning from solidarity: The miners' strike 1984–5', *Workers Liberty*. http://www.workersliberty.org/story/2004/06/17/learning-solidarity-miners-strike-1984-5.

DeWitt, John (1969) *Indian Workers' Associations in Britain*. London: OUP/IRR, p. 158–9.

Dromey, Jack (2010) 'Jayaben Desai obituary', *Guardian*, 28 December. http://www.guardian.co.uk/politics/2010/dec/28/jayaben-desai-obituary.

Dummett, M. (Chair) (1980) 'Southall 23 April 1979: Report of the Unofficial Committee of Enquiry'. London: National Council for Civil Liberties.

Eade, J., Ullah, A. A., Iqbal, J. and Hey, M. (2006) *Tales of Three Generations of Bengalis in Britain*. London: Nirmul Committee.

Eagleton, Terry (2011) *Why Marx Was Right*. New Haven, CT: Yale University Press.

Fanon, Frantz (1990) *The Wretched of the Earth*. London: Penguin, p. 188.

Farrar, Max (2001) 'Global Capitalism, Culture and the Politics of World Revolution'. Paper delivered to THE CLR JAMES CENTENNIAL CONFERENCE, CLR James at 100: Global Capitalism, Culture and the Politics of World Revolution, The University of the West Indies, St Augustine, Trinidad, 20–23 September 2001.

Fekete, Liz (2004) 'Anti-Muslim racism and the European security state', *Race & Class*, Vol. 46, No. 1, July, pp. 3–29.

Fisk, Robert (2012) 'The provocateurs know politics and religion don't mix', *The Independent*, 13 September. http://www.independent.co.uk/voices/comment/the-provocateurs-know-politics-and-religion-dont-mix-8131297.html

Foundation 2000 (1995) *Disturbances in Manningham: A Community Response – The Voices Must be Heard*. Bradford: Foundation 2000.

Friends of Anwar Ditta (1980) 'Anwar's Story', AD240. www.tandana.org

Fryer, Peter (1987) *Staying Power: The History of Black People in Britain*. London: Pluto Press.

Fukuyama, F. (1989) 'The End of History', *The National Interest*, Summer.

Fun-Da-Mental (1994) *Seize the Time* LP. Mammoth Records.

Gilroy, Paul (1987a) 'The myth of black criminality', in P. Scraton (ed.) *Law, Order and the Authoritarian State: Readings in Critical Criminology*, Milton Keynes: Open University Press.

Gilroy, Paul (1987b) *There Ain't no Black in the Union Jack: The Cultural Politics of Race and Nation*, London: Hutchinson.

Gilroy, Paul (1990) 'The End of Anti Racism', in J. Donald and A. Rattansi, *Race, Culture and Difference*. London: Sage Publications.

Gilroy, Paul and Lawrence, Errol (1988) 'Two-tone Britain: white and black youth and the politics of anti-racism', in Philip Cohen and Harwant S. Bains (eds), *Multi-Racist Britain*. Basingstoke, Macmillan Education, pp. 121–55.

Guru, Surinder (1987) *Struggle and resistance: Punjabi women in Birmingham*. Ph.D. Thesis, University of Keele.

Hall, Stuart (1991) 'Old and new identities, old and new ethnicities', in A. D. King (ed.), *Culture Globalisation and the World System: Contemporary Conditions for the Representation of Identity*. Minneapolis, MN: University of Minnesota Press.

Handa, Amita (2003) *Of Silk Saris and Mini-Skirts: South Asian Girls Walk the Tightrope of Culture*. Toronto: Women's Press.

Hann, D. and Tilzey, S. (2003) *No Retreat: Street Fighting Men*. Preston: Milo Books.

Harman, Chris (1981) 'The Summer of 1981: a post-riot analysis', *International Socialism*, Vol. 2, No. 14, Autumn, pp. 1–43. http://www.marxists.org/archive/harman/1981/xx/riots.html#n5

Hasan, Mehdi (2012) 'In defence of Britain's multiculturalism', *Al Jazeera*, 2 August. http://www.aljazeera.com/indepth/opinion/2012/08/2012819528793336.html

Hassan, Laila Salim (1982) 'Peerless' *New Statesman*, May.

Hayes, M. and Aylward, P. (2000) 'Anti-Fascist Action Radical resistance or rent-a-mob?', *Soundings*, Issue 14, Spring, pp. 53–63.

HCAR (1978) 'ANL Carnival, they did pass', *CARF*, No. 6.

Hendessi, Mandana (1989) 'In Conversation', in Southall Black Sisters (eds), *Against the Grain: Southall Black Sisters 1979–1989*. Southall: Southall Black Sisters.

Heseltine, Michael (1981) 'It Took a Riot', government report, August. http://www.estatesgazette.com/pdf/It-Took-A-Riot.pdf

Hiro, Dilip (1991) *Black British, White British: A History of Race Relations in Britain*. London: Grafton Books, pp. 139–40.

Home Office (1981) 'Racial Attacks: Report of a Home Office study'. London: Home Office, November.

Huntington, Samuel P. (1993) 'The clash of civilizations?', *Foreign Affairs*, Summer.

Husbands, Christopher (1983) *Racial Exclusionism and the City*. London: Allen and Unwin.

Imtiaz Atif (2005) 'Pursuing equality', online article from blog *Bradford Muslim: Notes on life in a Multicultural City*, 12 November. http://bradfordmuslim.blogspot.co.uk/2005_11_01_archive.html

IPYA (1977) 'Report and Agenda for the General Meeting held on 13 October', Saathi Centre Archives, Indian Progressive Youth Association.

IRR News Team (2012) 'Miliband's Progress?', interview with A. Sivanandan, Institute of Race Relations, 19 December. http://www.irr.org.uk/news/milibands-progress/

IRR (1987) *Policing Against Black People*. London: Institute of Race Relations.

Jackson, P. (1992) 'The racialization of labour in post-war Bradford', *Journal of Historical Geography*, vol. 18, no. 2, pp. 190–209.

JCAR (1982) *Racialist Violence in the UK 4/2/82*, 4 February. London: Joint Council Against Racism.

Jenkins, Roy (1966) Speech to National Committee for Commonwealth Immigrants, 23 May.

Johal, Sarbjit (1993/4) 'The Burnsall Strike – A Glimpse of the Future', *Inquilab*, South Asia Solidarity Group. http://www.southasiasolidarity.org/peoplesstruggles/labourmovements.html

Josephides, Sasha (1990) 'Principles, strategies and anti-racist campaigns: the case of the Indian Workers' Association', in H. Goulbourne (ed.), *Black Politics in Britain*. Aldershot: Avebury.

Joshua, J., Wallace, T. and Booth, H. (1983) *To Ride the Storm: The 1980 Bristol 'Riot' and the State*. London: Heinemann.

Kabir, Alamgir (1965) 'The growing campaign against Pakistanis in Britain', Peace News, 19 March.

Kalra, Sanjay, Hutnyk, John and Sharma, Ashwani (1996) 'Re-sounding (anti)racism, or concordant politics? Revolutionary antecedents', in Sanjay Kalra, John Hutnyk and Ashwani Sharma (eds), *Dis-Orienting Rhythms: The Politics of the New Asian Dance Music*. London: Zed Press.

Shukra, Kalbir (1998) *The Changing Pattern of Black Politics in Britain*, London: Pluto Press, pp. 56–9.

Kalra, Virinder (2000) 'Vilayeti Rhythms: Beyond Bhangra's Emblematic Status to a Translation of Lyrical Texts', *Theory Culture and Society*, Vol. 17, No. 3, pp. 83–105.

Kirk, N. (2000) *Northern Identities: Historical Interpretations of 'The North' and Northernness*. Aldershot: Ashgate.

Kundnani, Arun (2001) 'From Oldham to Bradford: the violence of the violated', in IRR, 'The Three Faces of British Racism: a special report', *Race & Class Special Edition*, Vol. 43, No. 2. http://www.irr.org.uk/2001/october/ak000003.html

Kundnani, Arun (2007) 'Integrationism: the politics of anti-Muslim racism', *Race & Class* Vol. 48, No. 24, pp. 24–44.

Kundnani, A. (2008) 'Islamism and the roots of liberal rage', *Race & Class*, Vol. 50, No. 2, pp. 40–68.

Leamington ARAF (1978) 'Anti-racist Anti-fascist committee newsletter', November, No. 3, p. 12.

Leech, Kenneth (1980) *Brick Lane 1978: The Events and their Significance*. London: Stepney Books Publications.

Leeds Other Paper (1982) 'Self defence is No Offence: How the Bradford twelve won their freedom', JA69. www.tandana.org

Lerman, Anthony (2010) 'In defence of multiculturalism', *Guardian*, 22 March. http://www.guardian.co.uk/commentisfree/2010/mar/22/multiculturalism-blame-culture-segregation

Macey, Marie (1999) 'Class Gender and Religious influences on changing patterns of Pakistani Muslim male violence in Britain', *Ethnic and Racial Studies*, Vol. 2, No. 5, pp. 845–66.

Mahamdallie, Hassan (2007) 'Muslim working class struggles', *International Socialism*, Issue 113, 30 January. http://www.isj.org.uk/index.php4?id=288&issue=113

Mahmood, Saba (2006) 'Secularism, hermeneutics, and empire: the politics of Islamic reformation', *Public Culture*, Vol. 18, No. 2, pp. 323–528. DOI: 10.1215/08992363-2006-006.

Maira, Sunaina (2002) *Desis in the House: Indian American Youth Culture in New York City*. Philadelphia, PA: Temple University Press.

Majid, Anouar (1995–96) 'Can the postcolonial critic speak? Orientalism and the Rushdie affair', *Cultural Critique*, No. 32, Winter, pp. 5–42.

Malik, Kenan (2010) *From Fatwa to Jihad: The Rushdie Affair and Its Legacy*. London: Atlantic Books.

Malik, Naeem (2012a) Statement sent to the *Evening Standard*, following the release of *The Innocence of Muslims*.

Malik, Naeem (2012b) 'NGO's and their position in the Global administration of the empire', *Viewpoint*, online issue No. 150, 10 May. http://www.viewpointonline. net/ngos-and-their-position-in-the-global-administration-of-the-empire.html

Mamdani, Mahmood (2005) *Good Muslim, Bad Muslim: America, the Cold War, and the Roots of Terror*. London: Pantheon.

Manchester Evening News (2011) '"You behaved like a pack of wild animals": Judge speaks out as more youths appear in court over Manchester riots', *Manchester Evening News*, 10 August. http://menmedia.co.uk/manchestereveningnews/ news/s/1455765_you-behaved-like-a-pack-of-wild-animals-judge-speaks-out- as-more-youths-appear-in-court-over-manchester-riots

Marley, Bob and Tosh, Peter (1973) 'Get Up, Stand Up', *Burnin'*, Bob Marley and the Wailers. Island Records.

Mehmood, Tariq (1983) *Hand on the Sun*. London: Penguin.

Mehmood, Tariq (2003) *While There is Light*. Manchester: Comma Press.

Mehmood Ali, Tariq (2008) 'Marginalisation, resistance and the road to fictional visibility', *South Asian Cultural Studies*, Vol. 4, No. 1, pp. 3–11. http://blogs. edgehill.ac.uk/sacs/files/2012/08/Document-3-Ali-T.-M-Marginalisation- Resistance-and-the-Road-to-Fictional-Visibility.pdf

Melucci, Alberto (1980) 'The new social movements: a theoretical approach', *Social Science Information*, Vol. 19, No. 2, May, pp. 199–226. DOI: 10.1177/053901848001900201.

Mercer, Kobena (1998) 'Welcome to the jungle: identity and diversity in postmodernpolitics', in Jonathan Rutherford (ed.), *Identity: Community, Culture, Difference*. London: Lawrence and Wishart.

Miles, A. and Phizacklea, A. (1984) *White Man's Country: Racism in British Politics*. London: Pluto Press.

Miles, Robert (1982) *Racism and Migrant Labour*. London: Routledge.

Miliband, Ed (2012) 'Building A Britain That Works Together', transcript of speech, 14 December. http://www.labour.org.uk/building-a-britain-that-works-together

Misty in Roots (1978) 'Ghetto of the City', in *Live At The Counter Eurovision* LP, Collectif d'Animation pour la Formation et l'information des Travailleurs.

Modood, Tariq (1990) 'British Asian Muslims and the Rushdie Affair', *Political Quarterly*, Vol. 61, Issue 2, April, pp. 123–246.

Modood, Tariq (1994a) 'The End of a Hegemony: The Concept of "Black" and British Asians', in John Rex and Beatrice Drudy (eds.), *Ethnic Mobilisation in a Multi-cultural Europe*. Aldershot and Brookfield, VE: Avebury.

Modood, Tariq (1994b) Political Blackness and British Asians, *Sociology*, Vol. 28, No. 4, November, pp. 859–76.

Modood, Tariq and Werbner, Pnina (1997) *The Politics of Multiculturalism in the New Europe: Racism, Identity and Community*. London: Zed Books, p. 130.

Moore, R. (1975) *Racism and Black Resistance in Britain*. London: Pluto Press.

Mukherjee, Tuku (1988) 'The Journey Back', in Philip Cohen and Harwant S. Bains (eds), *Multi-Racist Britain*. Basingstoke, Macmillan Education, p. 240.

NAYM (1983) 'Constitution and Summarised programme, Draft 3 of 11/9/83'.

NMP/AYM (Sheffield & Birmingham) (1984) 'Towards building an Independent Black Network', Minutes of meeting, 30 November.

Olende, Ken (2005) 'Roots reggae and resistance from Jamaica to Brixton', *Socialist Worker* online, 27 August. http://www.socialistworker.co.uk/art.php?id=7187

Page, Mike (1981) 'Relf launches race onslaught', *New Statesman*, 10 July.

Parekh, Biku (1990) 'The Rushdie affair: research agenda for political philosophy', *Political Studies*, XXXVIII, pp. 695–709.

Peggie, C. W. (1979) 'Minority youth politics in Southall', *New Community Journal of Ethnic and Migration Studies*, Vol. 7, Issue 2.

Phillips, Deborah (2001) The Changing Geography of South Asians in Bradford', Bradford Race Review Report, Supplementary Report 5, Bradford District implementation team. http://www.bradford2020.com/pride/suplimentary.html

Peirce, Gareth (2011) Speech by Gareth Peirce, Solicitor for the Bradford 12, given to 'Self defence is No Offence!', Bradford 12 Thirtieth Anniversary Commemoration, SOAS, London, 23 July.

Phillips, Trevor (2005) 'After 7/7: Sleepwalking to segregation', Speech given to the Manchester Council for Community Relations, Manchester, 22 September. http://www.humanities.manchester.ac.uk/socialchange/research/social-change/summer-workshops/documents/sleepwalking.pdf

PWA (1984) 'Aims and objectives 1984', *Paikaar: Journal of the Pakistani Worker's Association (Britain)*, Vol. 2, No. 4, Autumn, p. 21

PWA (1985) 'Britain Reports' *Paikaar: Journal of the Pakistani Worker's Association (Britain)*, Vol. 2, No. 4, Autumn, p. 19.

PWA (1985) 'Pakistan: in brief' *Paikaar: Journal of the Pakistani Worker's Association (Britain)*, Vol. 2, No. 4, Autumn, pp. 10–11.

PWA (1986) 'Pakistan: What Independence? What democracy?', *Paikaar: Journal of the Pakistani Worker's Association (Britain)*, Vol. 3, No. 3, pp. 4–7.

PWA (1986/7) 'The Murder of Ahmed Iqbal Ullah', *Paikaar: Journal of the Pakistani Worker's Association (Britain)*, Vol. 3, No. 4.

PWA (1986/7) 'Untouchable! Voices of the Dalit Liberation Movement', *Paikaar: Journal of the Pakistani Worker's Association (Britain)*, Vol. 3, No. 4, p. 15.

PWA (1989a) 'Racism and the Rushdie Affair', *Paikaar: Journal of the Pakistani Worker's Association (Britain)*, Vol. 6, No. 2/3, p. 7.

PWA (1989b) 'Racist Murders; Organise, fightback', *Paikaar: Journal of the Pakistani Worker's Association (Britain)*, Vol. 6, No. 2/3, p. 5

Race & Class (1975) 'Editorial', *Race & Class*, Vol. 16, No. 3, pp. 231–2. DOI: 10.1177/030639687501600301.

Race Today (1983) 'Reflecting on the trial of the decade: The Bradford 12', in 'The Struggle of Asian Workers in Britain' pamphlet. Brixton, London.

Race Today Collective (1976) 'Defend Manningham', *Race Today*, May.

Ramamurthy, A. (2004). 'Secular identities and the Asian Youth Movement', The Pakistan Workshop, Rook Howe, The Lake District.

Ramamurthy, A (2006) 'The politics of Britain's Asian Youth Movements', *Race & Class*, Vol. 48, No. 2, October, pp. 38–60.

Ramamurthy, Anandi (2011a) 'South Asian mobilisation in two northern cities: a comparison of Manchester and Bradford Asian youth movements', *Ethnicity and Race in a Changing World*, Vol. 2, No. 2, pp. 26–42.

Ramamurthy, Anandi (2011b) 'The Asian Youth Movement in Manchester', *Journal of North West Labour History*, No. 36, pp. 31–6.

Ramdin, Ron (1987) *The Making of the Black Working Class in Britain*. London: Wildwood House.

Rattansi, A. (1992) 'Changing the Subject? Racism, Culture and Education', in J. Donald and A. Rattansi (eds), *'Race', Culture and Difference*. London: Sage, pp. 11–48.

Renton, Dave (2006) *When We touched the Sky: The Anti-Nazi League 1977–1981*. Cheltenham: New Clarion Press, pp. 51–73.

Rodrigues, Jeff (1981) 'The Riots of '81', *Marxism Today*, October, pp. 18–22.

Rose, John (1976) 'The Southall Asian Youth Movement', *Notes of the Month*, *International Socialism* (1st series), No. 91, September, pp. 5–6. http://www.marxists.org/history/etol/newspape/isj/1976/no091/rose.htm

Rowe, M. (1998) *The Racialsiation of Disorder in Twentieth Century Britain*. Aldershot: Ashgate.

Russell, Dave (2004) *Looking North: Northern England and the National Imagination*. Manchester: Manchester University Press.

Sahgal, Gita (1989) 'When I became involved', in Southall Black Sisters (eds), *Against the Grain: Southall Black Sisters 1979–1989*. Southall: Southall Black Sisters.

SASG (1989a) *Asian Culture: Black Resistance*. London: South Asia Solidarity Group.

SASG (1989b) 'Unspoken Verses' Leaflet. London: South Asian Solidarity Group, April, p. 1.

SASG (2005) 'Fighting Multinationals, Racism and Anti-Union Laws', online article. London: South Asian Solidarity Group, October. http://www.southasiasolidarity.org/2011/08/04/fighting-multinationals-racism-and-anti-union-laws/

Scarman, Lord Leslie (1986) *The Brixton Disorders 10–12 April 1981: the Scarman Report*, Harmondsworth: Penguin Books.

Sharma, Sanjay (1996) 'Noisy Asians or "Asian Noise"', in Sanjay Kalra, John Hutnyk and Ashwani Sharma (eds), *Dis-Orienting Rhythms: The Politics of the New Asian Dance Music*. London: Zed Press.

Sharma, Sanjay, Hutnyk, John and Sharma, Ashwani (1996) *Dis-Orienting Rhythms: The Politics of the New Asian Dance Music*. London: Zed Press.

Shukra, Kalbir (1998) *The Changing Pattern of Black Politics in Britain*. London: Pluto Press.

Silver, Steve (1999) 'Echoes of the past', *Searchlight*, July. http://www.searchlightmagazine.com/index.php?link=template&story=102

Singh, Europe (1974) 'The Black Worker in Britain' book review, *International Socialism*, No. 73, December, p. 29. http://www.marxists.org/history/etol/newspape/isj/1974/no073/singh.htm

Singh, Marsha (1984) 'Education and race: a reply by Marsha Singh' essay in reply to Honeyford's Salisbury Review, 21 March, SC105. www.tandana.org

Sivanandan, A. (1976) *Race Class and the State: The Black Experience in Britain*. London: Institute of Race Relations.

Sivanandan, A. (1982) *A Different Hunger: Writings on Black Resistance*. London: Pluto Press.

Sivanandan, A. (1987) Speech at Church of the Ascension in support of Viraj Mendes, 20 March.

Sivanandan, A. (1990) *Communities of Resistance: Writings on Black Struggles for Socialism*. London: Verso.

Sivanandan, A. (1991) 'A Black Perspective on the War', *Race & Class*, No. 32, p. 83.

Smith, Evan (2010) 'Conflicting narratives of black youth rebellion in modern Britain' *Ethnicity and Race in a Changing World: A Review Journal*, Vol. 1, Issue 3 (July), pp. 16–31.

Solomos, John (1989) *Race and Racism in Contemporary Britain*. London: Macmillan.

Stark, Dave (1982) *A Report on Racist Violence in Bradford – 1981*, unpublished document written for the legal defence team of the Bradford 12.

Street, John (1986) *Rebel Rock: The Politics of Popular Music*. London: Blackwell.

Sullivan, Martin (2007) ' "Secular Muslim" backs Cameron', online article, *Islamophobia Watch*. 1 February. http://www.islamophobia-watch.com/islamophobia-watch/2007/2/1/secular-muslim-backs-cameron.html

Taylor, Charles (1992) *Multiculturalism and the Politics of Recognition*. Princeton, NJ: Princeton University Press.

Taylor, Stan (1982) *The National Front in English Politics*. London: Macmillan.

The Asian Times (1984) 'Asian Youth forge Belfast Links', MH161. www.tandana.org

Thomas, Devon (1984) 'Black initiatives in Brixton', in John Benyon (ed.) *Scarman and After: Essays Reflecting on Lord Scarman's Report, the Riots and their Aftermath*. Oxford: Pergamon Press.

Thomas, Paul and Sanderson, Pete (2011) 'Unwilling citizens? "Muslim" young people and national identity', *Sociology*, Vol. 45, No. 6, pp. 1028–44. DOI: 10.1177/0038038511416161.

Touraine, A. (1981) *The Voice and the Eye: An Analysis of Social Movements*. Cambridge: Cambridge University Press.

Van Dikj, Teun A. (1991) Racism and the Press. London and New York: Routledge.

Visram, Rosina (2002) *Asians in Britain: 400 Years of History*. London: Pluto Press.

Waddington, David (1992) *Contemporary Issues in Public Disorder*. London and New York: Routledge.

WAF (1990) 'Newsletter', No. 1, November, Women Against Fundamentalism.

Walker, Martin (1977) *The National Front*. London: Fontana.

Weller, Paul (2009) *Mirror for Our Times: 'The Rushdie Affair' and the Future of Multiculturalism*. London and New York: Continuum International Publishing.

Williams, Maxine (1979) 'The Anti-Nazi League and the Struggle Against Racism' RCG pamphlet. London: RCG Publications.

Williams, Raymond (2001) *The Long Revolution*. Peterborough, Ontario: Broadview Press.

Wilson, Amrit (1982) 'Evidence of racialism examined', *New Statesman*, 11 June.

Wilson, Amrit (2006) *Dreams, Questions, Struggles: South Asian Women in Britain*. London: Pluto Press.

Wilson, Amrit (2011) Speech at Bradford 12 Thirtieth Anniversary Commemoration, 23 July, SOAS, London.

Wilson, Kalpana (2012) *Race Racism and Development*. London: Zed Books, p. 234.

Winlow, Simon (2001) *Badfellas: Crime, Tradition and New Masculinities*. Oxford: Berg.

Workers Film Association (2011) *Memories of Struggle and Solidarity in the 1980s*, DVD.

Yaffe, David (2001) 'The labour aristocracy and imperialism. Part 4: the end of the post-war consensus', *Fight Racism! Fight* Imperialism, No. 164, December 2001/January 2002.

INTERVIEWS

Ahmed, Ijaz. Pakistani Workers' Association (conducted by Dave Rogers) (6 August 1987).

Ali, Shanaaz. Member of UBYL (2006).

Amin, Jayesh. Member of UBYL and Bradford 12 defendant (2006).

Bassi, Balvinder. Member of Birmingham Asian Youth Movement (March 2012).

Bassi, Bhupinder. Member of Birmingham Asian Youth Movement (2006).

Bundey, Ruth. Solicitor for Bradford 12 defendent Anwar Ditta (2006).

Dar, Mukhtar. Member of AYM (Sheffield), Pakistani Workers' Association (2006).

Ditta, Anwar. Anwar Ditta Defence Campaign (2006).

Fero, Ken. Migrant Media and United Friends and Family Campaign (2012).

Grover, Suresh. Member of Southall Defence Campaign, and Southall Monitoring Group (2006).

Harrison, Dave. Journalist and member of Bradford 12 Campaign (2011).

Hussain, Saeed. Member of UBYL, Bradford 12 defendant (2006).

Husayn-Ali-Khan, Matloub. Member of AYM (Sheffield) (2005).

Ismail, Aneez. Overseas Student Campaign Sheffield and Sheffield Students Union Black cauacus in 1970s (2006).

Johal, Sheera. Member of Birmingham Asian Youth Movement and Indian Workers' Association (M-L) (2006).

Kabir, Quamrul. Member of Asian Youth Movement (Manchester) (2005).

Kelemen, Paul. Anti-racist activist, member of Bangaldesh Divided families Campaign, Oldham CARF (2006).

Loft, Mike. Member of Oldham CARF (2006).

Mann, Kuldeep. Member of AYM, Manchester (2006).

Mehmood, Tariq. Member of Asian Youth Movement (Bradford) and United Black Youth League, Bradford 12 defendant, member of Pakistani Workers' Association (2006, 2007).

Mehta, Bharat. Member of Haringey Action Group (2012).

Nawaaz, Aki. Member of Fun-Da-Mental, and Fair Justice for all Campaign (2012).

Purewal, Balraj. Member of Southall Youth Movement (2006).

Qadir, Anwar. Member of Asian Youth Movement (Bradford) (2006).

Qureshi, Fahim. Member of Luton Youth Movement, member of Pakistani Workers' Association (2012).

Rashid, Jani. Member of Asian Youth Movement (Bradford) (2007).

Rashid, Noorzaman. Member of Asian Youth Movement (Bradford) (2006).

Shaikh, Nilofer. Asian Youth Movement (Manchester) (2006).

Singh, Gurnam. Member of Asian Youth Movement, Bradford, (2006).

Singh, Jasbir. Member of AYM (Sheffield) and Newham Monitoring Project (2006).

Singh, Marsha. Member of AYM (Bradford), MP for Bradford West 1997–2012 (2006).

Stark, Dave. Member of Bradford Trades Council, anti-fascist campaigner, Bradford 12 Campaign (2007).

Wilson, Amrit. Founding member of AWAZ, member of OWAAD, Bradford 12 Support Group, South Asia Solidarity Group (2006, 2012).

Zulfiqur, Mohsin. Member of Asian Youth Movement (Manchester), member of Pakistani Workers' Association (2006).

Index

Printed in Great Britain
by Amazon